# Applied Sociological Perspectives

# Applied Sociological Perspectives

Edited by
R. J. ANDERSON
W. W. SHARROCK

London
GEORGE ALLEN & UNWIN
Boston              Sydney

**George Allen & Unwin (Publishers) Ltd,**
**40 Museum Street, London WC1A 1LU, UK**

George Allen & Unwin (Publishers) Ltd,
Park Lane, Hemel Hempstead, Herts HP2 4TE, UK

Allen & Unwin, Inc.,
9 Winchester Terrace, Winchester, Mass. 01890, USA

George Allen & Unwin Australia Pty Ltd,
8 Napier Street, North Sydney, NSW 2060, Australia

First published in 1984
Second impression 1984

---

**British Library Cataloguing in Publication Data**

Applied sociological perspectives.
1. Sociology
I. Anderson, R. J. (Robert John)
II. Sharrock, W. W.
301      HM51
ISBN 0-04-301167-5
ISBN 0-04-301168-3 Pbk

---

**Library of Congress Cataloging in Publication Data**

Main entry under title:
Applied sociological perspectives.
Includes index.
1. Sociology—Addresses, essays, lectures.   I. Anderson,
R. J.   II. Sharrock, W. W. (Wes W.)
HM51.A65  1984      301      83-25801
ISBN 0-04-301167-5
ISBN 0-04-301168-3 (pbk.)

---

Set in 10 on 12 point Bembo by Setrite Typesetters
and printed in Great Britain by Billing and Sons Ltd, London and Worcester

# Contents

# Introduction

First and foremost, this is a book for students. It was conceived and written with their needs and interests in mind. More than that, it has been designed for those students who are just beginning to study sociology and who need introductory guidance through what might otherwise appear to be a forbidding maze of arguments, debates and substantive areas. Because of this, we have had two major concerns: we have placed a premium on clarity and simplicity, and we have restricted the range of topics to be covered. We have included only those substantive areas which, in our experience, are the ones most usually covered in introductory courses and the ones which are of most interest to students when they come to sociology. Indeed, it is often the case that they take up sociology precisely because they are interested in these topics. Our policy of deliberate simplification, while being primarily a means to ensure clarity and, we hope, understanding, has had two consequences. It has meant that each of our contributors has had to pass over, allude only briefly to, or even ignore altogether many intriguing and provocative questions as well as whole bodies of findings and studies, which they would have liked to have dealt with, but which would have led them well beyond their remit and the space which they were allocated. By concentrating only on the basic facts and what is at issue in their sociological interpretation, our contributors have been able to ensure that the essentials have been covered adequately and systematically.

The second consequence is to be seen in the restricted nature of the references provided in the text. We have opted to dwell on a limited number of themes and arguments rather than massive documentation. However, for those students who feel that they would like to grapple with the questions and debates in more detail, we have provided a bibliography of further reading at the end of each chapter. Students are encouraged to dip into these readings as their fancy takes them.

The desire to maintain simplicity and clarity and the restricted selection of topics has gone hand in hand with two other general strategies we have pursued. We have tried to be even-handed in presenting the variety of theories, positions and arguments that are covered. It is not our intention to use this book as a means of persuading students that only one kind of sociology is worth doing and that all others are unsound, illogical, partial and distorting. Individual contributions may well speak strongly on behalf of particular points of view, but the collection, as a whole, does not. For us, the one feature of sociology which all students ought to be introduced to right at the beginning is that arguments over and choices between methods and theories are not just rife but characteristic. To suppress them is to do both the student and sociology a disservice.

This leads us on to a last introductory comment. This collection was designed to be complementary to and supplemented by a general text such as E. C. Cuff and G. Payne (eds), *Perspectives in Sociology* (London: Allen & Unwin, 1983; 2nd edn) which provides the detailed, theoretical expositions necessary for a complete appreciation of the arguments presented here. For us to have endeavoured to cover both the theoretical background and reviews of the substantive areas would have made this volume far too large, far too unwieldy and far too expensive. It is expected that students will read the contributions we have collected here in conjunction with the appropriate sections of such a 'theory' text.

While each of the chapters was written as a free-standing entity, none the less many of them share common themes and even arguments. It is to be hoped that on finding these resonances and recapitulations, students will come to see sociology as a body of knowledge and endeavour and not as a mere compendium of discrete topics and interests.

R.J.A.
W.W.S.

# Acknowledgements

Table 3.1 on page 52 is reprinted with permission of Macmillan Publishing Company from *Sociological Ambivalence* by Robert K. Merton, copyright © 1976 by The Free Press, a Division of Macmillan Publishing Co. Inc.

Figure 5.1 on page 95 is reprinted with permission of Macmillan Publishing Company from *Outsiders* by Howard S. Becker, copyright © 1961 by The Free Press of Glencoe.

Figure 9.1 on page 177 is reprinted with permission of Oxford University Press from *Power and Poverty* by Peter Bachrach and Morton S. Baratz, copyright © 1970 by Oxford University Press Inc.

Acknowledgments

# Applied Sociological Perspectives

Chapter 1

# Should 'Sex' Really Be 'Gender' – or 'Gender' Really Be 'Sex'?

LIZ STANLEY

## Introduction

Many analyses of the existence of differences and inequalities in society can be seen, somewhat simplistically, to involve a 'nurture' as opposed to a 'nature' interpretation. The 'nurture' analysis argues that such phenomena have social bases and social origins, not 'natural' or biological ones, and even that how we ordinarily understand 'nature' and 'biology' is itself a social construction which changes over time. In arguing this, three main kinds of evidence tend to be used: evidence concerning variations between different cultures, evidence concerning variations over time in one specific culture, and evidence concerning variations within one specific culture at one point in time. As they have grown and developed, there have been marked changes in how the social sciences analyse inequalities. This can be seen particularly clearly in relation to racial inequalities; and here the change has been from a greater reliance on biological, 'nature' arguments to a now general rejection of these in favour of social, 'nurture' ones. A similar kind of change has also been occurring in relation to the treatment of sex differences and inequalities, the subject of this chapter.

It can be accepted without much argument and documentation that 'sex' is indeed a prominent feature in the organisation of society. The degree and nature of separation between 'male' and 'female' characters, roles and activities vary from one society to another, but some degree of separation is a feature of all. Sociologists have often emphasised the fact that this separation of males and females is a form of 'division of labour', and have thus drawn attention to the ways in which male and female roles complement each other: males do the hunting and females the cooking; females do child care and domestic activities and men the non-domestic work, and so forth. Recently, however, this kind of conception has come under question, along with other theoretical accounts which see social divisions as contributing to a harmonious integration of social parts within a unified whole. The consideration of male/female relationships is in the process of being re-conceived, so that the 'specialisation' of men's and women's roles is seen less in terms of complementarity and more in terms of inequality and exploitation.

## DIFFERENCES AND INEQUALITIES

The most basic belief common to all feminists is that relations between the sexes are those of inequality rather than simply differentiation. A system of stratification is involved which persists over time, is systematic and involves a hierarchy between females and males. Indeed, 'belief' in quotation marks is more appropriate, because it is not seen as such within feminism but as an entirely factual and demonstrable statement closed to debate. Critics of feminism have pointed to this as evidence of feminism's rigidity, its fanaticism, and so forth. Of course this misses the point, for this is tantamount to criticising mammals for being warm-blooded, or monetarist economists for thinking that control of the money supply is the key to the control of the economy. In other words, the criticism derives from an essentially different philosophical framework.

What can for the sake of simplicity be referred to as the 'non-feminist' viewpoint includes at least three major arguments concerning women's inequality. The first denies that inequality exists. Women may be treated *differently*, this argument suggests, but their contribution is *equally valued*. Here the example of childbirth and child-rearing as a valued women's contribution is frequently contrasted with men's contribution to the world of work. The second states that women *are* unequal, but *necessarily* so. This is because women are seen to be innately and biologically different, and this leads them into a style of life which is unequal. Here arguments about sex differences in brain structure and functioning, in various psychological attributes and in particular intelligence, are frequently used. The third considers both sex differences and sex inequalities outside the frame of reference adopted, which is concerned with the sex- and gender-free aspects of social life. Here ideas about science and the like are frequently to be met with.

Making a direct rejoinder to these arguments is rarely productive. And so, rather than trying to do so, it seems more useful to turn to an outline of the evidence and arguments used by feminists in identifying and analysing inequalities. These involve, among others, those (1) involved in paid employment, (2) arising from the nature of domestic labour and child care and their relations to production, (3) resulting from the relation to power and politics as traditionally defined, (4) within the educational and examination system, (5) affecting health, illness and social welfare as well as (6) those built into the structure of language and (7) into the operations of all the academic disciplines.

The evidence amassed about inequalities experienced by women is now immense; indeed it is so vast that it could not possibly be thoroughly reviewed here. However, this evidence can be reviewed another way, by discussing it in outline around the main dimensions of women's situation analysed by feminism. It is convenient to do so around the distinction which can be drawn between different kinds of unequal treatment: between 'discrimination', 'exploitation' and 'oppression'.

## DISCRIMINATION, EXPLOITATION AND OPPRESSION

'Discrimination' is the singling out of women, both individually and as a group, for unequal and inferior treatment from legal, civil and social rights and possibilities available to men. Here the focus is on the 'equal rights' aspect of feminist analysis. Included here are all legal disadvantages experienced by women by virtue of being women. It focuses on actual practices rather than solely the formal rights that exist, although women's exclusion from these is also and obviously a matter of concern. The civil rights aspect is concerned not only with business practice but also with practice within the public sector, including education. 'Social rights' are much harder to pin down and define; but included here seem to be things which are much less 'rights' and much more possibilities — for example, the possibility of engaging in various social activities without unwanted interference.

'Exploitation' involves the utilisation of discriminatory practices against women, both individually and as a group, in order to obtain disproportionate economic gains for other groups or categories of people. It concentrates primarily on paid employment, but it also includes home work and unpaid forms of work such as housework. Thus the notion of 'gain' here is a broad one and relates to the total workings of the economic system (for example, by relating the role of housework to the workings of the economy more generally). Often the exploitation of women is difficult to separate out from exploitation related to race, for many low-paid women workers come from non-white ethnic groups. However, it is worth pointing out that research in America has established that a pay and promotion hierarchy exists there, with white and then non-white males at the top, and white and then non-white females at the bottom; and it seems likely that a similar situation exists in Britain also.

'Oppression' involves the use of coercion, force and tyranny in order forcibly to constrain women, both individually and as a group. It includes sexual harassment, rape, sexual murder, torture and more everyday acts of violence in the form of batterings. Acts of oppression are acts of social and sexual terrorism in which women's actual and possible behaviours, both as individuals and as members of a group, are policed by the threat and practice of force. This is very often the dimension of women's situation which many people find most difficult to accept the existence of. To a large extent, however, battering and rape have been accepted as real problems in many women's lives; and sexual harassment is being increasingly documented, particularly in relation to paid employment. In addition, from time to time irrefutable instances of mass sexual terrorism against women percolate through to news agencies; however, the mass media often refuse to report these, as in the case of the mass rape of Bangladeshi women, and rape and worse used by men from all sides against women during the Vietnamese conflict.

In practice, the kind of separation between dimensions of women's situation that appears above is not possible. One instance will demonstrate what is meant here. Sexual harassment at work involves oppression; it also involves exploitation, as women's responses can be used to keep them economically as well as socially subservient to the sexually harassing male. As a consequence it can also involve a denial of social and legal and sometimes civil rights as well.

There are, as noted above, those who deny the very existence of such things, but they are, presumably, in a relatively small minority; and the main debate concerns various and different ways of interpreting the nature of causation. Some believe that such things are inevitable and irremediable, for the supposition is that the differentiation between women and men is deeply rooted in biology; and this position is, of course, opposed by those who suppose that sexual differentiation is socially created and therefore mutable. That is, obviously 'biology' *does* figure in human social relationships and *is* consequential for relations between the sexes as well as for other social relations. However, the crucial question concerns precisely what *kind* of part is played by biological factors; and it is to a discussion of this that we now turn.

## The Social Construction of Biology

### THE ARGUMENT

The basic argument is whether 'sex' (our 'maleness' or 'femaleness', the biological basis of sex differentiation) causes 'gender' (culturally ascribed notions about 'femininity' and 'masculinity'), or whether and to what extent 'gender' is a social construction. Two polarised positions on this can be described as 'biological essentialism' and 'social constructionism'. Paradoxically, it has more often been natural scientists working on these questions who have taken an unequivocally social constructionist line, while most academic feminists have occupied the so-called 'middle ground' of arguing for social constructionism which takes place on a biological base.

'Biological essentialism', then, argues that the social roles and psychological attributes of females and males in relation to a whole range of behaviours and personality traits are biologically determined. This position differs from what is known as 'biological reductionism', for the essentialist view is that what exists now is a *direct* product of biological factors still operative, while the reductionist view says they are the *indirect* product of biological factors no longer operative.

The feminist response has identified biological essentialism in the social and natural sciences as importantly involved in the maintenance of 'biology is destiny' ideas within commonsense views on this topic. It is, however, equally possible and equally likely that scientific views are the product of commonsense ones rather than the other way around. The feminist response has thus gone about dismantling what has been seen as 'popular ignorance' with an attack on scientific conservatism and prejudice, through the use of a very wide body of evidence drawn from various disciplines; these main kinds of evidence are now outlined.

## THE EVIDENCE

Previously reference has been made to the fact that fifteen years or so of feminist activity in the social sciences and elsewhere has resulted in a huge amount of work of various kinds. Again, because of this it is impossible fully to account for all the research involved. And so, instead of this, brief overviews are presented of this work under three headings. These are variations between cultures, variations in one culture over time, and variations in one culture at one point in time.

### (1)  Variations between cultures

Here the main body of work is anthropological in origin and concerns a very wide range of different cultures indeed. This evidence suggests that 'sex' forms a universal categorisation in all known societies; and in all known societies it also involves a hierarchy in which it is men and men's activities and attributes which are the more highly valued. Earlier work which had claimed the existence of totally non-stratified societies to a large extent now recants this view and accepts that within it the anthropologist had been 'blind to sex', in the sense of simply 'overlooking' women's inequality.

In addition, anthropological work has pointed out the fascinating and, for feminist theories of women's oppression, crucial fact that within this what is believed to constitute maleness and femaleness is subject to seemingly endless variation. Some of the best examples of this come from the work of Margaret Mead and in particular her *Sex and Temperament in Three Primitive Societies* (1935), where she describes three cultures, all existing in close proximity to each other but which nevertheless have very different constructions of 'gender'.

In addition, there is now an increasing amount of anthropological work which focuses on the different, and not so different, meanings attached to various behaviours in other cultures, which can be used to illustrate similar ones in our own. One example of this is in the work of Yolanda and Robert Murphy among the Mundurucu, where group rape is an explicit and widely used means of controlling women's behaviour (Murphy and Murphy, 1974). Another is in the work of Margery Wolf in rural Taiwan, which examines the role that gossip plays among seemingly powerless women in order to gain power (Wolf, 1974). Both of these examples concern sex-related behaviours which occur in our own culture, but which may be seen and understood very differently in others; and it is precisely from both the similarities *and* the differences that we can learn.

The overall import of this kind of research is that 'gender' is a lot more complex than it at first may appear; that it is variously constructed; and that even the 'same' behaviours may be seen and understood very differently in different cultures. Because of this it has formed a very important plank in feminist writings concerned with 'gender'.

### (2)   Variations in one culture over time
The key discipline involved here is history, and in particular both economic and social history. Within work here two different, and sometimes opposing, strands can be discerned. Perhaps the more significant, certainly in terms of the volume of work available, is that which is concerned with the changes brought about by capitalism in the economic and social roles of women and men.

Sheila Rowbotham's *Hidden from History* deals with the hidden history of women, hidden because mainstream history has not seen women's lives as either significant or interesting (Rowbotham, 1974). It examines changes brought about by capitalist development but also by developments within capitalism. In some ways it exemplifies the central Marxist tenet that in a sense 'gender' as a hierarchy of social value is a product of capitalism. However, in some other respects it just as clearly shows some of the differences between Marxist and Marxist-feminist analysis. For one thing, it is centrally concerned with women's place both in history (and the discipline of history) and in Marxist theory itself. And for another, it is written in a very different style. It deliberately sets out to make its own arguments and even 'facts' redundant, in the sense that it necessarily skims over the surface of the things it discusses; for the failings of history as a discipline have ensured that all that exists, with regard to women's lives, *is* surface.

Rowbotham's work has been superseded as more research has been done on the vast number of issues, problems and very wide time-period touched on in her book. Nevertheless, in a sense its central argument remains alive and flourishing, for whether men and women were different but not 'genders' before capitalism has not been satisfactorily 'answered'. Indeed, the second strand in historical writings illustrates fairly clearly the fact that it is unanswerable in any final sense, for neither question nor 'answer' is to be seen as theory-free. This second strand addresses itself, in a direct sense, to the question of women's and men's situation in pre-capitalist and capitalist periods.

Alan Macfarlane's *The Origins of English Individualism* rejects various of the key Marxist arguments about the nature and origin of capitalism on the basis of very detailed historical researches (Macfarlane, 1978). Macfarlane points out that most of the characeristics associated with 'capitalism' existed in England certainly as far back as the fourteenth century; and therefore that work which dates it as a seventeenth- and eighteenth-century phenomenon in fact results from theoretical imperialism rather than close attention to historical fact. It also deals with, among other things, women's situation in the geographical locations he is concerned with; and emphasises that in the 'pre-capitalist' period women were controlled and the subject of discrimination, but also that they could and did inherit, run businesses, and the like. In other words, their situation was complex, much more complex than Marxist and Marxist-feminist theory usually recognises.

In a quite different vein, Dale Spender's *Women of Ideas* points out that, as far back historically as one cares to research, women's resistance to various aspects of their situation can be found (Spender, 1982). Concerned with finding 'feminist writings', that is, those of women who offered a conscious critique of women's situation as a systematic phenonenon, she establishes that as far back as her research went (the early seventeenth century) organised groups of women were concerned with analysing women's situation as the result of discrimination, exploitation and oppression.

Different again, *The Diaries of Hannah Cullwick*, a Victorian maid-servant, show that the stereotype of the Victorian woman is precisely a stereotype, and a class-based one at that (Stanley, 1984). Hannah Cull-wick was almost entirely 'unwomanly', in the sense that she was im-mensely strong and went freely about the roughest parts of Victorian London without molestation, but also cherished herself as a worker and resisted all attempts to confine her in terms of 'feminine' dress, behaviours and attitudes. Moreover, these diaries make it clear that she was by no means atypical in doing so; and that vast numbers of other Victorian working women lived their lives in a very similar fashion.

The first strand in historical work outlined here stresses uniformity, both within pre-capitalist periods and then within capitalist ones. The second is in seemingly marked contrast, with its stress on variation within any particular period. However, it is useful to note that a tension can be perceived within the first strand, a tension between the empirical material used and the theoretical framework in relation to which this is used. Out of this seems to be coming a 'new generation' of Marxist and Marxist-feminist historical work, which utilises a rather different notion of 'theory' and which is much more dialectical in its approach.

### (3)   *Variations in one culture at one point in time*

There are obvious points of connection between the second of the two strands in historical writings and work which is specific to 'now' in our culture, because in both is to be found evidence of, simply, *variation*. 'Gender' may vary between cultures and over time – but that it varies in the here and now too is the overall conclusion which can be drawn from this body of work.

The idea that there is a sharp biological demarcation of males from females with an associated and automatic segregation of behaviour patterns has come into question as research has revealed that such boundaries are somewhat less sharp and determinate than has been imagined. Women and men are not always nor emphatically distin-guished from one another either biologically or psychologically, though social structures may treat people as though they must be distinguished from one another in sharp and discontinuous ways. 'Intersexuality' is a case in point.

There are various different forms of 'intersexuality' or cases where the sex of someone's upbringing and one or more of their biological sex characteristics do not match. The interlinked characteristics which con-stitute 'biological sex' are: chromosomal constitution, gonadal structure (whether ovaries or testes), morphology of external genitalia, morphology of genital ducts (whether Mullerian or fallopian tubes and uterus, or

Wolffian or vas and prostate), and, sometimes included, hormonal status (preponderance of oestrogens over androgens, or androgens over oestrogens). All these five characteristics are organic; however, hormonal status by itself is an insufficient indicator of intersexuality as there is an enormous range in relative distributions of oestrogens and androgens throughout the population.

At least fifteen different forms of intersexuality exist. However, the best known are probably 'Kleinfelter's syndrome' and 'Turner's syndrome'. Kleinfelter's syndrome involves chromosomally XXy males with undescended testes, vaginal openings which are blind-ended and a normal 'male' hormonal status although the androgens are interpreted in the brain as though they were oestrogens; and people with this syndrome function as normal although infertile and period-less females. Turner's syndrome involves chromosomally XO people, brought up as ordinary but 'slow' females but who in fact do not have a 'true' chromosomal sex as 50 per cent of the genetic sex material is absent.

Cases of intersexuality, particularly Kleinfelter's syndrome and other cases involving perfectly ordinarily functioning 'males' and 'females', have come to the attention of the medical profession primarily because of infertility, lack of menstrual periods, or more general 'sex problems' such as the experience of discomfort during heterosexual intercourse for people with Kleinfelter's. Clinics dealing with such cases are the 'practice' of which medical cytogenetics (research into the genetic structure of cells) is the 'theory'. In the early days of counselling, intersexed people were sometimes told that they were 'really' a different sex from that they experienced themselves as. Reactions to this included nervous breakdown and suicide. Since then counselling has changed and now it is likely that careful questioning will try to elicit whether 'patients' are happy members of their 'sex' of upbringing. If they are then they will often not be told that they are 'really' another 'sex' but instead that they are infertile for physiological reasons of various kinds. For the last fifteen years or so medical cytogenetics textbooks too have made it perfectly clear that for these natural scientists 'gender', social sex and psychological sex, are all entirely matters of upbringing. And this happened at a time, it should be remembered, when even to hint as much in the social sciences was to be seen as 'unscientific'.

The implications of this natural science research/practice are perfectly clear – that 'sex' is important, but not as important as social factors. However, exactly how 'gender' is produced is still a matter for great conjecture. The kind of natural science work just outlined filtered through to the social sciences only comparatively recently and disputes still rage between people who differently interpret its meaning.

*Applied Sociological Perspectives*

In particular, whether and to what extent psychological sex differences are a product of biological sex differences in the functioning of the brain has been one site of dispute. Corinne Hutt, a physiological psychologist, has argued that the evidence both of cytogenetics and of intersexuality instead shows the deterministic result of biological sex (Hutt, 1972). Thus it can be seen that Hutt interprets the same evidence very differently from the view of it outlined above and that current among practitioners. However, it is worth noting that her argument tends to focus on andro-genised females (that is, organically normal females who have been subject to large doses of androgens while in the womb) and uses as a control a group of Turner's syndrome females, themselves decidedly atypical, 'passive' and super-stereotypically 'feminine'.

A key feature of Hutt's argument is that the brain is itself sex differ-entiated and it is this which gives rise to many differences in psychological and so social functioning. However, Hutt takes as a given the existence of a wide range of psychological sex differences, a 'fact' disputed in other work. Of particular importance here has been the work of Maccoby and Jacklin, which has reviewed the then-existing psychological sex research literature (Maccoby and Jacklin, 1975). Many interesting points are made by Maccoby & Jacklin concerning the quality and focus of much of the research, but also about the main overall conclusions to be drawn from it. Generally, they suggest, almost all the popularly supposed sex differences in psychological functioning could not be demonstrated in research, which often tried very hard indeed to find them. They argue that the only psychological sex differences which research supports the existence of are four in number. First, females have greater verbal abilities than males. However, this difference begins to show only at around the age of 11; and so its often assumed biological basis must be doubted. Secondly, males have greater visual-spatial abilities than females. However, this difference begins to show only at around the age of 13; and so the often assumed biological basis of this too must be doubted. Thirdly, males have greater mathematical abilities than females. This too only manifests itself at around the age of 12; and its biological basis is again in doubt. Fourthly, males are more aggressive than females. This difference begins to manifest itself at around the age of 3, when social play begins.

Maccoby and Jacklin are willing to consider the possibility that this last psychological difference between males and females may have a biological basis. However, they also note that its existence neither means that all males are more aggressive than all females nor that male aggression is immutable. In other words, they suggest that although biology may be important it can be changed, modified and indeed completely overturned in particular societies or particular groups within a larger society (an example might be men who are Quakers and women who are political terrorists in our own society).

## SOME CONCLUSIONS?

Both biological essentialists and social constructionists claim that the weight of evidence is on *their* side; and this highlights something of the practical difficulties involved in the operations of science within the social sciences. That is, it is most certainly easy to find evidence which categorically supports the essentialist position but it is just as easy to find categorical rejections of it; and similarly so with the constructionist position.

That being said, it seems that the general trend has been towards a much greater acceptance of constructionist ideas about biological sex. Paradoxically, constructionism is found more within certain of the natural sciences involved in research and counselling in this area of practice than within the social sciences. And interestingly, a large number of academic feminists have eschewed constructionism in favour of the 'middle ground' of arguing that social construction takes place, but on a given biological base of physiologically determined traits, attributes, and so forth. This is a variation within the position earlier referred to as 'biological reductionism'. Nevertheless, the overall trend is still that 'sex' should really be considered as, to a large extent, 'gender'. Perhaps ideas about 'normal science' and what is and is not thought to be professionally acceptable in the social sciences play a part here, for while much of academic feminism is to be found in this middle ground, feminists outside academic life are to a large extent constructionists.

Since the differentiation between females and males is seen as something socially sustained, much research concerned with explaining this has emphasised the 'coercive' aspect of socialisation, the extent to which gender identities are *imposed* upon people, through internalisation by the child during primary socialisation and reinforcement by social control mechanisms. Power certainly operates in the construction and allocation of sexual identities, but the next section suggests that such an interpretation of it is not only too crude but also sets up a particular reading of the nature of interconnection between 'gender', 'sex' and 'biology' which can be similarly characterised.

## 'Biology', Rationality and 'Sex' as a 'Natural Order'

### SCIENTIFIC AND EVERYDAY RATIONALITIES

In the last section some of the now vast body of evidence which has been used in debates concerning the 'sex/gender controversy' has been outlined; and the general tenor of conclusions to be drawn from this were summarised as an increasing acceptance that 'sex' should really be construed as 'gender'. However, 'gender' is conceptualised in much social science theory and research as a set of 'internalised' traits, attributes, behaviours, and so forth. Much recent work on 'socialisation', whether by feminists or not, has focused on what is known as 'primary socialisation' (sometimes referred to as 'sex role socialisation'); and is concerned with the period from birth until the age of about 4 or 5, during which, it is assumed, 'gender' is somehow 'laid down' through the pattern of interaction between the child and its social and physical environment. Much of this work has been located within psychology or a sociology very heavily influenced by psychology. There is, however, another sociological way of understanding 'gender' and around which some extremely interesting work has been carried out. Some of this will be outlined later; and around this an alternative way of understanding the persistence of biological considerations will be discussed.

Within the general movement of social scientific opinion towards various versions of social constructionism there has been a sometimes implicit and sometimes explicit judgement of 'popular opinion', with its continued support of essentialism. Essentially this support is depicted as irrational or perhaps 'pre-scientific', for it is seen to fly in the face of scientific facts of the kind earlier outlined. However, such assessments of 'popular' as against 'scientific' not only treat both as having the same purposes and goals but also treat the realm of the scientific as by definition more advanced in its understandings, modes of procedure, and so forth.

Instead of seeing everyday and scientific theorising as competing forms of explanation, the philosopher Schutz prefers to see them as different attitudes, each with different purposes, procedures and desired outcomes (Schutz, 1967). In everyday life, our 'commonsense knowledge' is practical and contingent on what Schutz calls 'projects', our concern with various features of the here and now rather than the pursuit of 'truth'. In this sense scientific knowledge is not 'practical' at all because it is not dependent on everyday knowledge and standards but those specific to 'science'. Behaving in a 'scientific' way in everyday life, unless acknowledged and licensed as such through the recognition that this is indeed 'science', can lead to behaviour being seen as odd, eccentric, or even as a kind of madness.

An alternative way of seeing and understanding the persistence of biological invocations in relation to 'sex' and 'gender' is to see these as part of everyday theorising and thus as practical, contingent, purposeful and rational, rather than as the result of ignorance and confusion which will dissolve on receipt of 'scientific fact'. 'Gender' is conceptualised in psychological, rather than sociological, terms in most of the relevant literature. That is, 'gender' is seen as internalised behaviours, traits and the like which are then later 'released' into various social situations.

This can be seen as a kind of 'psychological essentialism', which may not be biologically determined but is certainly deterministic. However, sociology sees social life as *inter*subjective, as the result of negotiation and interaction, and not as the release of something 'inside'. It argues that the social world is one shared in common between us and to be seen as a human social construction rather than as a multiplicity of inner worlds. Thus the way into an alternative understanding of biological invocations is through reconceptualising 'gender' in more sociological terms.

### 'GENDER' IN SOCIOLOGICAL TERMS

In *Gender Advertisements* Erving Goffman examines various features by which 'gender' is pictorially constructed in a range of media advertisements (Goffman, 1976). However, as well as demonstrating the very stark way in which 'gender' and 'power' overlay each other in these, Goffman also emphasises that advertisements deal with an obviously unreal world, unreal in various ways. One feature of its unreality is the starkness of 'gender advertisements'; and Goffman argues two things out of this. One is that 'gender' in this form is an atypical feature of social interaction; most everyday behaviours are equivocal, and stark and unequivocal instances of 'gender' and of other forms of behaviour are rare. The other is that the atypicality of 'gender' does not mean its unimportance; indeed rather the reverse. By presenting images which stand out in the way that these do, gender advertisements mark out 'ideals' and these feed back into the construction of 'gender' in everyday life.

A discussion of male–female, and parent–child, conversational interactions by Candice West and Don Zimmerman in 'Women's Place in Everyday Talk' (West and Zimmerman, 1977) notes both the interactional construction of 'gender' and also its close similarity to other forms of power. West and Zimmerman note in particular that men in conversation with women, and adults in conversation with children, 'do power' in comparable ways through interruptions and other ways of disturbing turn-taking sequences in conversational structure.

Both Goffman and West and Zimmerman stress the interactional construction of 'gender' rather than its release into social situations and that the specific mechanisms by which this occurs can be analysed by close attention to detailed pieces of recorded interaction. Harold Garfinkel's work concerned with 'Agnes', an apparently intersexed person, is ostensibly in a different vein (Garfinkel, 1967). One of Garfinkel's concerns is with the role that 'passing', or 'achieving and securing . . . rights to live as a normal, natural female', plays in Agnes's life. However, an implication of Goffman's and West and Zimmerman's work is that 'passing', with its attendant possibility of failure, is a feature of 'gender' for 'normal' males and females also, although the 'taken-for-grantedness' of interactional response somewhat differs, along with the specific consequences of failure.

Garfinkel treats Agnes as an intersexed person concerned with the management of what she perceives to be her natural, original, real 'sex', and only residually as someone who might be actually involved in the production (through the use of hormones) of her 'real sex' attributes; and indeed this possibility becomes more residual over time. However, an appendix deals with Agnes's disclosure to Garfinkel's medical collaborator that she was in fact not intersexed. In essentials, as Garfinkel notes, the practical accomplishment by Agnes of her intersexuality was achieved in a specific setting through the establishment of a determinate account of 'Agnes and her past', whereby alternative accounts are ruled out.

In this work, the usually symbiotic relationship of 'sex' and 'gender' (and whatever the culturally specific content of 'gender') is demonstrated. By establishing claims to her 'real sex', Agnes also achieves a determinate reading by others of her behaviours as 'gender' (and this in its turn reinforces the claims to her 'real sex') rather than 'effeminacy' or other terms which deny a correspondence between them and 'real sex'. In a sense, then, 'gender' 'works' because of the assumption of various links, most importantly between 'gender' and 'sex', and between 'sex' and ideas about 'natural orders'.

### 'SEX' AS A 'NATURAL ORDER'

The idea of a 'natural order' is one which includes the notion that what is 'natural' is also given, fixed, determined and non-volitional, and is thus *not* socially constructed, changing and volitional. 'Sex' construed as a natural order is thus conceptualised in ways which cut out the possibility of conceptualising it as 'really' 'gender', really socially constructed and so mutable. Moreover, implicit within ideas about 'natural orders' is a way of treating and understanding alternative, non-natural, conceptualisations. These are indeed seen as 'non-natural', as unnatural in the sense that they fly in the face of what is self-evidently fixed, given, and so forth.

'Sex' as a natural order includes more than ideas about our 'biological selves' and our social behaviours and attributes. It also importantly includes ideas about people as sexual beings in the sense of 'doing sex', 'having sex'. That is, the 'naturalness' of 'sex' extends to, indeed crucially includes, sex as innately heterosexual reproductive behaviours. 'Sex' in the strictly biological sense is thereby not only an outcome of 'doing sex' but also what this is naturally 'for'; and a number of interesting pieces of work have taken up this idea and explored it by looking at sexual behaviours and 'sexual roles' and their relationship to 'gender'.

At this point it becomes possible to return to the question of the persistence of biological invocations in the explanation of sex differences and sex inequalities; and to examine this around the ideas briefly summarised above.

Biological invocations persist because these are rooted in a supremely rational way of interpreting and constructing what it is to be a man or a woman in our society. Commonsensically 'gender' is instead seen as 'sex' because in a practical sense this explains a great deal more, and is much more useful, than the other way around. Ordinarily, normally, typically, 'sex' has a great deal more explicatory power, for it is linked in with ideas about 'sexual orientation' and thus into 'doing sex' as reproductive behaviour. This 'correspondence theory', as it is known, states that ordinarily a correspondence is assumed between 'sex', 'gender', 'sexual orientation' and 'reproductively sexual behaviour' with, standing behind these constituent elements, the notion that these constitute a 'natural order'. In a sense these form an 'impermeable theory', one not amenable to modification through, for example, new evidence. It constitutes an internally consistent self-fulfilling prophecy in which 'contrary evidence' is instead treated as a confirmation of the theory because its very existence demonstrates its own unnaturalness and thus irrationality.

Here it is instructive to consider that, very frequently, feminists are construed as failed 'real women', who hate men and want to castrate them, and who deny not only biology as related to 'sex' but also as related to the assumed ideas that 'doing sex' is necessarily penetrational and that childbirth and child care are necessarily central in women's lives. In this can be seen the implicit argument that feminists deny the natural order of 'sex' and are thus not only unnatural in doing so, but unnatural in themselves. 'Sex' as a natural order is also an order involving *power* and its distribution; and feminists and feminism threaten the present distribution of power within this order. Responding to the message of feminism in terms already set within the notion of a 'natural order', however, removes this threat because one consequence is that the debate opened up by feminism is thereby depoliticised by being taken out of the realm of the social and mutable and back into the realm of the natural and immutable.

The recent growth of interest in the social position of women is obviously, from what has been said above, connected with the rise of the feminist movement; and it is feminists who have made much of the running in attempting to explain the persistence of sexual differences and their associated inequalities. In the remainder of this chapter some of the principal theories that have arisen in this connection are outlined. The failure of sociology and other sciences to give much attention to the position of women until feminists did so is something which might be seen as a consequence, not merely of sexist oversight, but of the intrinsic nature of social science thinking; and the female and feminist critiques of the social sciences are outlined.

## Feminist Theories of Women's Oppression

Until comparatively recently feminist theoretical work has been concentrated on the production and refinement of explanations of *why* women are oppressed. The theories touched on here are thus essentially causal, sometimes monocausal, theories. Their prime concern is with establishing the cause(s) of oppression as the necessary first step in removing it. Each of them is concerned with 'gender' because each challenges the 'biology is destiny' argument, although some do so only indirectly.

### MARXIST-FEMINIST AND SIMILAR THEORIES

The inclusion of Firestone's (1970) work in this group of theories will surprise some, for it is usually seen as the main example of radical feminist work. Explaining its presence here provides a useful introduction to these theories. Firestone identifies the cause of women's oppression as childbirth because from this flows various social consequences, particularly the assumptions that women are incapacitated by childbirth and that they must be responsible for child care. Her 'answer' is to argue for the necessity of different forms of childbirth outside the female body.

Thus far Firestone's work has little in common with Marxism-feminism; but its style and form introduce points of commonality. Her intention is to 'turn Marx on his head' by using the Marxist dialectic and historical materialism, but replacing 'class' with 'sex class'. Apart from her use of 'the Marxist method' her work has other features in common with Marxism-feminism. It has often been criticised as 'biological reductionism'. However, as Firestone herself notes, identifying biological sex as the first and primary division of labour started with Marx and Engels. In addition there are grounds for suggesting that historical materialism itself constitutes a form of biological reductionism.

The notion of a 'sexual division of labour' provides a key logical link between Marxism and Marxism-feminism, for it suggests that it is essential to capitalism that there are 'sexed places' within the market and not just 'empty places'. Without such a link Marxism-feminism would be simply Marxism. There is a recognition that in pre-capitalist periods a sexual division of labour existed, although one without the value judgements about 'men's-' and 'women's-work' found in capitalism. But explaining *why* it was that men and women in pre-capitalist times carried out different economic tasks requires reference to some kind of biological explanation (as with Engels's work, 1972, which sees the motivation as economic but the basis as biological), and thus to biological reductionism.

## LIBERAL FEMINIST AND SOCIALISATION THEORIES

This group of theories is often criticised for failing to provide any explanation of women's oppression. This is because 'causal explanation' is usually defined as necessarily including an historical dimension. However, a clear, although in a narrow sense 'ahistorical', exposition of the causal origins of women's oppression is contained within them. The notion of 'socialisation' provides the central explanation of the perpetuation of oppression. Within its constituent practices children learn prescribed and proscribed social roles, including those pertaining to gender, and these are later enacted in social life. Of course this notion of 'origins' is different from that found in the first group of theories, for it locates a different kind of 'past' in which origins are to be found, focusing on pre-birth, pre-infancy and infancy.

These are essentially learning theories, and their utilisation of pre-birth explanations may seem out of character. Two comments may be of use here. One is that many writings of this kind hedge their bets — they retain a minimal notion of 'sex' as a causal agent; and this was earlier referred to as a 'middle ground' position between constructionism and essentialism. The other involves the idea that various factors outside the womb can influence what goes on within it and thus the later social life of its occupant.

## RADICAL FEMINIST THEORIES

A common thread in this group of theories is their distinctive interpretation of 'oppression' and 'responsibility'. 'Oppression' involves both the idea and the threat of sexual force as a means of keeping women 'in line'. Power is identified as the knowledge that force exists and will be used if necessary; but for as long as power is effective power then force need exist only at the level of threat. So far this analysis has much in common with radical analyses of power within the social sciences. However, radical feminism focuses on sexual power while these social science analyses seem to focus on everything but. Radical feminist analysis also sees men as responsible for women's oppression.

Radical feminism argues that women are oppressed by men in the sense that although it may not be the majority of men who 'work' the system of oppression, nevertheless by not actively opposing it the rest of men passively support it and so permit it to continue. Some men may indeed oppose women's oppression in a variety of ways, but until all men as a group do so the argument remains valid.

### OTHER ACADEMIC FEMINIST WORK

Not all feminist work is concerned with the refinement of causal explanations of women's oppression. Some is concerned with 'filling in the gaps' in social science work, which has almost exclusively focused on men and men's activities. And some has taken the form of analyses of the nature and practice of the social sciences themselves. One of the first examples of this was the 'female critique', which argued that so-called 'science' either ignored women or else misrepresented women's lives by examining them around sexist assumptions and ideas. But as its proponents themselves emphasised, the 'female critique' was 'normal science' in its aims: it retained allegiance to traditional and conventional ideas about the role and form of the social sciences.

There are other and more fundamental criticisms to be made of the 'science' view of social science than appear in the 'female critique'. These are often referred to as the 'critique of positivism'. Some, indeed a growing number, of academic feminists now support and add to this more fundamentally critical body of ideas; and their work has been termed a 'feminist critique' of the social sciences. It is also useful to note that feminists outside academic life since the early days of this present feminist movement have adopted a more radical stance than is represented in the 'female critique'.

## References: Chapter 1

Engels, F. (1972), *The Origin of Family, Private Property and the State* (London: Lawrence & Wishart).

Firestone, S. (1970), *The Dialectic of Sex* (St Albans: Paladin).

Garfinkel, H. (1967), *Studies in Ethnomethodology* (Englewood Cliffs, NJ: Prentice-Hall).

Goffman, E. (1976), *Gender Advertisements* (London: Macmillan).

Hutt, C. (1972), *Males and Females* (Harmondsworth: Penguin).

Maccoby, E., and Jacklin, C. (1975), *The Psychology of Sex Differences* (London: OUP).

Macfarlane, A. (1978), *The Origins of English Individualism* (Oxford: Blackwell).

Mead, M. (1935), *Sex and Temperament in Three Primitive Societies* (London: George Routledge).

Murphy, Y., and Murphy, R. (1974), *Women of the Forest* (New York: Columbia University Press).

Rowbotham, S. (1974), *Hidden from History* (London: Pluto Press).

Schutz, A. (1967), *Collected Papers Volume 1: The Problem of Social Reality* (The Hague: Martinus Nijhoff).

Spender, D. (1982), *Women of Ideas* (London: Routledge & Kegan Paul).

Stanley, L. (1984), *The Diaries of Hannah Cullwick* (London: Virago).

West, C., and Zimmerman, D. (1977), 'Women's place in everyday talk', *Social Problems*, vol. 24, pp. 521–44.

Wolf, M. (1974), *Women and the Family in Rural Taiwan* (Stanford, Calif.: Stanford University Press).

# Further Reading

Archer, J., and Lloyd, B. (1982), *Sex and Gender* (Harmondsworth: Penguin).

Delamont, S. (1980), *The Sociology of Women* (London: Allen & Unwin).

Oakley, A. (1981), *Subject: Women* (London: Fontana).

Sayers, J. (1982), *Biological Politics* (London: Tavistock).

A further useful source of documentary material is the *Equal Opportunity Commission*, Quay Street, Manchester.

## FEMINIST THEORIES OF WOMEN'S OPPRESSION

### *(a)   Marxist-feminist and similar theories*

Mitchell, J. (1971), *Women's Estate* (Harmondsworth: Penguin).

Rowbotham, S. (1973), *Woman's Consciousness, Man's World* (Harmondsworth: Penguin).

### *(b)   Liberal feminist and socialisation theories*

Friedan, B. (1963), *The Feminine Mystique* (Harmondsworth: Penguin).

Greer, G. (1970), *The Female Eunuch* (London: Granada).

Oakley, A. (1972), *Sex, Gender and Society* (London: Temple Smith).

### *(c)   Radical feminist theories*

Brownmiller, S. (1975), *Against Our Will: Men, Women and Rape* (Harmondsworth: Penguin).

Daly, M. (1978), *Gyn/Ecology* (London: Women's Press).

Millett, K. (1969), *Sexual Politics* (London: Abacus).

Chapter 2

# Social Stratification

## PETE MARTIN

### Introduction: the Universality of Inequalities

To the layman, it often seems as if sociologists are obsessed with the subject of social class. The topics of inequality and social stratification were among the central concerns of the founding fathers of the subject, and modern social researchers have displayed a continuing preoccupation with such matters. A steady stream of research reports and journal articles has appeared, dealing with such topics as the distribution of wealth and power, class structure and social mobility; in Britain, the last few years have seen the publication of the Oxford Mobility Study – one of the largest-ever investigations into aspects of inequality in British society.

So, before discussing the results of some of these studies, it is appropriate to consider briefly why the topics encompassed by the term 'social stratification' should have become so important for sociologists. The basic idea is simple enough: in all known societies there is some measure of inequality in the way that scarce and valued resources are distributed. Most obviously, there is a great deal of variation in the amounts of wealth held by individuals, in the power they have to influence others and in the prestige they enjoy in the community. Thus the image of societies as stratified – like layers of rock – suggests the pattern of inequalities which may be observed, with the rich and powerful at the top, the poor and helpless at the bottom and a variety of layers and levels in between. Such a hierarchy is often evoked in everyday speech, as when we hear talk of the 'middle class', the 'elite', the 'lower orders', or our 'station in life'.

Why, then, are these patterns of inequality of such great interest to sociologists? First, as we have already suggested, they seem to be universal: a fundamental aspect of all known societies. Even in modern industrial countries where there is, in principle, enough wealth to ensure that everyone has an adequate level of nourishment, clothing and housing, it has become evident that extremes of wealth and poverty are a persistent feature of the social order.

A second reason why sociologists have been so concerned with social stratification arises from one of their basic perspectives on human society. The vast majority of people are remarkably similar in terms of their biological characteristics and physical attributes; our societies, on the other hand, are to a considerable extent organised on the basis of elaborate systems of differences and distinctions which we employ in deciding what 'type' of person we are dealing with. (It can make a very great deal of difference if your skin is slightly darker than someone else's, if your IQ score is 95 rather than 105, or if you call yourself an 'Arab' rather than a 'Jew'.) The making of such distinctions is at the heart of the process which has come to be known as social differentiation. In theory, social differentiation could be based on any criteria whatsoever – from trivial physical characteristics to deeply held beliefs. But in practice, as members of particular cultures we learn to make some distinctions rather than others. Those based on age, sex, economic class, race and religion have been especially prevalent. Processes of differentiation may occur informally, when we describe a person as 'elderly', for example, or formally, as when someone achieves the status of 'graduate' or 'colonel'.

For the purposes of sociological analysis, patterns of social stratification may be regarded as processes of social differentiation which have become institutionalised. That is, certain ways of distinguishing between people have become established as valid or appropriate, and the resulting processes of differentiation have become part of the normative structure of a society. Thus, the characteristics of the stratification system in any society largely reflect the sort of criteria on which institutionalised social differentiation is based. In modern British society we are accustomed to talking of social stratification in terms of 'social classes' based largely on economic differences, but, in other times and places, stratification has been based mainly on other criteria such as race, religion, or age. And some pattern of stratification based on sex seems to be a characteristic of most societies (cf. Chapter 1 above).

The image of societies as stratified like layers of rock, while a useful metaphor, should not be taken too literally. It is apparent, for example, that social classes are not fixed or self-contained entities which can be easily described or measured. As we shall suggest below, there is a good deal of 'social mobility' both between and within the conventional class categories, and any attempt to specify the boundaries of a class presents some tricky problems. Moreover, the nature of social classes, and their relationships to each other, are liable to change and transformation. In Karl Marx's classic account, social change was seen largely in terms of the inherent conflicts between classes. Whereas in feudal societies the nobility was dominant by virtue of its possession of land, the development of industrial production greatly reduced the importance of land as a factor in the creation of wealth, and generated a new ruling group – the capitalist class – whose ownership of manufacturing industries gave it control over the predominant sector of the economy. Moreover, industrial production itself gave rise to further changes in the pattern of stratification: far fewer people worked on the land, many more became industrial wage-workers, and – later – wholly new groups of administrators, managers and technical specialists emerged. So not only is there considerable movement between the 'layers' of the stratification hierarchy, but these layers themselves are liable to expand and contract, change places, emerge from nowhere and disappear altogether.

In Marx's view, of course, changes in the stratification pattern of a society were, ultimately, a consequence of changes in its 'mode of production'. But his general account also demonstrates that such changes may come about either as a result of some people's deliberate efforts to pursue their interests, or the inability of others to defend theirs. Political parties, for example, are organisations pursuing certain policies or defending particular interests. Classically, this is illustrated by the opposition between those promoting the interests of labour, on the one hand, and capital, on the other. It is evident that the outcome of their perpetual struggle will have a considerable influence on the pattern of stratification: for example, in determining the relative shares of wealth which accrue to workers and their employers. More generally, and this is a point to which we will return, it seems that interest groups tend to form on the basis of the criteria of social differentiation mentioned above.

Whereas a Marxian approach to stratification emphasises the economic basis of social classes, some sociologists – following Max Weber – have argued that the other criteria of social differentiation may be equally important. Such 'status' factors as age, sex, religion and race may give rise to interests which cut across the fundamental lines of class division. Moreover, such factors may be important in providing individuals with a sense of identity: thus a woman may see herself as a Catholic or a mother, for example, rather than as a wage-worker; or a lad may prefer to project his status as a 'United supporter' rather than that of unemployed. So some Marxists have seen such identities as aspects of 'false consciousness', which prevent people from appreciating the real nature of their economic position. The important sociological point, however, is that such identifications may be a source of the ideas and beliefs which influence people's actions, regardless of whether they are correct or not.

It is evident, too, that people's interests may predispose them to think about matters such as social class in significantly different ways. Academic researchers are no exception: there is no precise definition of 'social class' which everyone will accept. Indeed, the very idea of a 'class structure' depends on the imposition of certain categories on a complex and constantly changing social world, in accordance with the assumptions and preconceptions of the analyst.

Finally, returning to the theme with which we began, it will be apparent that the sociological evidence concerning stratification and patterns of inequality is somewhat at odds with political ideologies which emphasise the virtues of a more equal or even egalitarian society. Anthropological studies have cast considerable doubt that there is a harmonious and relatively egalitarian condition, to which we may some day revert: even the simplest societies display quite complex patterns of stratification. Nor does it seem, as studies of state socialist societies have shown, that the abolition of private property inevitably leads to a just and equal social order. There is also evidence, some of which we discuss below, suggesting that even quite deliberate attempts to reduce inequalities in Western capitalist societies have been remarkably ineffective. This last point has been a persistent theme in much recent research. The coming of the so-called 'affluent society' did not produce the trend towards equality that many had predicted. But it also seemed clear that advanced capitalist societies were not displaying the process of 'polarisation' into two opposed social classes that was implied by the classic Marxist model.

A great deal of recent sociological research, then, has been concerned with the investigation of social stratification in modern industrial societies; with trends in the distribution of income and wealth, with poverty, social mobility and the overall 'shape' of the class structure. It is with such topics that we shall be concerned in the remainder of this chapter.

## Explaining Social Inequality: The Functionalist Tradition

Since some form of social stratification is an important feature of every known society, it would seem appropriate to explain inequality in terms of functionalist theory. After all, the basic premiss of functionalism is that regularly recurring patterns of social activity are maintained because they make some contribution to, or fulfil some function in, the overall working of a society. What positive contributions might patterns of inequality make to the functioning of societies? In contrast to egalitarian political theorists, functionalists argued that inequality is inevitable and necessary in societies primarily because it motivates people to try to achieve the most functionally important positions, which are the most highly rewarded ones. It is, they argue, vital for society as a whole that such positions are filled by sufficiently talented and capable people. So stratification is, in the words of Davis and Moore, 'an unconsciously evolved device' (1967, p. 48) by which such people are led to compete for the top jobs, lured by the prospect of greater wealth and prestige. Conversely, less talented people will be progressively eliminated in the competition, and will end up in occupations more suited to their abilities. In this way, then, a rough equivalence is assumed to be established between individuals' abilities and the functional importance of the jobs they do.

As applied to modern industrial societies, the functional theory of stratification seems at first sight to be quite plausible, though, as we shall see presently, further scrutiny reveals some major difficulties. It is undeniable that there is a broad range of inequality in the distribution of wealth, income and prestige, and that a large-scale talent competition is organised through the institutions of formal education. Moreover, there is a positive correlation between the level of a person's educational qualifications and his or her occupational level, in so far as that is indicated by income and social prestige. However, as we hinted above, the results of detailed studies have not been particularly favourable to the funtionalist interpretation. This can best be illustrated by considering certain major implications of the theory.

## THE DISTRIBUTION OF INCOME AND WEALTH

It is implicit in the functional theory of stratification that the development of modern industrial societies will produce a considerable reduction in the extremes of wealth and poverty, and a trend towards the concentration of incomes around the middle of the range. First, the theory assumes that the distribution of rewards and benefits is principally the result of competition in the labour market. So eventually, sufficient people will have been motivated to obtain qualifications to create a surplus of candidates for the most highly rewarded positions. According to market principles, this excess of supply over demand will reduce the rewards offered by such positions. On the other hand, organisations which depend on people doing unpleasant and unpopular jobs will have to offer greater inducements for people to do them. In the long run, then, such processes will reduce high rates and increase low ones.

Secondly, the functional theory suggests that modern industrial societies are increasingly dependent on a labour force which is much more skilled than that required in earlier phases of industrial development, when the major need was for physical strength or for docile machine-minders. It is estimated that before the First World War more than three-quarters of the British labour force were in manual work; the data collected for the Oxford Mobility Study indicated that by the 1970s the figure may have fallen to around 45 per cent (Goldthorpe *et al.*, 1980, p. 44). Hence a much greater proportion of the labour force is now in intermediate and middle-class occupations, and it was argued that this change in the shape of the occupational structure would be reflected in the distribution of incomes.

However, it is now clear that, although certain processes of redistribution have occurred, there is little evidence of a significant trend towards greater quality of incomes. The Royal Commission on the Distribution of Income and Wealth (Cmnd 7595, 1979) estimated that in 1949 the top 10 per cent of income-earners received 33 per cent of all income; by 1977 this had fallen to 26 per cent. But, significantly in the present context, the share of income going to the bottom 50 per cent remained fairly constant, at around 25 per cent over this period. In other words, any losses suffered by the top 10 per cent were offset by gains made by the next 40 per cent. Overall, the Commission concluded that 'if the decline in the share of the top 1% is ignored, the shape of the distribution is not greatly different in 1976–77 from what it was in 1949', and that it 'shows a remarkable stability from year to year' (ibid., p. 17). Moreover, it does not appear that income tax policy made any significant difference to the shape of the distribution: in 1976–7, for example, the lowest-paid 10 per cent received 2.5 per cent of all income before tax, and 3 per cent after tax.

Similar conclusions have been reached by those who have investigated poverty. As Noble puts it: 'Over 6 million people were living on or below supplementary benefit level in 1977 and almost another 4 million were within 20 per cent of it. On this official measure then, at a conservative estimate almost a fifth of the population could be considered to be in poverty or on the margin of it' (Noble, 1981, p. 254). Such figures reinforce the arguments of those who have suggested that most poverty is not the result of 'exceptional circumstances' such as illness or unemployment. As A. B. Atkinson has put it, poverty is a 'normal expectation' for many old-age pensioners, low-paid workers and single-parent families. Moreover, as both unemployment and the proportion of retired people in the population have increased considerably, these 'structural' causes of poverty can be expected to become even more important. Atkinson's conclusion is uncompromising: 'After the social security legislation of the past seventy years, one might have expected to see a considerable decline in the numbers of those for whom poverty was a normal expectation, and that it would only remain a problem for those with exceptional needs, but this has not happened' (Atkinson, 1975, p. 201).

The question of poverty inevitably leads us to consider the manner in which wealth is distributed. As in the case of incomes, it does seem at first sight that there has been a considerable reduction in the extent to which the ownership of wealth is concentrated in the hands of a small minority. It has been estimated by Noble, for example, that the proportion of total personal wealth owned by the richest 1 per cent of the British population has fallen from over 60 per cent in the mid-1920s to less than 25 per cent in the late 1970s. However, closer examination of the data suggests that this trend may not be as far-reaching as it seems. It is evident, in fact, that a great deal of the redistribution of wealth has occurred within the richer strata of society: thus the proportion held by the top 10 per cent was still as high as 58 per cent in 1978. And there is very little evidence of a major trend towards redistribution outside the top 25 per cent of wealth-owners. The share of this group was 87 per cent in 1966 and 83 per cent in 1978. Even more striking is the fact that the poorer 50 per cent of the population owned 3.5 per cent of personal wealth in 1966, and 5 per cent in 1978. Slight changes there may have been, but hardly an inexorable trend towards equality. Indeed, having reviewed the available data, Noble concludes that the redistribution among the richer half of the population is primarily the result of a decline in the value of stocks and shares (which belong overwhelmingly to the rich), in relation to the increasing value of houses (which are a major component of 'smaller fortunes'), and the simultaneous expansion of home ownership. Whereas less than 10 per cent of householders were owner-occupiers in 1914, the figure for 1979 was 55 per cent (Noble, 1981, pp. 244–5).

But while possession of a house is indeed an important element in a family's wealth, as Noble points out this does not give the owner significant economic power. Further, research has shown that only a small minority of the very rich achieve their wealth through hard work, luck, or savings: the majority have inherited substantial fortunes. So it is quite innaccurate to view such wealth, as the functional theory does, as a reward for making some important contribution to society: great fortunes are still largely acquired by accident of birth. And as we have seen, there is little evidence of a general trend towards a more equal distribution of personal wealth: what is apparent is the success with which both the rich and the moderately well-off have defended their advantages.

The interpretation of evidence on such sensitive matters as income, wealth and poverty presents some difficult problems. Ultimately, much depends on the values and assumptions which are brought to the task, whether by official agencies or academic researchers. Some have been concerned to stress the way in which certain income differentials have been reduced over the last half-century, while others emphasise the massive inequalities which still persist. What we wish to suggest in the present context is that such redistribution as has occurred need not be seen as part of a more general trend towards equality; rather, such changes have come about as a result of particular political and economic circumstances which have favoured them. Moreover, the most striking conclusion to emerge from research into the distribution of income and wealth is the general stability displayed by patterns of inequality, however these have been measured.

This general stability does not mean, though, that the structure of inequalities is static and inflexible. On the contrary, Guy Routh has argued, on the basis of an exhaustive review of income inequalities, that the apparent regularities in the distribution of incomes are simply the outcome of a perpetual struggle among individuals and occupational groups to maintain or improve their positions, or to make up lost ground. As he puts it: 'It is not perhaps very surprising that those who share a common occupation should be dedicated to the maintenance of its status relative to other occupations: the misteries of the Middle Ages were so engaged, as are the trade unions and professional bodies of the present day' (Routh, 1980, p. 198). In Routh's view, the historical evidence simply does not support the idea that rates of pay are determined by the simple 'supply and demand' considerations of economic – or functionalist – theory: even major increases in unemployment do not cause drastic reductions in the incomes of those who remain in work. Rather, rates and claims primarily reflect prevailing notions of what is the reasonable and proper reward for a job, in relation to others with which it may be compared. Routh's argument thus rests on the fundamental sociological insight that the way in which people act depends on how they define the situation they are in; they do not simply respond to economic "forces" or functional "needs". So far as incomes are concerned, 'Orderly patterns are maintained through the tensions of perpetual disequilibrium, the system powered by moral energy: the pursuit of what is right and fair' (ibid., p. 204).

## SOCIAL MOBILITY

A second general trend which was predicted by the functionalists was that the process of social differentiation in industrial societies would come to depend more on individuals' talents and achieved qualifications, and less on their social background and ascribed qualities. The ever-increasing need for professional and technical specialists, it was argued, would make it essential that people with the appropriate abilities were identified and trained, regardless of their sex, race, or social origins. In Britain, successive governments in the postwar years carried out policies which were intended to bring about such a situation: it was hoped that by reforming the educational system, and spending more money on it, there would be greater equality of opportunity, and ultimately a more 'meritocratic' society. Subsequent research, however, has demonstrated that such an aim is still far from realisation. Indeed, as with the distribution of income and wealth, what is striking is the stubborn persistence of class, race and sex differences in educational attainment (cf. Chapters 1, 3 and 4 in this volume).

However, although these findings have significant and perhaps troublesome implications as far as social policy is concerned, they do not allow us to conclude that the social structure has remained rigid, with each social class reproducing itself in every new generation. Full-time education is not the only means by which people are channelled to their occupational destinations, and the achievement of qualifications by part-time study has been of considerable importance as an 'alternative route' into higher-status occupations. Moreover, many people experience considerable changes in the course of their occupational careers. There are, too, still some well-rewarded jobs for which educational qualifications are largely irrelevant, and some areas of the economy which are not dominated by large organisations with formal recruitment procedures. The Oxford Mobility Study, by examining individuals' social origins, education and occupational careers, enables us to identify some of the major ways in which these are related, and hence some of the overall patterns of social mobility in British society.

The study was based on a representative sample of 10,000 men in England and Wales, who were interviewed in 1972. For present purposes, we may emphasise two of the general conclusions which emerged. First, the data indicate that during the last fifty years or so British society has been characterised by a relatively high level of social mobility. Thus, for example, more than 7 per cent of the sons of manual workers had obtained 'class I' (higher professional and managerial) occupations. Due to the size of the 'manual' categories, this meant that by 1972 well over a quarter of all men in class I jobs had come from working-class homes. The extent of such mobility, Goldthorpe argues, suggests that the higher levels of the occupational structure have been much more open to new recruits than has commonly been supposed. However, when we turn from the absolute volume of mobility to the relative chances of men from different classes, a somewhat different picture emerges: sons of men in the top two occupational classes were nearly four times as likely to attain such occupations themselves as were the sons of manual workers. So, judging in terms of *relative* chances of social mobility, it cannot be concluded that British society has become any more 'open' during the period in question. On the contrary, the data suggest that this pattern of unequal opportunity has remained remarkably stable.

The second general conclusion is that the mobility patterns which have been observed are mainly a result of changes in the occupational structure. After all, the expansion of higher-level managerial, administrative and technical jobs, and the contraction of manual ones, has made a considerable volume of 'upward' mobility inevitable: 14.3 per cent of the fathers were in class I or II occupations, but 26.5 per cent of their sons (Goldthorpe *et al.*, 1980, ch. 2). In the present context, we can now see one of the main reasons why many studies have found a rather loose relationship between educational attainment and occupational level. As Goldthorpe suggests, until the 1960s these higher level occupations were expanding much more rapidly than the provision of higher level educational courses, so 'indirect' routes into top jobs were of considerable significance. More recently, however, the situation may have altered decisively. Since the 1970s moderate economic growth has given way to stagnation and even decline. In these new circumstances, it is highly unlikely that the expansion of higher-level jobs will continue, and with increasing competition for desirable jobs, formal qualifications may well become more important. But Goldthorpe is not inclined to conclude that this will, at last, produce a trend towards meritocracy. On the contrary, such a situation is one in which upper- and middle-class families are likely to use their superior resources to maintain the class position of their offspring, thus reducing the opportunities for upward mobility.

Goldthorpe's conclusions concerning social mobility may serve to reinforce our earlier arguments concerning economic aspects of inequality. There is no simple trend which may be expected to produce a consistent pattern of social change. The pattern of inequalities at any given time must be seen as the outcome of an implicit competition for scarce and valued resources. Legislative reforms or institutional changes which are designed to alter the pattern of inequality may be frustrated by the ability of powerful and wealthy groups to resist them. In Goldthorpe's terms, attempts at reform often underestimate 'the resistance that the class structure can offer to attempts to change it; or, to speak less figuratively, the flexibility and effectiveness with which the more powerful and advantaged groupings in society can use the resources at their disposal to preserve their privileged positions' (Goldthorpe *et al.*, 1980, p. 252).

## Explaining Social Inequality: Conflict Approaches

It should be evident by now that the expectations derived from the functionalist model have not been sustained by the results of empirical research. There is no apparent trend towards an equalisation of incomes or towards a reduction in the gulf between rich and poor; on the contrary, although the absolute value of British incomes has risen substantially since the Second World War, patterns of relative inequalities have displayed a remarkable stability. Nor does it seem as though the predicted trend towards a more 'meritocratic' society has gone very far.

In view of the apparent inadequacy of the functionalist model, it is hardly surprising that in much recent sociological work there has been a concern to develop more satisfactory explanations of these observed patterns. Given the inherent dilemmas of sociological theorising, it was inevitable that many such efforts should display the elements of a 'conflict' model of social order. As we have seen, both Routh and Goldthorpe were led to interpret their findings in terms of a continuing struggle among social groups as they attempted to defend or challenge the *status quo*. Although a variety of conflict perspectives has been formulated, it is possible to distinguish two main forms, which derive from the ideas of Karl Marx and Max Weber respectively.

### MARX AND THE CONFLICT OF CLASSES

Marx's discussion of the development of capitalist society is well known and will not be presented in detail here. In the present context, however, the aspect of his general analysis which requires emphasis is the idea that the process of capitalist development will tend to produce two fundamental classes whose interests are opposed. Marx argued that ownership of the means of production would increasingly become concentrated in the hands of a small, all-powerful capitalist class while the rest of the population, lacking capital, would be forced to sell its labour to survive. In Marx's scheme, then, a tiny bourgeoisie would come to confront a huge proletariat who could maintain themselves only at subsistence level. Members of the latter group, however, would eventually come to an understanding of their collective subordination and, given the inherent instability of the system, would be able to overthrow the capitalists in revolutionary action. The outlines of a conflict model have seldom been drawn more clearly.

In the century which followed the publication of *Das Kapital* in 1867, it seemed to most observers that the class structures of the advanced capitalist societies were not exhibiting a tendency to polarisation along the lines that Marx had suggested. It was true that the ownership of enterprises became more concentrated and that the 'petit bourgeoisie' declined greatly, being swallowed up by big business on the one hand and wage labour on the other. But, unquestionably, the most notable trend was the emergence of a 'new' middle class of managerial, administrative and technical specialists. Westergaard and Resler (1976) calculated that in 1921, 24.5 per cent of male employees in Britain were in these professional, managerial and clerical occupations; by 1971 the figure was 37.4 per cent. For women the figures are 31.7 and 54.3 per cent respectively. In the same period, as we have seen, the proportion of manual workers was consistently falling. Such changes scarcely seemed to fit the pattern envisaged by Marx; indeed, at first sight they seem to suggest that the functionalist account, with its stress on the growth of relatively skilled and specialised jobs, is more in accordance with the facts. So in the 1950s and 1960s many social and political theorists tended to regard Marx's analysis simply as a set of predictions which had not been supported by the evidence of history. Indeed, it was widely felt that the growth of the middle class, coupled with the general increase in the real value of incomes, was contributing to a process of 'embourgeoisment' in British society.

However, research results offered little support for the 'embourgeoisment' thesis, and further challenges to it have been produced by several authors who have examined the growth of the 'new' middle class. In Britain, Westergaard and Resler argued that much of the apparent growth of 'non-manual' groups in the labour force simply reflects the large increase in the numbers of women in clerical or sales work: from 16.3 per cent to over 38 per cent of all women workers in the period 1921–71. Such jobs, they argue, are in general poorly paid and routine, and offer little scope for either promotion or the exercise of real responsibility. Thus the growth of such jobs cannot be taken as an indication of the expansion of a 'new' middle class. As far as men are concerned, the increase in the overall proportion of 'white collar' jobs has been more moderate. Moreover, again as Westergaard and Resler argue, it is mistaken to regard the conventional manual/non-manual distinction as indicating a real difference in the class situation of employees. In their view, intermediate and lower-level 'white collar' jobs are increasingly coming to resemble proletarian ones in terms of the income and working conditions which they offer. Occupants of administrative, clerical and lower managerial posts, it is held, do not generally participate in the decision-making processes of the organisations which employ them, and in recent years their incomes have fallen relative to those of both higher non-manual, and manual groups. Furthermore, the increasing automation of office procedures is likely to lead to greater proletarianisation in 'white collar' work.

So whereas earlier authors were concerned with the possibility of 'embourgeoisment', the contrasting implication of Westergaard and

Resler's argument is that the labour force is undergoing a process of proletarianisation in modern Britain. On the one hand there is the small percentage of the population who, as we have seen, remain the substantial owners of capital, and those to whom they delegate responsibility for running the system. On the other is the vast majority who do not own any substantial wealth, who must sell their labour in order to live and who, whatever their level of earnings, have no significant role in the exercise of power.

A similar argument has been presented by Braverman (1974) in relation to the American occupational structure. Braverman's initial point is that the alleged raising of occupational skill levels in advanced capitalist societies is largely illusory. True, there are more professionals and scientists, more engineers, administrators and technical specialists; but these categories still only include a minority of the working population, around 15–20 per cent in the USA. For most of the remainder, the development of capitalist production, with its emphasis on the rationalisation of work and its inherent tendency to automation, has progressively reduced the extent to which genuine skills are required in the performance of jobs. Craft skills, for example, are increasingly eliminated by the availability of cheap mass-produced goods. And people in the most numerous 'white collar' jobs – routine clerical, sales and administrative work – are mostly required to perform repetitive and mindless tasks which reduce them to the level of the machines which will soon replace them. So Braverman argues that a wholesale process of 'de-skilling' has occurred, and that in view of their working conditions and reward levels between two-thirds and three-quarters of the labour force 'appears readily to conform to the dispossessed condition of a proletariat' (Braverman, 1974, p. 403).

Arguments such as those of Braverman, and Westergaard and Resler, suggest that although mass immiserisation has not been the inevitable outcome of capitalist development, the underlying tendency towards polarisation is still in evidence. This thesis, however, has been disputed by some who have pointed to the results of research into social mobility. As we have seen, the Oxford Mobility Study revealed that men in higher-level occupations had come from a wide range of social backgrounds: more than a quarter were the sons of manual workers. Such evidence has been taken to indicate that access to powerful and privileged positions at the commanding heights of the occupational structure is not closed off to people of humble origins. Even though the latter are not represented in top jobs in anything like their due proportion, enough of them do achieve such positions to undermine the idea that such positions are the exclusive preserve of an elite. Thus Goldthorpe has criticised the 'closure' thesis which suggests that 'access to the higher levels of the class structure is tightly controlled' so that 'a marked homogeneity of social origins' is evident in such high places (Goldthorpe *et al.*, 1980, p. 45).

Nevertheless, on Goldthorpe's own admission, the data of the Oxford study seem insufficient to invalidate the two-class model as formulated by Braverman, or Westergaard and Resler. The bourgeoisie, as described by Marx, included only that small fraction of the population who were owners of significant wealth, and who through it wielded great economic and political power. Such a description is hardly consistent with the 14.3 per cent of respondents who were classified as 'Class I' in the Oxford Mobility Study. Moreover, Goldthorpe concedes that 'more specialised' studies have given some support to the closure thesis, and further that 'if an elite is distinguished within our Class I in terms of high income . . . then in this case evidence much more suggestive of closure in recruitment is to be found than when Class I is considered as a whole' (Goldthorpe *et al.*, 1980, p. 46).

To this it may be added that the sample survey, which was the basic research instrument used in the Oxford study, is not a particularly suitable means of investigating elites, their activities and their influence. First, it is an essential feature of this method that social groups are sampled according to the extent of their representation in the population; inevitably, then, there will be very few rich people in the study. Secondly, it is highly likely that a disproportionate number of such people will decline to participate in the research, or be unavailable to do so. (The overall response rate in the Oxford study was 81.8 per cent.) In the present context, the significant point about elites or dominant economic classes is that they are held to exercise a measure of power out of all proportion to their numbers; it follows that a sample survey is unlikely to yield much useful knowledge concerning such top people or their careers. Studies of specific high-status groups or individuals, however, may in fact be more productive precisely because they are unrepresentative of the general population.

Contrary to widespread opinion, then, recent research has not completely invalidated Marx's idea of an inherent tendency towards class polarisation in capitalist society. In this context, Marxists make a distinction between the *appearance* of a graded hierarchy of incomes and authority, and the reality of an underlying structural conflict between the agents of capital and the interests of labour. Similarly, the façade of democratic political institutions is held to mask the sovereignty of the money market. In a system which is fuelled by the investment of capital, decision-making will ultimately reflect the requirement to produce adequate returns for the few, rather than the needs of the many.

However, even if it is accepted that there is a 'structural' strain towards polarisation in advanced capitalist societies, only the most committed of Marxists could comfortably claim that any of these societies have yet arrived at the point of revolutionary class confrontation envisaged by Marx himself. Is it simply a matter of time? Or are there significant social processes which have inhibited the transformation of antagonistic economic groupings into real social classes? Some of these issues have been explored by sociologists working in the tradition established by Max Weber, and it is to their work that we now turn.

## THE WEBERIAN TRADITION

The essentials of a Weberian approach to the analysis of social stratification may be discerned in Weber's brief remarks entitled 'Class, Status, Party' (Weber, 1948). Like Marx, Weber begins by granting fundamental importance to the economic divisions – 'class' factors – evident in any society. However, Weber argued, the evidence does not suggest that real societies are perpetually riven by conflicts between antagonistic classes. On the contrary, the pages of history contain countless stories of servants who have died for their masters, peasant armies fighting for their lords and workers who vote for bourgeois political parties. Thus it is evident that people's actions may be motivated and regulated by non-economic factors, such as religious beliefs, customary practices, or loyalty to the community. Weber suggests, therefore, that it is necessary to emphasise 'status' factors, such as religion, race, or sex, in the process of group formation; such factors can create a web of conflicts and loyalties which overlays economic divisions.

It is also apparent that significant conflicts of interest may develop within the major economic classes: between landowners and industrial capitalists, for example, or between craftsmen and unskilled workers. Moreover, the existence of conflicting interests does not inevitably give rise to antagonistic social groups or classes: the emergence of 'parties' – organised groups actively pursuing particular interests – depends on the extent to which people are aware of their common interests, the resources they can mobilise, the capabilities of their leaders, the strength of potential opponents, and so on.

Seen from a Weberian perspective, then, the pattern of stratification in a society is the outcome of a perpetual struggle for advantage amongst a plurality of groups, which may coalesce on the basis of economic or other interests. Such a view forms the basis of Frank Parkin's analysis of contemporary industrial societies. Parkin's critique of Marxist approaches rests on his claim that 'the contours of a stratification order cannot be read off from the fact that a given society has a capitalist mode of production – understood as a system rooted in private property and market relations' (Parkin, 1979, p. 8). Racial and religious divisions, for example, are of fundamental importance in the stratification of some capitalist societies. The system of apartheid in South Africa shows how white capitalists and workers can unite to maintain the subordination of blacks and to exclude them from positions of wealth and power. In Northern Ireland, Protestant and Catholic workers' organisations confront each other with bitter hostility. Such situations demonstrate how these status factors may override class ones in the development of personal identities, the process of group formation and the creation of political institutions.

Clearly, other status factors may be important in the process of social differentiation. We have already noted the persistence of substantial sex differences in incomes and patterns of employment (cf. Chapter 1 above). It is consistent with Weber's approach that improvements in the legal and economic position of women have largely been achieved as a consequence of the formation of specific interest groups which have forced the issues into the political arena, as well as deliberate efforts to make women more aware of their collective disadvantages. The occasional eruption of nationalist sentiments also serves to illustrate the persistence of status factors which, while often dormant in contemporary industrial societies, are always available as actual or potential bases for the expression of sectional interests. The influence of religious ideologies, too, remains far from negligible.

It is also evident that social differentiation on the basis of race remains a persistent characteristic of industrial societies. John Rex's studies in the Birmingham area have led him to the conclusion that immigrants from the 'new Commonwealth' countries do not occupy similar economic positions to those of white workers, and that the differences are 'not simply quantitative but qualitative and structural, with the immigrant situation being characterised by a different kind of position in the labour market, a different housing situation, and a different form of schooling' (Rex and Tomlinson, 1979, p. 276). As a consequence of their exclusion from good jobs and opportunities for advancement, the immigrant communities have had to develop their own strategies of self-defence. Among Asians, 'individuals may aim at capital accumulation and social mobility' and 'in the West Indian community it may take the form of withdrawal from competition altogether with emphasis on the formation of a black identity . . .' (ibid.).

In the present context, Rex's analysis usefully illustrates two points: (1) the way in which similar economic situations of black and white wage workers need not be experienced as an identity of interests, or give rise to collective action. Indeed, Rex refers to immigrant minorities as a separate, underprivileged, 'underclass'; (2) the ways in which the 'immigrants' themselves are highly differentiated. Asian and West Indian groups have quite different cultural and historical traditions, which are reflected in their distinctively different adaptations to the problems of settling in Britain.

Status factors, then, may generate interests and political movements which are independent of pure class considerations. Moreover, as Weber suggested, inherent tendencies towards differentiation and conflict exist *within* the major classes. In the dominant economic group, for example, the aim of 'finance' capitalists to secure the best possible returns on investments may conflict with the interests of those engaged in manufacturing, for instance by channelling investment funds into the latters' foreign competitors. In the middle class, a distinction has generally been made between the 'old' middle class – entrepreneurs, shopkeepers, 'small businessmen', professionals, and the like, and the 'new' middle class of salaried employees: managers, administrators, teachers, accountants, technicians, engineers, and so on. However, even this group cannot be regarded as homogeneous, since its members may vary greatly in skills and qualifications. Following Weber, Anthony Giddens suggests that such employees vary considerably in their 'market capacity' – their ability to obtain rewards for their labour (Giddens, 1973, p. 103). In the present context, the significance of such differences is that they provide actual or potential bases for the formation of interest groups within the 'middle class'.

Similarly, it is difficult to translate the category 'working class' into any coherent or observable collectivity. As we have seen, Braverman argues that the class interests of most manual and non-manual employees are becoming increasingly similar, and thus that more than three-quarters of the population should be regarded as 'proletarian'. But the theoretical coincidence of interests does not seem to generate any observable trend towards solidarity among this 'class'. On the contrary, much of the data considered earlier indicate that occupational and other interest groups have acted, often with considerable success, to *maintain* economic differentials and customary distinctions. The way in which the pattern of wealth-holding has developed may be of considerable significance in this context. For while it is undeniable that the great majority of people are not the owners of substantial capital, the main forms in which their wealth is held – houses and pension rights – does give them a direct interest in the prosperity of the dominant financial institutions. Home-owners and those with valuable pension entitlements may well have to sell their labour on the market, but they are unlikely to see themselves as proletarians who 'have nothing to lose but their chains'.

Braverman's view of the development of the proletariat may be contrasted with that of another Marxist, Nicos Poulantzas, who has argued that the true working class now consists only of those workers who are 'productive' (as opposed to 'unproductive') and engaged in 'manual' (as opposed to 'mental') labour (Poulantzas, 1975). On this basis, the working class is reduced from Braverman's 75 per cent-plus to nearer 20 per cent of the labour force. The contrast between these two analyses may serve to highlight both the problems encountered in any attempt to employ the concept of 'class' in a specific historical situation, and the way in which the assumptions which different authors bring to their analyses have a major influence on their conclusions.

Two general points emerge from these considerations. First, as Parkin argues, the term 'exploitation' need not be restricted, as in the Marxist usage, to the economic process by which the capitalist acquires the 'surplus value' created by the worker. Rather, relationships are exploitative if members of one group exclude others from power, wealth, or any other scarce resources, whatever the social basis of their domination. Secondly, one implication of Parkin's argument is that the sociological analysis of stratification should begin with a consideration of real conflicts, interest groups and political processes as opposed to those which are predicted only on the basis of general theories. In short, the aim should be to fit theory to the facts, rather than vice versa.

As we have suggested, the influence of Weber's ideas is apparent in Parkin's discussion of stratification. The dominant class is held to be the 'bourgeoisie', who maintain their position (like all ruling groups) primarily by strategies of 'social closure': that is, they attempt to 'maximise rewards by restricting access to a limited circle of eligibles' (Parkin, 1979, p. 44). There are two main methods by which they do this. First, through the institutions of property, which are supported by the state, the bourgeois class can retain control of productive resources; thus they exclude others from the exercise of economic power and deny them the opportunity to accumulate wealth. An important example is provided by the laws governing inheritance, which – as we have noted – is the principal means by which people become wealthy in Britain.

The second basic strategy of 'social closure' is the restriction of access to top positions in the occupational structure to those who have the required educational or professional qualifications. Following Weber, Parkin argues that the need for such 'credentials' cannot be explained simply in terms of the technical demands of occupations. Rather, educational requirements increase as professions and other social groups themselves seek 'social closure': to maximise their rewards and security by restricting entry to a strictly limited number of newcomers. The strategy of 'credentialism' is doubly effective in that children of the upper socio-economic groups are disproportionately successful in obtaining higher-level educational qualifications (cf. Chapter 4 below). If, as Parkin argues, the attainment of such qualifications depends on the possession of 'certain class-related qualities and attributes', then it is easy to see how high occupational positions can be passed from one generation to the next even though educational selection is formally 'meritocratic'.

Collins (1977) has presented a similar argument in respect of the USA. What formal qualifications really represent, he argues, is the extent to which a person has acquired, or failed to acquire, the culture of the dominant status group. In the United States this has been the white, Anglo-Saxon, Protestant business elite. Members of this 'WASP' group have succeeded in establishing their values and standards in the organisation and content of schooling. Thus members of other class, religious and racial groups are inherently at a disadvantage in the school system, and the schools themselves have been an effective means of perpetuating the dominance of the WASPs: their own children will tend to obtain higher levels of qualification than others, and so facilitate their own progress into higher-level occupations. In addition, deference towards the WASP culture will be inculcated in the rest of the population: their language, for example, will be presented as the 'proper' mode of speech (just as 'BBC English' is in Britain). So the socially acquired characteristics of WASP children are treated in schools as if they were naturally given abilities, and for members of other status groups to succeed, it is necessary for them to adopt the values and standards of the WASPs.

Collins's argument serves to illustrate the way in which 'credentialism' may operate as a basic strategy of social closure. Similar arguments have been advanced in respect of more specific occupational groupings: the 'professions', for example, have been regarded as groups which have successfully claimed a relatively high degree of autonomy. Professional bodies are able to define appropriate standards of work performance, to control recruitment and often to define the level of their members' rewards. The implication is that such arrangements are likely to benefit the 'professionals' more than their clients; it is also evident why numerous occupational groups have aspired to 'professional' status. (The idea is a familiar one: it was George Bernard Shaw who suggested that 'all professions are conspiracies against the laity'.) Trade unions, too, are bodies which aim to protect and further their members' interests: thus they are inevitably brought into conflict with employers, and often with each other. The general picture, then, which emerges from the Weberian perspective is one in which a multiplicity of interest groups are in perpetual competition; conflict, both implicit and explicit, is thus seen as a normal condition of society, and social order as the outcome of an end-less struggle among the contending forces.

## CONFLICT PERSPECTIVES AND THE ANALYSIS OF MODERN SOCIETIES

As we noted at the start of this section, there is no single 'conflict theory', but a variety of approaches to the analysis of social organisation, with concerns ranging from the dynamics of interpersonal relations to the formation of nation-states. However, the Marxist and Weberian perspectives have been predominant in the study of social stratification, and we shall conclude this section by considering two general issues which emerge when they are contrasted.

First, the Marxian version involves the idea that the same process of historical change which gave rise to the bourgeoisie and the proletariat will eventually lead to revolutionary conflict, the overthrow of the former by the latter and the establishment of a new, classless, society. This kind of 'evolutionary' theory was widely held in the nineteenth century when Marx was writing, and in modern times the idea that social change ultimately brings 'progress' is still commonplace. For present purposes, we may simply note that in the Weberian perspective there is no implication that historical change has any particular direction, nor of an inevitable pattern. This is not to say that such change is in any way random – Weber himself often emphasised the continuing tendency towards the 'rationalisation' of social life – but simply to suggest that the circumstances of any historical situation are unique, so that the ultimate pattern of change is not predetermined. Hence, for example, although many societies have experienced the transition from agricultural to industrial modes of production, Weberians point out that this transition has occurred in very different ways and in widely different circumstances (and seldom in accordance with the pattern suggested by Marx and Engels in the 'Communist Manifesto'). As a result, stratification patterns and institutional structures vary significantly in industrialised and industrialising societies. As we have seen, the same arguments may be used to suggest that there is no inexorable trend towards equality in industrial societies. Nor is there much evidence of a movement towards some sort of harmonious 'classless' society. Marx may well have been correct in perceiving the ultimate instability of the capitalist economic order, but there is little reason to assume that its collapse will bring about a new utopia. Indeed, in recent years there has been increasing concern about the possibility of 'de-industrialisation' in Britain, and the prospect of not only relative, but absolute economic decline.

The second theme centres on the number and nature of the social classes identified by the two perspectives. It was suggested above that the Marxian assumption of two basic antagonistic classes is, in certain important respects, sociologically unsatisfactory. Real social groups and movements cannot easily be categorised in terms of this division alone, and conflicts too often seem either to cut across the boundaries of the classes, or to occur within them. However, Weber's emphasis on the importance of status factors and differing 'market capacities' also leads to problems. Taking such factors into account could lead us to identify 'a cumbersome plurality of classes', as Giddens has put it (Giddens, 1973, p. 104). But, as Giddens argues, the important sociological task is to examine the ways in which this potentially infinite variety of interests is translated into real social structures and processes. It seems, therefore, that our understanding of the processes of stratification will gain more from the examination of real individuals and groups in particular 'conflict' situations than from efforts to define class boundaries on the basis of 'armchair theorising'.

## Conclusion

In this chapter we have considered a process of reorientation in the sociological study of stratification in industrial societies, from a period in which much research reflected functionalist assumptions to a more recent concern with conflict and the pursuit of interests. By way of conclusion, certain implications of this shift of emphasis may be noted.

First, the stratification studies demonstrate the way in which each of these general orientations leads to the formulation of distinctively different research problems. Researchers working within the functionalist tradition were generally led to adopt a sort of 'underdog' orientation. To them the central problem appeared to be why some groups consistently lost out in the distribution of scarce resources. Thus there were numerous attempts to explain the educational failure of working-class, or black, children in terms of their own alleged deficiencies or the presumed inadequacies of their culture. There were, too, many studies of those afflicted by poverty. From a 'conflict' point of view, however, the careers of middle-class 'overachievers', and the activities of wealthy and powerful people, are equally problematic. As R. H. Tawney once put it, 'what thoughtful rich people call the problem of poverty, thoughtful poor people call with equal justice the problem of riches' (quoted in Field, 1979, p. 1). The implication, clearly, is that the sociological analysis of stratification must focus on those processes which produce success and failure, wealth and poverty, power and impotence, in regular and patterned ways.

Secondly, while the term 'conflict' is useful in alerting us to the actual or potential competition for scarce resources, its use may be somewhat misleading. Certainly, as we are daily aware, there are overt conflicts of interest between groups and institutions in any society. But from a sociological point of view, at least as much significance must be attached to activities which, to the individuals concerned and to the observer, may seem quite normal, prosaic and routine. Of particular interest are the activities of those who are in a position to impose authoritative definitions on economic, political and cultural matters. Once again, then, it may be suggested that more can be learned by examining the activities of the powerful than by documenting the situation of the powerless.

Thirdly, while it would be difficult to exaggerate the influence of Marx's thought in this field, we have suggested that the fundamental concepts of class and class conflict are not always easy to reconcile with empirically observed patterns of stratification. Thus the Marxian model (and, indeed, the functionalist one) must themselves be regarded as 'images' of society which analysts bring to their investigations, and which may have a major influence on the outcome of their research. Not only do functionalists and Marxists 'see' society in different ways, but even within the same basic orientation there may be major divergences. (For Braverman the proletariat is huge, for Poulantzas it is tiny.) In this context, we wish to emphasise two general points: (1) that such perspectives cannot be accepted as neutral or objective descriptions of the social order – their use is, rather, an active process of definition in which certain categories are imposed on the social world; (2) that our understanding of social stratification is likely to be advanced more by examining the activities of real people than by sophisticated attempts to redefine the world in accordance with general theories.

## References: Chapter 2

Atkinson, A. B. (1975), *The Economics of Inequality* (London: OUP).

Braverman, H. (1974), *Labour and Monopoly Capital* (New York: Monthly Review Press).

Collins, R. (1977), 'Functional and conflict theories of educational stratification', in J. Karabel and A. H. Halsey (eds), *Power and Ideology in Education* (New York: OUP), pp. 118–36.

Davis, K., and Moore, W. E. (1967), 'Some principles of stratification', in R. Bendix and S. M. Lipset (eds), *Class, Status and Power* (London: Routledge & Kegan Paul), pp. 47–53.

Field, F. (ed.) (1979), *The Wealth Report* (London: Routledge & Kegan Paul).

Giddens, A. (1973), *The Class Structure of the Advanced Societies* (London: Hutchinson).

Goldthorpe, J. H., *et al.* (1980), *Social Mobility and Class Structure in Modern Britain* (Oxford: OUP).

Noble, T. (1981), *Structure and Change in Modern Britain* (London: Batsford).

Parkin, F. (1979), *Marxism and Class Theory: A Bourgeois Critique* (London: Tavistock).

Poulantzas, N. (1975), *Classes in Contemporary Capitalism* (London: New Left Books).

Rex, J., and Tomlinson, S. (1979), *Colonial Immigrants in a British City* (London: Routledge & Kegan Paul).

Routh, G. (1980), *Occupation and Pay in Great Britain 1906–79* (London: Macmillan).

Royal Commission on the Distribution of Income and Wealth (1979), *Report No. 7*, Cmnd 7595 (London: HMSO).

Weber, M. (1948), 'Class, status, party', in H. H. Gerth and C. W. Mills, *From Max Weber* (London: Routledge & Kegan Paul), pp. 180–95.

Westergaard, J., and Resler, H. (1976), *Class in a Capitalist Society* (Harmondsworth: Penguin).

# Further Reading

Abrams, P. (ed.) (1978), *Work, Urbanism, and Inequality* (London: Weidenfeld & Nicolson).

Collins, R. (1975), *Conflict Sociology* (London: Academic Press).

Martin, P., and Sharrock, W. W. (eds) (forthcoming), *Class, State, and Power in Modern Britain* (Harmondsworth: Penguin).

Reid, I. (1981), *Social Class Differences in Britain*, 2nd edn (London: Grant McIntyre).

Scott, J. (1982), *The Upper Class – Property and Privilege in Britain* (London: Macmillan).

Chapter 3

# Racial and Ethnic Relations

## ROD WATSON

This chapter will attempt to answer two questions. First, why are sociologists interested in racial and ethnic relations? Secondly, how do sociologists analyse the phenomena of racial and ethnic relations? Let us begin
by making some crucial distinctions between the *biological facts* and the
*social facts* of race.

The 'biological facts' referred to below are the findings of professional
biological scientists. Whilst these biologists disagree on some aspects of
race, they do agree that all human beings, *homo sapiens*, originate from a
common stock (Baxter and Sansom, 1972, pp. 68–73). The subdivisions
we call 'races' are simply subsidiary and secondary in nature; the biological features which all human beings have in common are far more
basic and far more numerous than those which are held to distinguish the
different races. The biological features which 'distinguish' human races
are often quite visible, with skin colour being an obvious example. Skin
colour is a 'biological' feature in that it is genetically transmitted. There
is, however, no evidence that distinctive mental or psychological traits are
genetically transmitted along racial lines.

Biologists also tell us that 'pure races' (populations of genetically
homogeneous human types) do not exist, and that consequently we
cannot divide the different human populations into clear-cut and simple
racial types. Biological differences *within* virtually all given human populations are likely to be as great as, or even greater than, the differences
*between* human populations. The genetic diversity of the species *homo
sapiens* is such that they cannot easily be classified on the basis of hereditary
physical traits in the straightforward way that, say, many animals can be
so classified. Migration of and interbreeding between different human
groups adds to the complexity of the biological picture; and many major
aspects of migration and interbreeding cannot be analysed in biological
terms but must be analysed sociologically. Migration and interbreeding

involve social phenomena, often being related, for instance, to persecution or intermarriage respectively. These social phenomena can be analysed by sociologists and other social scientists; biologists have no central interest in such phenomena.

Biologists say that we can only talk about the biological aspects of race in the most careful and limited way. However, ideas about the 'facts of race' are not merely biological or held only by professional biological scientists. They are also social, held by ordinary members of society. Whatever the biologists claim, many lay members of society believe that there *are* 'pure races' of human beings and that there exists a clear-cut typology of races. Moreover, many of these society members also believe that there exists a set of clear-cut typical psychological characteristics for each 'race'. For instance, people may believe that members of a given 'racial group', as they define it, have less (or more) intelligence than members of some other racial group. Or people may believe that the typical character, personality, or temperament of one racial group differ from those of another racial group. Thus, for instance, black people are sometimes seen as more emotional and spontaneous, more musical, or as characterised by 'natural rhythm' and the like, than are white people. The fact that the disciplines of biology and psychology offer no scientific justification for such beliefs may well have little effect on them.

These beliefs about race are eminently social in nature; that is, they are jointly held and sustained (and perhaps modified) by a group of persons. Such beliefs are transmitted from generation to generation through people's cultural capacity to communicate them as part of the socialisation of the young and of other newcomers to the group. Moreover, people are likely to act on the basis of these racial beliefs. If someone believes that members of a given racial group are less intelligent than his own group then he is quite likely to treat them that way when, say, meeting them in the street. Furthermore, that person may also feel inclined to support proposals to introduce some special, and perhaps separate, educational arrangements for this 'less intelligent racial group'. If large numbers of people hold and act in patterned ways upon such beliefs about race, then society itself is likely to be shaped, to some degree, by this. Societies may, for instance, develop distinctive social roles for members of different racial groups, along with different rights, obligations, rewards, opportunities, and the like. This frequently results in the racial minority having a very poor social and economic position in the society, as well as being subject to other forms of racialist treatment. In this case, any visible biological racial characteristic such as skin colour may be taken as 'role signs' (Banton, 1967, ch. 4), that is, emblems of the role in society to which the member of that racial group is conventionally assigned and treated accordingly. Here we see that biological and social facts intertwine; the sociologist's interest is not in the biological fact of race as such but in what members of society *make* of the biological fact, and, derivatively in how social arrangements are shaped by this.

The socially − (collectively) − held beliefs about race often incorporate notions of 'racial hierarchy'. In other words, they contain ideas about the 'superiority' or 'inferiority' of this or that racial group. This purported superiority or inferiority may take on many forms − moral superiority/ inferiority, physical superiority/inferiority, intellectual superiority/ inferiority, and so on. Very often, members of a given racial group believe that their own morality or their own capacities are superior to those of other groups; this is what sociologists term 'ethnocentrism'. Further- more, some racial groups may have the power to impose their version of racial hierarchy on other groups, so that the organisation of the society itself is at least in part shaped by this notion of racial hierarchy. This, in turn, may reinforce society members' notion of hierarchy, for they can now point to an actual racial hierarchy in society. Members of the society may then treat this racial hierarchy as a natural order, as inevitable given the alleged biological differences between races, or as 'right and good' given the alleged moral differences between races. Here we can readily see the way in which people's beliefs about 'the facts of race' are entangled with moral judgements about race. Notions of superiority and inferiority of different groups of human beings are essentially evaluative, not simply factual.

However, the scope of the sociology of racial and ethnic relations is not restricted to the analysis of the relations between physically differing racial groups. A physically different group may be a 'minority group' (irrespective of whether or not it is a numerical minority) because of its low position on the social hierarchy, but other minorities may not be notably different from other groups in the society in terms of hereditary physical characteristics. Other groups may find themselves in a minority position on a social hierarchy largely because they have a culture, language, national origin, or religion which differs, to a greater or lesser degree, from the dominant groups in that society. These groups are often termed 'ethnic groups'. In our own society, the Jewish, Italian, Polish, Irish and many other minorities are cases in point. In addition, the 'group' of black people in Britain are, of course, by no means a culturally homogeneous category of persons, since different sub-groups have different geographical origins, cultures, languages, dialects and creoles; here again we see how the seemingly simple biological categorisations of race are immensely complicated by social facts such as culture, language, religion, and the like, and it is the sociologist's job to explore these. Add to this the complexities of the mixing of cultures and the 'cultural borrowing' owing to patterns of conquest, colonisation, migration, and so on, and the picture becomes quite formidably complicated!

To conclude this section, we can say that the professional biologist talks about the genetic facts of race in a cautious and circumspect way. The sociologist looks at the social facts of race; the social facts to be examined include society members' collectively held beliefs about the biological aspects of race (which may show remarkably little similarity to the biologist's evidence) and also the cultures, religions and languages of the various groups in society. Finally, and crucially, the sociologist examines the degrees and ways in which the dominant groups of society set themselves apart from the different racial and ethnic groups and accord them what is often a highly disadvantageous social and economic position in society. This issue, too, involves the 'social facts of race and ethnicity', and many sociologists would claim that this particular issue must be their central concern. These sociologists share ordinary people's concern about the existence of racialism and the wide range of other social problems associated with racial and ethnic relations in society.

Having said that all sociologists are concerned with the 'social facts of race and ethnicity' it must also be said that sociologists are far from unanimous in their analyses of racial and ethnic relations. They differ in their characterisation of racial and ethnic relations and in which of the 'social facts of race and ethnicity' they emphasise. They differ, for example, as to whether or not they focus on the social problems associated with racial and ethnic relations.

The source of these analytic differences amongst sociologists largely boils down to the picture they have of society (or of social order). Some sociologists see society as a social system which is based on a set of moral values which virtually everyone in the society shares. Others see society as characterised not by a single set of values but by differences and divergences of values and by great disparities in power, economic resources, and so on. Yet other sociologists see society not as a large-scale entity, as an overall 'system', but as being built up from the actions and interactions of society members. It is obvious that the analytic treatments accorded by sociologists to racial and ethnic relations will vary according to which picture or 'model' of society is espoused. To espouse one model of society will involve a focus upon some social phenomena rather than others. This, in turn, necessarily affects the sociologist's characterisation not only of racial and ethnic relations but also of the social problems associated with these relations.

## Order-Consensus Approaches to Racial and Ethnic Relations

Order-consensus approaches are quite diverse in nature. Indeed, one might usefully refer to them as a 'family' of approaches. This family's main features are that social order (society) is possible because virtually all society members share the same moral values, the values which define (say) 'the British or American way of life'. Any diversity of values within the society are limited and contained within this consensual framework. People are socialised into conformity with these values, and external social controls such as the police and public opinion also operate to maintain their conformity. In this way people's actions fit together in an orderly way, and when this occurs people can be said to be adjusted to or assimilated into society.

Social problems occur when large numbers of people cease to conform to society's morality and when inordinately large amounts of deviance occur. This happens when, because of rapid social change, socialisation agencies cease to function adequately and/or external controls on behaviour break down. This is termed 'anomie' or 'social disorganisation'. The resultant deviant conduct of large numbers of inadequately socialised or inadequately controlled ('maladjusted') people feeds into and escalates this social disorganisation, which may be local or societal in extensiveness. A very large number of sociological approaches to racial and ethnic relations fall within the framework of order-consensus assumptions.

Let us now see how this basic model of society and social problems is applied in the sphere of racial and ethnic relations.

Social disorganisation, say order-consensus theorists, is typically found in those areas of society where social change is most rapid. This social change is usually found in cities, which may change owing to overall growth or contraction, or owing to economic factors, changes in land use, successive waves of migration into or between cities. Some areas of cities may be far more subject to change than others. For instance, inner city areas are particularly subject to social change; other areas of the city may be more stable, as may the rural communities beyond the city limits. It is in the inner city areas, which are often termed 'zones in transition', that many racial and ethnic minorities are found, owing to their poor economic circumstances. Here, the dominant values of the society, promulgated by school, church, neighbourhood, community and settlement groups, and the like, are constantly subject to challenge from subsidiary value systems — value systems espoused by immigrant, rural, or foreign-born people or value systems that are part of the criminal groups and delinquent gangs in the area.

Robert E. L. Faris is a 'Chicago School' sociologist who, decades ago, examined the nature of social disorganization (Faris, 1948). He regarded a successful 'social organisation' (such as a community) as being characterised by social stability and the complementarity and interdependence of people's roles and conduct. To use a simile, he saw social organisation as a functional unit akin to a team. This teamwork required the crucial elements of (a) a consensus on moral values as expressed in shared customs and shared folk knowledge (beliefs about the world), and (b) trust between members of the social organisation. Social organisations were seen by Faris as similar to commercial banks; they could only exist and succeed if people trusted them and had confidence in them; these build up a group morale in the society, which is crucial for stable social organisation and for stable personality organisation, since individual personality stability depends upon social support. The trust and co-operation involved in a successful organisation served to mitigate the competition between society members, overlaying the competitive relations between people with a web of social bonds.

Conversely, social disorganisation involves a relative breakdown in the social bonds engendered by trust and co-operation. Competition becomes more intense and more visible. People become much more aware of being directly in competition with each other and the feeling of threat accompanying this undermines people's sense of belonging to a society. Such disorganisation can be the root of many of the social problems pertaining to racial and ethnic relations. For instance, the disorganisation can give rise within one racial or ethnic group to hostile rumours concerning another racial or ethnic group. These rumours may be that the second group has murdered a member of the first, that members of the second group have raped a female from the first group, or that there has been a fight between two gangs of different races, perhaps involving the 'invasion' of one racial group's 'territory' by members of another group. Or, perhaps, white police officers may be believed to have harassed or assaulted members of a minority group.

Such rumours embody and indeed sharpen and intensify hostile images held by one group of another. These images are often termed 'stereotypes' – grossly oversimplified, exaggerated and distorted pictures and beliefs about another group. Ideas about Jewish people being greedy and ruthlessly competitive, Irish people being dull-witted, black people being lazy, are all stereotypical. As social disorganisation escalates, these stereotypes work to break down any remaining bonds and co-operation, and competition between individuals and between groups becomes much more extreme. It also becomes, in the most literal sense, more visible. When someone with a black skin takes a job which a white person had just been fired from, then the competition between individuals and groups becomes all too visible; indeed, the competition between individuals comes to be seen as a competition between racial groups. The same applies when people are applying for council housing, or even queuing for buses and public facilities of various kinds. The sharpening of hostile stereotypes held by some racial and ethnic groups of others, may even trigger off some form of mass action such as race riots, racial lynchings, or 'race wars'.

Faris gives many examples of the ways in which social disorganisation can involve severe racial turmoil. This turmoil can be triggered off by what seems to be a relatively trivial incident, but one which becomes a 'flashpoint' for all the pent-up racial tension which in a socially disorganised, intensely competitive situation have been building up for a considerable time beforehand. Faris writes of the Chicago racial disturbances of 1919, where the 'flashpoint' occurred when a black person accidentally swam into the part of Lake Michigan that white people claimed was their preserve by a common understanding with black people. This incident developed into a fight which in turn escalated into a 'race war', a week of violent interracial clashes resulting in the deaths of thirty-eight persons, the injury of 537 others and 1,000 homeless and destitute. Finally, the militia had to be brought in to suppress the violence.

However, prior to the 'triggering' incident a huge 'reservoir' of threat, tension and insecurity had been building up in that area of Chicago. First, black people began openly competing with whites for housing, and had moved into housing areas which traditionally had been 'reserved' for whites. Secondly, black people who had recently migrated from the rural areas of the 'Deep South' into the vast urban expanses of Chicago began competing with whites for jobs; this competition became highly visible when employers began to use blacks to break white workers' strikes. In addition, black people (including the new residents) felt increasingly threatened by marauding gangs of white youths who 'invaded' black areas. All this compounded the sense of resentment among black people that their migration north had not met with the improvement in socio-economic conditions they had sought and expected. This increasingly sharp competition, frustration and insecurity gradually broke down any remnants of the web of mutual confidence, complementarity and interdependence which, Faris argued, forms the foundation of successful social organisation, and set the scene for a large-scale violent outbreak.

Other analysts such as Suttles (Suttles, 1968) have toned down the somewhat extreme picture of social disorganisation presented by Faris. Based on a study of a multi-ethnic urban zone, Suttles sees such areas as characterised by what he calls 'ordered segmentation' involving patterns of association and interaction based on intra-ethnic and intra-familial trust and inter-ethnic and inter-familial distrust. Yet other members of the Chicago School, notably Park and Stonequist, emphasised the 'marginality' of various racial, ethnic and particularly immigrant groups and persons of mixed racial descent, observing how all their members were caught between two cultures (their ethnic culture and the 'mainstream' culture), feeling that they belonged to neither culture; this, in turn, produced identity problems and anxiety (Stonequist, 1937).

A major analyst of race relations in the order-consensus tradition is Gunnar Myrdal, a Scandinavian social and economic scientist who conducted a mammoth research investigation into black–white relations in the USA in the early 1940s (Myrdal, in Rose, 1964). The resultant two-volume study was entitled *An American Dilemma*. Myrdal claimed that virtually everyone in the USA, including black Americans, shared and genuinely endorsed American cultural values, the values which found their formal expression in the American Constitution – the belief in liberty, free speech, the equality of human beings, equal opportunity and the right to justice and to pursue happiness. These values, claimed Myrdal, were the values of the American 'melting pot' which successive waves of immigrants had gradually accepted and had consequently been increasingly assimilated into the 'mainstream' of American life. From this picture, one might imagine that there would be few if any social problems of racialism, racial disadvantagement, and so on, in the USA. However, Myrdal noted that these problems did indeed exist, and consequently asked 'how could this be?'

Myrdal's answer was that white Americans, particularly those in the Deep South, had an additional set of values – white 'in-group' values that underpin exclusively white customs, beliefs, and the like. These are the ethnocentric values that constitute the basis of white racial supremism, irrationality, intolerance and discriminatory treatment of black people, including the denial to blacks of the equal opportunity to achieve economic success. These values of white in-group living contrast with the values of the 'American Creed'.

Thus, says Myrdal, many white Americans are presented with an inner moral dilemma, namely: on a given occasion of interracial contact, do they follow the values of the American Creed or the values of 'white in-group living'? Often, the actual behaviour is a compromise between the two sets of values; often, too, the values of the American Creed are totally abdicated. Either way, there is a (partial or total) rejection of the values of the Creed. This results in the according to the black American of an inferior status – something that violates the American Creed. This, says Myrdal, frequently causes great anxiety and guilt feelings amongst white Americans.

White Americans attempt to resolve these conflicts by resorting to what Myrdal terms 'popular beliefs' and stereotypes about black people. The essence of these beliefs is that blacks have failed to avail themselves of equal constitutionally guaranteed opportunities and rights or *would* fail were those opportunities and rights offered. This preserves the whites' *prima facie* adherence to the American Creed whilst at the same time denying black people such opportunities and rights. This 'resolution' also, of course, works as a self-fulfilling prophecy, when the conduct of whites based on these beliefs and stereotypes serve to keep blacks down in the lower reaches of the stratification system, and this lowly position works spuriously to validate the whites' conclusion that they were 'right all along' to see blacks as 'losers'. However, it is the popular beliefs which result in 'keeping blacks down', thereby providing false 'evidence' for their initial 'correctness'. Myrdal thought that increased education into more scientific beliefs about race, and into the American Creed, would gradually erode these self-fulfilling prophesies and the racialism through which they were sustained.

Another order-consensus theorist, Robert K. Merton, has spelled out and specified Myrdal's analysis in a more logically exhaustive form. Like Myrdal, he focuses on the aspect of the American Creed which lays emphasis on equal access to opportunity (Merton, 1976). Again, like Myrdal, he sees this and other values of the American Creed as inadequately institutionalised in US society, especially in some regions such as the Deep South. Many people evade adherence to the moral values of the Creed. Merton also draws more sharply than Myrdal the distinction between racial or ethnic prejudice (hostile attitudes to members of a given racial or ethnic group) and discrimination (actual behaviour or practices which work against one or more minority groups). One can be prejudiced against, say, black people without actually involving oneself in conduct which overtly discriminates against blacks. Finally, Merton makes a similar distinction to that made by Myrdal when he says that much depends on people's beliefs and attitudes to the actual Creed and secondly on their actual conduct in relation to the Creed, their ways of putting it into practice. Out of all this, Merton develops a typology of ethnic prejudice and discrimination (summarised in Table 3.1).

Type 1, the unprejudiced non-discriminator, adheres to the American Creed both in belief and practice, whatever the circumstances. Merton says these people are often referred to as 'all-weather liberals'. Type 2, the unprejudiced discriminator, is unprejudiced in attitudinal terms but discriminates in his conduct in certain circumstances, such as where it is more expedient or profitable (for example, a shopkeeper who fears that a black shop assistant will lose him business amongst his discriminatory customers). This type of person will tacitly acquiesce to the discriminatory practices of others, and will sometimes actively discriminate in his own conduct, because he fears condemnation or ostracism by other discriminatory people. Often the person espousing this type of adjustment builds up great feelings of shame.

Table 3.1 *Merton's Typology of Ethnic Prejudice and Discrimination*

| Type of prejudice and discrimination | Attitude dimension (Prejudice/non-prejudice) | Behaviour dimension (Discrimination/non-discrimination) |
|---|:---:|:---:|
| Type 1  Unprejudiced non-discriminator | + | + |
| Type 2  Unprejudiced discriminator | + | − |
| Type 3  Prejudiced non-discriminator | − | + |
| Type 4  Prejudiced discriminator | − | − |

( + = conformity to the American Creed)
( − = deviation from the American Creed)

People who show the type 3 adaptation, the prejudiced non-discriminator or 'fair-weather illiberal', are the prejudiced people who do not discriminate in their conduct because they fear sanctions (for example, the legal sanctions of Equal Opportunity and Fair Employment laws, and so on) which might otherwise be visited on them. Like the fair-weather liberal of type 2, the person with this type of attitude is a creature of circumstance; however, the fair-weather liberal will not discriminate unless pressures 'force' him to do so, whereas racialism is ingrained into the character of the prejudiced non-discriminator. The underlying personality structure of persons who make up the type 3 adaptation differ radically from that of persons making the type 2 adaptation.

Finally, the person who shows the type 4 adaptation is what Merton terms 'the bigot, pure and unashamed', a person whose attitudes and behaviour constantly depart from the American Creed, whatever the circumstances. The person making this type of adaptation often belongs to a regional subculture where this adaptation predominates (for example, the Deep South of the USA) and obtains great psychological gains from his prejudicial and discriminatory practices.

Merton suggests that the fair-weather liberal may be 'treated' by changing social situations (through altering the 'mix' of positive inducements and social controls) to negate the profit from racialism, but that for the fair-weather illiberal the extension and intensification of social controls through legal sanctions are the only possible answer; this is even more the case with all-weather illiberals. Moreover, Merton claims that media propaganda against racism will not work to reduce prejudice and discrimination; such propaganda just seems to boost the morale of the all-weather liberals. Nor does a higher level of education necessarily reduce prejudice or discrimination. Unlike Myrdal, Merton tends to emphasise positive and negative sanctions (social rewards and controls) rather than socialisation. However, he does share the concern of Myrdal and other order-consensus theorists to institutionalise further the 'core values' of the society, thus reducing social disorganisation with all its attendant racial and other problems and reducing local subcultural departures from these 'core values'.

## Conflict Models of Racial and Ethnic Relations

Like order-consensus theories, conflict theories too are examples of 'structuralist' theories, which characterise 'society as a whole'. The picture given by the conflict model, though, emphasises inter-group tension and conflict based largely on differential access to property or wealth. The conflict group(s) with the lion's share of the wealth will thereby have more power and will emerge as the dominant group(s). They will increasingly seek to impose their values and culture on the subordinate groups, forcing them to act against their own (the subordinate groups') vested interests and culture and exploiting these groups' labour power. The subordinate groups may well become collectively alienated from these arrangements and try to resist such impositions. This resistance may be limited or radical, but may produce a social change in the distribution of wealth and power to a greater or lesser degree; indeed, conflict theorists see society as a dynamic, not a static, entity (Horton, 1966).

One of these groups may, by virtue of having ownership or control of such scarce resources, acquire a disproportionate amount of power and so emerge as the dominant or ruling group, with the other groups occupying a variety of subordinate social positions. Members of the dominant group will seek to institutionalise and legitimise their position of power over the others, and so will seek to impose through coercion or indoctrination their values on the other groups, who may try to resist and to retain their own values and vested interests. Social change occurs with a shift, sometimes radical, sometimes more modest, in the distribution of power as between conflict groups, and manoeuvrings between conflict groups ensure that the situation is constantly changing. The imposition of dominant group power on subordinate or minority group(s) will tend to alienate these groups by suppressing their vested interests, cultural values and way of life; that is, the members of the group will experience a collective sense of self-estrangement and coercion and might develop a common ideology and project of disalienation (revolutionary or otherwise).

Unlike order-consensus models the conflict models emphasise the centrality of economic processes, not of shared morals or values.

Just as order-consensus approaches are varied, conflict approaches are likewise quite diverse in nature. One major dispute among them with a particular relevance to racial and ethnic relations concerns the definition of the conflict groups. For instance, are British blacks or black Americans members of a conflict group we usually call the working class or proletariat, or as a racial group do they comprise a separate conflict group in themselves?

Oliver C. Cox (Cox, 1948), an eminent black American sociologist, has argued that the situation of the vast majority of black Americans can best be understood if we conceive them as being part of the propertyless American proletariat in a capitalist economy. Like many conflict theorists, Cox used a historical approach to show that American blacks were always workers whose labour was exploited for profit, which is exactly the position of all workers in that economy, regardless of colour. To understand the problem of black Americans is to understand their position as proletarians, members of the working class who, since they do not own and control the means of agricultural or industrial production, have to sell their labour in order to survive. The plantation slave system in the Deep South was a special case of black people being exploited by the rural capitalist bourgeoisie, the plantation-owners. Slaves were cheaper than other forms of labour (such as white indentured labour), and once bought were owned for life. Having no economic resources, not even a wage, they were powerless and thus constrained to be 'better workers'. Since virtually all slaves were black, they were more conspicuous if they escaped; here we have an example of race as a visible sign of a person's economic role. The slave system developed hand in hand with the colonial expansion of capitalism.

After formal emancipation, black people found themselves in a modified version of the plantation system; they were still expropriated and, frequently, heavily indebted to the white bourgeoisie – the owners and controllers of the plantations. During industrialisation and urbanisation large numbers of black people seeking higher wages moved north and, along with poor southern white immigrants, became part of the urban proletariat. There they began to attain some formal education, though, as with the education of workers everywhere, their education was limited in extent and was primarily vocational, that is, restricted to the acquisition of the self-discipline and skills required to be a worker. This allayed fears of better-off white people that blacks would get the education to improve their position beyond that of some whites. Broadly speaking, says Cox, the black proletariat shared many of the economic experiences and vested interests of the white working class, owing to their being in a similar overall social and economic position; both white and black workers had to respond to changes in the capitalist labour market. Revolts and protests of black people against their exploitation both before and after slavery were very similar to the revolts, protests and similar expressions of alienation of white people. The position of blacks in capitalism can best be understood if we regard blacks as being in pro-letarian situations. Cox says that the racial tensions between white and black proletarians were part and parcel of an attempt by the dominant classes to divide the proletariat amongst themselves in order to prevent a revolution or some other form of class-based collective action. Thus, the capitalist bourgeoisie would tend to give the white workers certain economic and other advantages over the blacks and would tend to sponsor white workers against blacks (by, for instance, reserving certain skilled manual jobs for whites). Thus, white workers' racialism was fostered for the economic ends of the white bourgeoisie who were in fact profiting both from white workers and (even more) the black workers who came to comprise a cheap labour force who were last hired in a capitalist boom and first fired in a slump. Indeed, Cox claims there was a strong tendency in US capitalism to proletarianise an entire race; to be black was to be identified as working class, and as on the lower echelons of the working class too, for example, as the pool of unemployed reserve labour.

In Britain, Sivanandan (Sivanandan, 1976) has produced a similar analysis of the situation of immigrants from Britain's former colonies in Africa, Asia and the Caribbean. He points out that immigrants were imported to Britain in the 1950s when their labour was required in the least skilled, least desirable and lowest-paid jobs in non-growth economic sectors such as the textile and clothing industries, engineering and foundry work, transport and communication, or as waiters, ancillary hospital staff, cleaners, porters, kitchen hands, casual workers, and the like. These workers were especially profitable for capitalism because they were 'ready made workers'; they had already been raised and educated at the expense of the underdeveloped nations they came from – nations, which had been kept underdeveloped and poverty stricken by colonialism and neocolonialism, and who could ill afford to bear the cost of raising people whose labour is eventually lost to a far wealthier colonising nation.

In addition, of course, these immigrants paid taxes to the country of immigration. Moreover, many immigrants arrived in Britain as unattached people, so the nation did not have to help bear the cost of raising or educating the immigrant's family. These things were, in effect, a corollary of a continuing process of economic colonisation. Immigrants were forced into the large metropolitan areas where housing shortages meant they had to pay high rents to slum landlords who profited from overcrowding their rented properties. In this sense, the economic gains of immigration were appropriated by capitalists but the social costs were borne by labour, especially the immigrants themselves. The competition with white workers for this property greatly increased racial tension, and in turn divided and even atomised the working class. As in the USA, members of minority groups in Britain were *de jure* or *de facto* increasingly subject to divisive racialist practices in the labour movement. The immigrants became a racial 'under-class', a specially disadvantaged segment of the working class.

Other proponents of the conflict model have challenged the claim that the socio-economic position, experience, or vested interests of black people can be equated with those of members of the white working class. Those analyses which came from the Black Power movement in the USA said that the 'class model' propounded by Cox and others was inadequate because the model seriously underestimates the power and pervasiveness of white racialist attitudes, beliefs and ideologies in setting black people apart. These critics of the class model have claimed that the USA is a society characterised by 'institutional racism', that is, racialism which is so fundamentally built into the organisation of the society that black people are profoundly separated from all whites – so much so that the black population constitutes what might, literally or metaphorically, be termed an 'internal colony' surrounded by the large-scale white society.

Two proponents of the Black Power movement, Stokely Carmichael and Charles V. Hamilton, applied the notion of the internal colony particularly lucidly to the problems of black people in the USA (Carmichael and Hamilton, 1968). They claim the racialist organisation of the USA is so ingrained in society that the chances that there will be any coalition between black and white workers in the foreseeable future – something that many of those who espouse the class model see as entirely possible – are in fact very slim indeed. Carmichael and Hamilton's argument suggests that in looking for economically based similarities in the class position of white and black workers, the proponents of the class model overlook some basic and far-reaching social and political, as well as economic, differences in the position of the two racial groups – differences which usually result in the white workers co-operating with middle-class and other dominant group whites in 'keeping black people down' so that the entire white community benefits economically, politically and socially from the subordination of blacks. As Black Power proponent Eldridge Cleaver put it, 'Black people are a stolen people held in colonial status on stolen land . . .'.

When writing of blacks as a colonised minority, Carmichael and Hamilton put the terms 'coloniser' and 'colonised' in quotation marks, arresting to the metaphorical application of the term 'colony'; after all the notion of colony is usually used to denote the domination by a metropolitan society of distant societies. However, they argue that there are sufficient similarities between the 'internal' and 'external' colonies to warrant the use of the term. Indeed, as Cox also points out, the historical processes of colonisation in both senses are inextricably linked. Colonies of both kinds exist primarily for the enrichment of the colonisers who, concerned only to exploit the colony, weaken its economic base and thus perpetuate its dependence. This is equally true, argued Carmichael and Hamilton, for the way the larger white society treats the black ghetto, the physical locus of the 'internal colony'.

Carmichael and Hamilton claim that the exploitation of the ghetto takes the form of white people – shop-owners, landlords, employers and public officials – coming into the ghetto from the outside and 'bleeding it dry' by 'raking off' the profits, or more accurately the surplus value by exploiting the one resource that black people have, namely, their labour power. Whites also 'cash in' on the basic human needs of black people for shelter, food, warmth, and so on. Because most black people are consigned to the spatial areas termed 'the ghetto' there may be great pressure on housing and so rents might be very high indeed. Welfare payments also keep black ghetto-dwellers in a state of colonial dependence, for welfare payments are only made if recipients accept certain restricting conditions. Wages are low in the ghetto, and blacks comprise a pool of cheap and dispensable labour. Prices, insurance premiums and interest rates for credit are all higher in the ghetto than in many middle-class white areas. All this makes it difficult for the black person to set up in business in the ghetto; most employers, public officials, and so on are white – a visible fact which increases blacks' alienation from the US economic structure. The wealth made in the ghetto is taken out by these whites and is used in (and supports) white, middle-class areas.

In the political sphere, blacks are in the numerical minority in the USA (unlike an 'external' colony where the local population far outnumbers the foreign colonisers) which means they are frequently outvoted, particularly as blacks are frequently divided amongst themselves. Few blacks hold national political office, and those who do seldom hold any real power; their presence comprises a 'token' representation of blacks. On the level of local politics, too, this 'tokenism' occurs, with 'black community leaders' – classic marginals – often simply being 'puppets' of the local white power-holders rather than having any autonomous power. Carmichael and Hamilton draw a parallel with the white colonialists' co-option of local chiefs to administer colonial politics in Africa.

These local 'neo-colonialists' of the ghetto are paid well to 'keep the lid on' the ghetto, to prevent disturbances, protests, and the like. They are aided in this by the police force, who in effect comprise a white 'colonial army of occupation', an alien force in the ghetto. As in 'external' colonies, the colonial relationship is ultimately maintained by force of arms.

Similarly, in social terms, being black is seen as a stigma in white society, where white cultural standards of beauty prevail. Often this stigmatisation has caused a great deal of self-hatred among blacks. Many of the cultural standards imposed on blacks are derived from white, Anglo-Saxon Protestant life (Hannerz, 1969). Many blacks find these standards alien, although there is great pressure to assimilate into the white cultural 'mainstream' – pressure which until the last two decades meant that some American blacks attempted to assimilate into white culture by using skin bleaches, hair straighteners, and so on, and by acquiring the visible symbols of white success.

Carmichael and Hamilton sketch out a general programme for casting off these alienating white economic, political and cultural impositions, thereby embarking upon a project of disalienation initiated by blacks themselves without any alliance with whites.

It can be seen that the proponents of the class and colonial variants deal with broadly the same features of society and therefore overlap considerably. They seem to differ in emphasis rather than anything else. Even Cox writes about the special position of blacks owing to their 'proletarianization as a race' in the USA. Sivanandan's works too show some parallels with the colonial model. Moreover, there have been some attempts to integrate the class and colonial variants just as there have been attempts to integrate some features of conflict models with some features of order-consensus models.

Often order-consensus models are seen as politically conservative or liberal-conservative models, emphasising harmony and stability in society, whereas conflict models are seen as espousing a radical version of the perspective of the minorities. Whilst the reader may make his own judgements on this issue, he should not be distracted from examining, in as detached a way as possible, the reasoning and the data involved in these models.

## Ethnographic and Interactional Analyses of Racial and Ethnic Relations

As in the case with the other perspectives outlined above, this category covers a diversity of approaches. All these approaches, however, are committed to the position that the most fundamental level of sociological analysis is that of social action and interaction. Instead of accounting for (for instance) racial and ethnic phenomena in terms of the large-scale arrangements of the society, the proponents of this set of approaches focus on the way in which people act and fit their actions together with those of others in order to form interactions. It is from these actions and interactions that the society is built up. Instead of working down 'from the top', these perspectives tend to 'work up from the ground floor', if they try to work up at all.

A distinctive feature of this set of approaches is that society members are seen as active interpreters of their everyday world, and their interpretations or definitions are built into their actions. People define a situation in a certain way, and act according to that definition. Part of this definition of the situation is how they define other people *in* that situation, in order to act towards them and with them. Consequently, these studies attempt to examine what definitions or interpretations people make of the situation and how they arrive at and apply these definitions and interpretations. The study of definitions or interpretations often requires that the sociological observer participate with or otherwise observe (perhaps with the use of a tape recorder or video recorder) the people under scrutiny in their natural mundane settings going about their everyday activities.

A major set of these analyses can be termed 'ethnographic studies', that is, participant observations of, say, minority group communities. Suttles's study (cited above) involves some ethnographic observations. A classic study is that of Ulf Hannerz, who examined some facets of a black ghetto community in the USA. He looked at various ghetto life-styles, the relations between the sexes, streetcorner myth-making and 'rapping', and a variety of other aspects of ghetto life and culture. He sees the major distinctive cultural aspects of the ghetto as female household dominance; a specific male role emphasising toughness, sexual activity and a considerable degree of alcohol consumption; a relatively conflict-ridden relation between the sexes; a constant fear of trouble and problems in the environment; an intense concern for the music of the group; and a comparatively hostile view of white America and its representatives.

Hannerz's characterisation of ghetto life-styles is formulated with considerable reference to how the ghetto residents themselves define them. For instance, mainstreamers conform quite closely in family life and other aspects of their life-style to mainstream American culture, being home-owners, houseproud, 'respectable' and 'conventional' in many other ways, with, for instance, both spouses being employed. By contrast the second type of life-style, that of the 'swingers', involves people who are usually younger than mainstreamers and often unmarried, with their (the swingers') life being organised around parties, visiting clubs, travelling, and so on, and flitting from job to job. The third category is street families, which are composed of the mother, daughters, daughters' children, and so on, often with no consistently present father. Adult male residents tend to be brothers, friends, or boarders. If there is a husband around, he is liable to be a 'common law' husband and many married couples of street families are separated but not divorced, divorce being too expensive. These families are economically badly off and vulnerable. The final life-style is that of streetcorner men, who tend to be unattached drifters, spending their lives gambling and drinking, many being alcoholics. Streetcorner men often sustain some sense of solidarity and mutual assistance but there are also constant arguments, usually about money. Hannerz therefore not only describes life-styles but also types of person to be found in this ghetto.

There are other types of ethnography, too. Some ethnographies are far less all-embracing than that of Hannerz. For instance, Elliott Liebow's study *Tally's Corner* (Liebow, 1967) looks in detail at one group in the black ghetto – a particular gang of streetcorner men. He observed their orientation to jobs and unemployment, their support for each other and their disputes, their social networks and a variety of features of their gender identity and sexual associations and activities. Liebow examines the 'theory of manly flaws' where streetcorner men publicly account for their marriage failures by reference to their weakness for alcohol and other women, whereas Liebow says that privately they know all too well that their marriage really broke up because of the unemployment that meant the men could not act as adequate providers for their families. This 'reality' was constantly disattended by the men when speaking of others as well as themselves, thereby warding off a sense of failure.

Other ethnographies focus on one activity or set of activities in the ghetto, for example, speech practices such as 'signifying', 'marking', 'rapping', 'capping', 'playing the dozens', 'toasts', and streetcorner folk-lore, story-telling and myth-making – styles that the boxer Muhammad Ali once made famous (Abrahams, 1970). Many of these myths incorporate a derogatory view of whites; indeed, although these studies might appear to focus on minority communities, one can obtain an all too clear view of the influence of white mainstream culture, including of course racialism, on the lives of minority groupers and on their outlook.

Other analysts have focused on the way in which society members' shared definitions and interactions incorporate a sense of the hierarchial relations between racial or ethnic groups. For instance, Herbert Blumer (Blumer, 1961), a symbolic interactionist, looks at racial prejudice in terms of the way in which people actively interpret their world, through shared symbols and definitions, rather than treating prejudice as a set of attitudes ingrained into individual personality. The commonly held interpretative scheme which serves as a framework for racial prejudice comprises (*a*) the racial identification made of oneself and others and (*b*) the way in which the identified groups are seen in relation to each other.

Within this framework, there are, says Blumer, four types of definitions which comprise superordinate group members' shared 'picture' of race relations and which incorporate this sense of group identity and position: (*a*) a sense of the superiority of the superordinate group with which one identifies. This may well include the belief in the laziness, deceitfulness, immorality, or stupidity of the subordinate group which, in short, involves the reactive definition of that group; (*b*) a belief among superordinate group members that the subordinate group is intrinsically different, that they are 'not of our kind'; (*c*) a feeling that the superordinate group should have proprietary rights over certain privileges, powers and advantages such as jobs and political office, with exclusive access to places like clubs, schools, churches, housing areas and recreational institutions as well as to certain symbols and trappings of high status and to certain areas of intimacy, familiarity and privacy – for instance, sexual contacts; and (*d*) a feeling among the superordinate group that the minority group wishes to appropriate these advantages and privileges. Overall, the subordinate group is seen as remote, a group of strangers; this sense may even permeate the personal encounters between members of different races.

This framework works as the basis for a vast number of interactions concerning race, both within and between the superordinate and subordinate racial groups, including interactions that involve the coercing, threatening, inciting, intimidating of others. Any group member who disavows this sense of group superiority runs the risk of self-alienation, ostracism, and the like. Race prejudice becomes manifest when there is a felt challenge to this sense of group position, where, for instance, some event of great collective significance occurs. The early manifestations of the Civil Rights movement provided several perceived challenges of this kind in the USA, and public figures often articulated this challenge, pointing out to whites that blacks were making unprecedented claims and gains.

This sense of group position may even be shared by the subordinate group. Harald Eidheim studies the inter-group relations on the northern coast of Norway between 'mainstream' Norwegians and the Lapps, who have their own language and ethnic identity (Eidheim, 1969). Eidheim found that the Lapps were acutely conscious of their subordinate position – a position which was so low, in the eyes of the superordinate group, that to be a Lapp was a social stigma, a 'discreditable' thing. This was evident in three types of social setting: (i) the Lappish closed sphere, (ii) the Norwegian closed sphere, (iii) the public sphere, where there is actual or potential interaction between Norwegians and Lapps. In the Lappish closed sphere, where only known and trusted Lappish identities are present, only Lappish is spoken. In the Norwegian sphere, only Norwegian is spoken. In the public sphere, Lapps speak Norwegian and attempt, if possible, to suppress information about 'discreditable' Lappish identity. If someone in the public sphere asks them a question in Lappish, they will reply in Norwegian. The Norwegians, in turn, look down upon any signs of Lappish identity, something of which the Lapps are acutely aware. Thus, if the Norwegian unexpectedly enters into a closed Lappish sphere, the Lapps' conversation will immediately switch to Norwegian, and Lappish topics will be avoided.

It is this social stigma which so often in history has attached to minority group membership, and has so frequently impelled minority groupers to try to pass as members of the superordinate group, by perhaps attempting to adopt the appearance and cultural orientations of superordinate group members who provide what Goffman calls the 'virtual identity', the measuring rod or ideal against which others are adjudged. Anyone manifesting any significant departure from the visual identity is liable to be stigmatised, that is, treated as in some way having a spoiled or blemished identity. Racial stigma (or, as Goffman, 1975, puts it, 'tribal stigma') is a special case as it is transmitted along lineages, though even in that case non-whites, for instance, may attempt to 'pass for white' (Watson, 1970).

For the interactional analyst, racial stratification is an *achieved* matter, and is by no means a necessarily smoothly-running affair. Everett C. Hughes (Hughes, 1945) shows, for instance, that society members occasionally encounter status contradictions, for example, cases where they are faced with, say, a black doctor. Both the 'black' and 'doctor' statuses are 'master statuses', that is, very powerful 'identity definers'. The contradiction occurs when the status 'black' is held very low in esteem and the status 'doctor' held is very high in esteem. A white patient who endorses these status positions may face an inner dilemma: do I treat this person primarily as a *black person* (thereby treating him in a patronising manner or worse) or primarily as a *doctor* (thereby treating him with respect and deference)? The doctor who accepts these status positions may have the same inner dilemma in reverse, as may the doctor's white colleagues who also have the same sense of group position.

How the dilemma is resolved depends greatly on the situation (that is, whether or not it is a emergency, or whether the doctor has some special skill). Often – though by no means always, of course – it results in self-segregation by the doctor or the patient, in which case the black doctor may be seen as a traitor or 'Uncle Tom' by fellow members of his race. Or the black doctor may be pushed into research, where he no longer has to encounter patients, or may be put in charge of an all-black team in a hospital. These interactional strategies may be termed 'stratification practices' through which persons are accorded positions in some social hierarchy.

A whole variety of communicative and interactional resources may be modified in order to effect racial subordination. Speier (1973, pp. 184–96) gives us the following example, an actual case of an encounter many years ago in the Deep South of the USA between a black doctor (D) and white police officer (P):

> P: 'What's your name, boy?'
> D: 'Dr. Poussaint. I'm a physician.'
> P: 'What's your first name, boy?'
> D: 'Alvin.'

Here the white policeman, in calling the black doctor 'boy' (at that time in the Deep South, a customary address-form used by whites for blacks), tries to downrank him by the invocation of an identification derived from the identity-collection 'stage of life'. In short, the black doctor is degraded in the age-grading system, being addressed as a child, not an adult. The black doctor attempts to reverse this downranking by invoking the fact that he is a doctor, which as an occupation is more highly ranked than a policeman, and therefore rebuffs the policeman's attempt at downranking. However, the policeman responds by again calling the black doctor 'boy', and by getting him to give his first name reinforces that downranking in the age-grading system; typically, adults can address children by their first name, and can by this and other cultural methods claim rights and control over them. Here, then, we see that racial subordination can be achieved in interaction by invoking identities other than race.

In conclusion, one can merely recommend that each of these perspectives is initially examined in an even-handed way, with an attempt to understand the manner in which proponents of each perspective attempt to understand the diverse and complicated domain of racial and ethnic relations. Each perspective, even in its most sophisticated form, intendedly selects and simplifies that complex domain so that sociologists can examine this or that aspect of racial and ethnic relations with as much clarity and precision as possible and so that they can constantly attempt to remain conscious of their assumptions and ways of analysing their data. It is not necessary to choose between the above perspectives; each perspective has its strengths and weaknesses, as adjudjed from the standpoint of proponents of other perspectives. However, if you do feel inclined to choose one perspective over the others, then such a choice should at least be made in the light of a proper understanding of the other sociological points of view.

# References: Chapter 3

Abrahams, Roger D. (1970), *Deep Down in the Jungle, Negro Narrative Folklore from the Streets of Philadelphia* (Chicago: Aldine).

Banton, M. (1967), *Race Relations* (London: Social Science Paperbacks).

Baxter, P., and Sansom, B. (1972), *Race and Social Difference* (Harmondsworth: Penguin).

Blumer, H. (1961), 'Race prejudice as a sense of group position', in J. Masuoka and P. Valien (eds), *Race Relations: Problems and Theory* (Chapel Hill, NC: University of North Carolina Press), pp. 217–27.

Carmichael, S., and Hamilton, C. V. (1968), *Black Power; The Politics of Liberation in America* (Harmondsworth: Penguin).

Cox, O. C. (1948), *Caste, Class and Race: A Study in Social Dynamics* (Garden City, NY: Doubleday).

Eidheim, H. (1969), 'When ethnic identity is a social stigma', in F. Barth (ed.), *Ethnic Groups and Boundaries* (Boston, Mass.: Little, Brown), pp. 39–57.

Faris, R. E. L. (1948), *Social Disorganisation* (New York: The Ronald Press).

Goffman, E. (1975), *Stigma* (Englewood Cliffs, NJ: Prentice-Hall).

Hannerz, U. (1969), *Soul Side: Inquiries into Ghetto Culture and Community* (New York: Columbia University Press).

Horton, J. (1966), 'Order and conflict theories of social problems as competing ideologies', *American Journal of Sociology*, vol. 71 (May), pp. 701–13.

Hughes, E. C. (1945), 'Dilemmas and contradictions of status', *American Journal of Sociology*, vol. 50, pp. 353–9.

Liebow, E. (1967), *Tally's Corner: A Study of Negro Streetcorner Men* (Boston, Mass.: Little, Brown).

Merton, R. K. (1976), 'Discrimination and the American creed', in *Sociological Ambivalence and Other Essays* (New York: The Free Press), pp. 189–216.

Rose, A. (1964), *The Negro in America: The Condensed Version of Gunnar Myrdal's 'An American Dilemma'* (New York: Harper & Row).

Sivanandan, A. (1976), *Race, Class and the State* (London: Institute of Race Relations).

Speier, M. (1973), *How to Observe Face to Face Communication* (Pacific Palisades, Calif.: Goodyear).

Stonequist, E. V. (1937), *The Marginal Man* (New York: Charles Scribner's Sons).

Suttles, G. (1968), *The Social Order of the Slum* (Chicago: University of Chicago Press).
Watson, G. (1970), *Passing for White* (London: Tavistock).

## Further Reading

Rex, J. (1970), *Race Relations in Sociological Theory* (London: Weidenfeld & Nicolson).
Schermerhorn, R. A. (1970), *Comparative Ethnic Relations* (New York: Random House).
Shibutani, T. and Kwan T. H. (1965), *Ethnic Stratification: A Comparative Approach* (New York: Collier Macmillan).
Zubaida, S. (1970), *Race and Racialism* (London: Tavistock).

# Chapter 4

# Education: Success and Failure

## DIANNE PHILLIPS

Sociologists have repeatedly documented the fact that inequalities in educational attainment are related to 'social factors' and, particularly, to patterns of social stratification – the lower classes do less well, educationally, than those above them. Despite efforts to open up educational opportunity and to reduce the strength of the link between stratification and achievement, the connection persists.

In seeking to interpret these relationships, sociologists have assumed that inequalities in achievement between classes or ethnic groups are not to be understood as a product of genetic or other inherent differences in the characteristics of individuals, but are to be seen as resulting from the relationship between groups and institutions within the context of social systems and, particularly, in the connection between the education system and the structure of stratification relationships.

In a society like ours, certain connections between education and stratification (in addition to those bearing upon the unequal distribution of educational achievement) are obvious; schools and other organisations have a prevailing 'middle class' character in terms of the social standing of the persons who staff them, the values they espouse and the social skills and attitudes preferred and inculcated within them.

The general disposition of many people, and not just of sociologists, is to regret the inequalities in education, or at least the fact that inequalities in achievement are shaped not by abilities, pure and simple, but by social characteristics, by circumstances other than the individual's specific capacity for achievement. A prominent preoccupation which governs the analysis of education as an institution is to see whether there is the possibility of reorganising the relationship between educational institutions and the encircling society in order to obviate this connection. Whether or not educational achievement can be dissociated from 'outside' characteristics depends of course on what the *nature of the relationship* between education and society now is, upon why stratification and achievement are connected. We shall distinguish four main alternative ways of interpreting the 'place' of educational institutions in society. These are

(1)   functionalism: education serves the needs of society;
(2)   education as a provider of opportunities;
(3)   education serves the needs of capitalism;
(4)   education serves the interests of bureaucracy.

This division into four views is to make it easier to grasp the outlines of a number of complex debates. The reader should be aware that alternative classifications are very possible and indeed the arguments are often cross-cutting and fit uneasily into these simplified categories.

In each case we shall (*a*) look at the account of the purposes, functions and possibilities of educational institutions, which invariably involves the relations to other social structures; (*b*) assess the picture of the nature and significance of educational attainment that is related to each view; (*c*) look at the criticisms that have been made of each viewpoint. Each view yields criticisms of the others, so, in this way, we can see how they relate to each other and sample some of the issues that divide them.

## (1)   Functionalism: Education Serves the Needs of Society

The broad character of the functionalist approach is well known and described in many places. Institutions are to be examined for the role they play in the society *as a whole* and, particularly, for the positive contribution they make to its unity and stability. Education is thus to be looked at in relation to the vital function of socialisation. If there is to be continuity in *any* society, then there must be a transmission from generation to generation of the culture of that society. *All* societies must have ways of socialising new members and *some* societies have differentiated educational institutions which are specialised agencies for socialisation, preparing people for life in the wider society.

The basic functionalist argument for the existence of educational institutions in some societies is derived from Durkheim and is a *developmental* one: 'simple' societies are characterised by a very limited division of labour' in *all* areas of life. If and when such societies begin to develop into more complex forms, they do so by enhancing the division of labour and by differentiating out institutions specialised in the fulfilment of certain functions. Education comes to take on a role that was previously filled in the course of family, work, religious and other activities.

The basic functionalist argument is elaborated by Parsons (1961), whose views are rather more complex and subtle than those usually credited to him or to functionalists generally. Parsons argues that education in *modern* society provides for both basic and differential socialisation. *Basic* socialisation has to do with the production of a type of person, one who is both committed to the society's cultural pattern but also an independent individual motivated to enjoy an organised part in society. *Differential socialisation* involves fitting individuals with the specialised knowledge, skills and attitudes that they will require if they are to be distributed amongst the highly specialised roles which make up the wider society. There has, then, to be a 'matching' of education's output with the 'needs' of the system, that is, if the system is to work, schools and the like must produce people with the kinds of skills, knowledge, and so on, that are the same as those required for fulfilment of social roles.

The existence of such a connection is assumed by other changes in the character of the system, particularly its tendency towards 'meritocracy', the treating of education and qualifications as the basic considerations in appointing people to positions (rather than social background or personal connections, and so on).

However, though educational qualifications (rather than, say, social class membership) have increasingly been the basis for determining one's position in the occupational hierarchy, it is also clear that social class has remained an 'indirect' determinant in the sense that the quality of one's educational attainment is likely to correspond to, or depend upon, one's social class origins.

How do the functionalists account for the persistence of *inequalities* (not just differentiation) in educational attainment? They do so by claiming that social roles in a modern society are not merely specialised in terms of the knowledge and skills required for their performance, but they also differ in terms of the levels and quality of skills needed. The abilities and tasks which make some of the more complex and difficult skills acquirable are not, themselves, teachable; from the point of view of the schools, people either do or do not have these abilities and it is the school's role to identify and develop the respective 'gifts' of pupils. Thus functionalist accounts of education link to the functionalist theory of social stratification. People in the educational system have talents – some possibly innate – and tastes, which, for functionalists, must be the determinants of their attainment. Schooling both develops these talents and certifies them for efficient recruitment.

## CRITICISMS OF FUNCTIONALISM

It is important to remember that functionalist theories are deliberately highly simplified and that they are not meant to correspond to the real world in a straightforward way. This is often forgotten in criticising functionalism. Objections to it often involve the mistaken assumption that showing that things in reality don't match the functionalist's theoretical picture shows functionalism to be in error. With this caution in mind, we can say that there are such discrepancies between the picture and the reality in the case of education to suggest that an *essentially different* picture may be needed.

Many of the criticisms argue that if education were to have functions to fulfil, it would not fill them very well. If education were supposed to develop people's abilities and to instil in them a commitment to society's culture, it would do neither of these things very well. The provision of educational resources is very unevenly distributed amongst social strata. In many areas of the educational system little real effort is made to develop whatever talents the pupils might have; little opportunity exists to provide all the resources that would be necessary to create the background against which children from the lower classes would have the same chance to develop any potential they might have to the same level as those from higher classes. The school is not in any case — or so the argument goes — attempting to instil a common culture but is seeking to impose that of one segment — the middle classes — on all, with the result that education simply 'turns off' many lower-class children who find that culture alien, even repellent. Rather than attracting children to that culture, schooling may be driving them away from it.

The idea that the school is developing talents for the benefit of society as a whole is one which requires (*a*) that educational achievement results from ability and (*b*) that the abilities cultivated in the educational system be distributed through the occupation system in a 'free market' way. But these assumptions come up against the observable fact that educational achievement is systematically related to social position and background, and against the problem that success in education is not clearly related to occupational attainment. Jencks *et al.* (1972) have even argued that social origin is far the most important influence in this and *that schooling counts for virtually nothing.*

## (2)  Education as a Provider of Opportunities

This second 'reformist' view is both in substantial agreement with, yet also a reaction to, the functionalist view. It suggests that there is no ideal complementarity between education and society, nor consensus on the efficiency or justice of the results. Given education's powerful potential for 'socialisation', may it not be seen as the instrument by which a society at once more equal, more just and more efficent, can be created? There need not be an inevitable conflict between the demands of social amelioration and the need for the efficient performance of the socialisation and 'recruitment' function. Thus there is a viable position which links easily to a gradualist model of social change. 'Education can compensate' (Halsey, 1980) can stand as its watchword. This view, then, taking as read a continuum of inequality in terms of life-style, housing, consumption patterns, concerns itself with the development of a common culture and agreed values while retaining the interest in 'economic efficiency'. Programmes of educational reform and expansion can lead to the amelioration of poverty, promote a more highly skilled workforce and, in the long run, work towards breaking down hereditary privilege.

In general, this view informed the post-Second World War educational debates and institutional battles in Great Britain. The system set up by the 1944 Education Act was increasingly criticised for failing to break the pattern whereby working-class children were perennially recruited to the lower bands. The 'comprehensive' movement of the 1960s and early 1970s reflected the idea that schools can and should change society. This view is an elaborate extension of the first, functional one, rejecting its adequacy as a picture of contemporary society, but retaining its idea of what education *should* do. The root of failure is simply 'that so far we have not tried hard enough' (Blackstone, 1980). Both views share a presumption of the effect and importance of schooling for society and its possibilities, therefore, for social breakdown and social transformation.

Among many of the original enthusiasts, the move to comprehensive education and the broader attempts to change society by enlarging the common culture and contact, produced disillusion and cynicism. Working-class children continued to 'fail' disproportionately and their representation in higher education continued to remain depressingly low.

Those who believe in the educational system as an instrument of social change do not necessarily reject the view that talent is one of the contributors to educational success. Indeed it often seems to be their ideal that differential success be based on ability alone; meritocracy is their goal. Obviously they consider that there are currently other factors affecting attainment than innate talents; these are socially imposed ones and should be eliminated. In general, they will tend to believe what cannot yet be demonstrated, namely, that genuine equality of opportunity, when social engineering removes the social factors in individual attainment, will result in a much greater measure of equality of achievement, and assume that such inequalities as then persist will be the result of ineliminable 'natural' differences of talent, and so on.

So, there is a twofold argument: that we can identify the systematic influence of social factors in individual achievement; and that changing these will contribute to the transformation of society more broadly. The social factors identified are those which tend to produce individual success and failure on the basis of membership of a social grouping, rather than on individual talent and effort. Naturally, social class differences have been taken to be central here.

In selective systems, with a fee-paying sector available, some parents will pay to keep a child in a particular kind of education. Also it has been argued that middle-class parents are more familiar with the procedures involved, clearer about the increased life-chances that derive from further years in education, and, in general, have more supportive households. All these features could lead to superior performance by their children. Thus sociologists talk of the 'social construction of failure', and the reproduction of the existing shape of society. In the selective system, there was, hence, a tendency, although not an absolute one, for grammar schools to become middle-class and for secondary modern schools to become primarily working-class. The politically successful campaign for comprehensive schools was based in the idea that non-selective schools would inhibit these processes of selection. However, it was soon argued (although the experiment has not yet had all that long to work) that the processes of selection were replicating themselves *within* comprehensive schools, and taking institutional form in systems that effectively, if not officially, 'streamed' children. Again middle-class children were taking a disproportionate share of the 'academic' streams.

The remarkable pervasiveness of these relations could be taken as a criticism of the view that schools can change society. But it can also be argued that understanding is improving, and that further social engineering in the schools will eventually produce the desired effects. This leads to an endless argument. Certainly attempts to improve educational attainment have yielded a better understanding of how schools interact with society in shaping levels of attainment. In these attempts two major ideas have been those of cultural variability and theories of classroom interaction.

Theories of cultural variability took two main forms: cultural deprivation and cultural difference. These arguments can be applied in much the same way to both social class and ethnic group differences: we shall refer mainly to social class here, the considerable application to the situation of ethnic groups being assumed to be apparent. Both propose that the economic distinction of social class expresses itself in cultural differences. In cultural deprivation accounts, the culture of the working classes handicaps children in contact with the culture of the society transmitted in the schools. Cultural difference accounts suggest that children who are obliged to master new cultural elements, when moving from one group to another, are faced with tasks additional to those who do not move. Further, this is a costly process in terms of the values and commitments of the home culture.

Cultural deprivation theory gets a poor reception from many anthropologists and sociologists who take it that the attempt to understand the diversity of human lives is not enhanced by the tendency to patronise ways other than one's own. There is often an *unduly* patronising assumption of the superiority of one's own culture to that of others, to the extent that one begins to assume that one's own range of preferences are definitions of culture and that anyone not falling in with those is 'cultureless'. Such a disposition to be complacent about the virtue of one's own ways can lead to insensitivity to the character and quality of lives that differ from them. There is thought to be something of this in cultural deprivation theory, owing to its tendency to assume unproblematically the straightforward superiority and desirability of the 'high culture' (art, music, and so on) appreciated by important segments of the middle classes in the Western world.

It is true that the working class do show relatively little taste for the 'high culture' which plays a large part in many middle-class lives, but cultural deprivation theory is criticised for obfuscating, by talk of *cultural deprivation*, the extent to which working-class lives are conditioned by *economic* disadvantage. It may be that the absence of books and other cultural artefacts from working-class homes does detract from the capacity to do well in school, but this is to draw attention to the extent to which consumption of middle-class cultural valuables is linked to a style of life which, in turn, requires sufficient economic stability to enable its pursuit. Working-class enthusiasm for high culture might well be incompatible with the conditions of a life lived in economic disadvantage, under the uncertainty resulting from bearing the brunt of social and economic change, and in a position where one is destined to be the recipient, not the giver, of orders and instructions.

The second objection is that the emphasis upon 'high culture' aspects and their absence from working-class life overestimates the extent to which the working class lack culture and underestimates the extent to which their way of life embodies a different culture from that of the middle classes.

One must beware of overly simplifying ideas about the unity and stability of a 'working-class culture' and its sharp distinction from that of other groups in the society. It must be recognised that it has become differentiated and varied under the historical influence of powerful social and religious movements, that it contains threads of working-class intellectualism and self-education, involvement in the social and political struggles of the wider society, and connection with institutions and organisations such as churches and sects, the Co-operative movement, trade unions and the Labour Party. Persistent local and community traditions and hobby-based leisure concerns add to the diversity, but one can still speak of a working-class culture which emphasises a commitment to community solidarity and mutual co-operation: values different from those individualistic, achievement-oriented ones which prevail in the middle classes.

These two arguments lead to the third, which is that cultural deprivation theory misunderstands educational failure by viewing it as the result of a lack of resources and by assuming alienation, troublesomeness, and so on, to be the reaction to failures and as a response to rejection by the education system. It does not see that working-class children fail not because they lack motivation to succeed but because they are motivated in other directions than those favoured by the school. The alienation from school is a rejection of an institution in which they never wished to participate, let alone succeed. It is an expression of values *at odds* with those promoted by the school, of an alternative culture which is ambivalent about the virtues of social mobility and often negative about the value of education, contemptuous of the attitudes and behaviour involved in it, prizing aggression, sexuality and leisure over the self-discipline, compliance and deferred gratification needed for doing well in school.

'Cultural difference theory' opposes 'cultural deprivation', and calls for an approach which shows more respect for cultures other than those of the middle classes, one which might broaden the curriculum to recognise and harness the cultural alternatives. In relation to black groups in the USA and immigrant populations in the United Kingdom, this is a frequent suggestion. But in general, this argument leads to deep suspicion about the whole of the 'compensation' view and scepticism about whether any conceivable change in the schools is going to be an effective agent for social change. Cultural difference theory leads to a view of schools as agencies of social stasis and reproduction.

One very popular theory illustrates some of these relationships. Basil Bernstein (1971) has attempted to argue for the contribution of ways of speaking to differential achievement in education. Although Bernstein's arguments have changed and are not always clear and consistent, they can be roughly summarised as attempting to draw a distinction between 'public' and 'private' codes of speech. In a group of close acquaintances, with considerable shared knowledge of one another, developed over a personal history in common, speech can be condensed, and elliptical: a single word can trigger an old joke or an interpretation. In public situations, where the participants may not know each other, or may have only very limited knowledge of each other, then there must be a more careful rendering explicit of what is said. The full resources of vocabulary, grammar and careful shades of meaning must all be employed, and elliptical uses avoided. Bernstein proposed that if these ways of speaking in social situations were regularly and differently employed by particular social groups, the differences would bring about a different receptivity to the same linguistic message. The ways of speaking, which when they become regularised he terms 'codes', reflect different social situations. The 'restricted' or private code reflects life in continuing personal groups with shared histories; the 'elaborated' or public code in more formal situations. So, an idealised working-class community will be one with greater emphasis on the restricted code; middle-class families will use it in appropriate situations, but will have also greater access and familiarity with the elaborated code.

Working-class children would be disadvantaged in school by the lack of familiarity with the elaborated code said to prevail there. Bernstein also claimed that cognitive consequences follow from differential familiarity with the two codes, and this would have implications for educational attainment. The restricted code was claimed to be poor in syntax, limited in vocabulary and inadequate for the expression of complex logical arguments. The formal lessons of the school require facility in 'elaborated' language. There is, then, a reference to cultural deprivation but in Bernstein's statements it is never straightforward. If it could be shown that working-class children do possess *some* familiarity with the essentials of the elaborated form, why does this argue for a lesser cognitive capacity? It has proved difficult to demonstrate that there are differential codes which are unequally distributed on a stratification basis (Edwards, 1976). Extreme claims of linguistic deprivation, particularly exemplified in claims about the disadvantaging role of black dialects in the USA, led linguists into massive counter-arguments. A famous paper by Labov (1973) argued that practices of speech which could be labelled 'restricted' were characteristically selected by 'working-class' children in the classroom and other formal contexts because they perceived such situations as threatening. Outside these situations the children's dialectal forms were wholly adequate for complex, logical arguments.

Bernstein himself has always insisted on the vigour and power of the restricted codes of working-class communities, and for its utilisation in appropriate ways in schooling. Such discussions are characteristic of cultural difference arguments. Should children be schooled in 'standard' languages permitting easy access to what is adjudged the valuable 'standard' cultural heritage, at the price of imposing additional learning tasks on them as opposed to children for whom these are already native modes? Should the situation be equalised by making native users of middle-class standard English versions learn, for example, creole dialects and the culture expressed in them? One factor which such discussions overlooked, but which the linguistic critics of deprivation theory had insisted on, was the ease with which children pick up new dialectal uses and add them to their repertoire, 'switching codes' from one situation to another. Hence it would come as no surprise to those critics to find that even the educational failures had no difficulty in picking up the rudiments of Jamaican creole, and the elements of a West Indian messianic religious cult (Rastafarianism), without any intervention from the schools. It is obviously important not to underplay the difficulties of frightened young children caught up in culture clashes but neither must one underestimate their capacity to cope and adapt.

In the pursuit of social factors in individual attainment, many sociologists attended to the close analysis of what happened in the classroom. An early influential study by Rosenthal and Jacobson (1968) applied the notion of the self-fulfilling prophecy to the ways in which children came to fail differentially. After a (claimed but criticised) equalising for intelligence, teachers were given what they were told were the IQ scores for particular children, but were in fact randomised scores. The measured IQ of children came to resemble what the teachers had been told to expect, more than their 'real' IQs. The teachers, this suggests, were consciously or unconsciously modifying their behaviour in relation to children they associated with particular scores, with the consequence that the children 'failed' or 'succeeded' in the light of a 'prophecy', and the teacher's expectations based on that. The study has been extensively criticised for poor methods, and has not been replicated successfully despite attempts to do so. But it did encourage the examination of the detailed processes of the assessment of ability in the classroom and school. Success or failure depends, as much as anything, on delicate and drawn-out processes of negotiation and interaction between staff and pupil, teaching colleagues, teachers and pupils, administrators, and so on, on the basis of variable but persistently used conceptions of ability employed by those 'educational decision-makers'. Thus conceptions like 'bright', 'articulate', 'co-operative', formed early in a child's school career by particular teachers or informal consensus, can be linked to middle-class membership and familiarity with formal occasions, and to cues like styles of dress, cleanliness and politeness, and can then operate to produce teachers' judgements of those qualities, as a continuing matter. Practices of reporting, and bureaucratic dossiers, can be used to create pictures of children which can reflect such inputs, and reputations, once created, can be difficult, or impossible, to live down. We scarcely need, in the face of such factors, to invoke cognitive deprivation. If (possibly defensive and aggressive) children react to such processes by suspending interest and co-operation, the effect becomes self-fulfilling.

### CRITICISMS OF 'EDUCATION AS A PROVIDER OF OPPORTUNITIES'

The critics of the view that education can compensate for society and finally change it, argue that experiments in changing the schools, though limited in relation to the size of the problem being tackled, have met with little success so far. The world and its economy are also changing and have greatly altered the socio-economic environment of education with changes in the industrial base and new processes of technological job replacement. Political changes, too, inhibit the experiments with schooling, but it is clear that the encouragement of culture contact and extended education has not changed patterns of wealth, nor seriously disrupted existing patterns of social recruitment and mobility (cf. Chapter 2 above). There have been expansions of opportunity as with the recruitment of those of working-class origins to the enlarged bureaucracies of the last fifty years, and education has played an important part in qualifying people for mobility. But this was historically a 'one-off' event; expansion is now altogether slower and comparable opportunities simply do not exist. Above all, wealth-holdings have only diffused within the families of the wealthy, and sharp differences continue to reflect the patterns of capitalism. Education has failed to create one society, to open the avenues of social mobility, or to enlarge a consensus.

Optimism about the capacity of education to change and to produce changes was very much dependent upon optimism about the way in which industrial societies would generally be developing, and has lately faded. There is now much more willingness to believe that real changes in education are only possible if there are drastic changes in the nature of society as a whole. Hence the liberal radicalism of this view tends to give way to the suggestion that schools cannot change society, but are necessarily agencies of social stasis, change and reproduction. This brings together criticisms of both the 'functionalist' and 'reformist' views.

## (3) Education Serves the Needs of Capitalism

Educational institutions are largely under the control of, or subordinate to, more powerful and fundamental social arrangements. These are most frequently conceptualised as the economic structures, and particularly the relations of production, of capitalist society, that is, arrangements of rights to property, and the control of industrial production and activity. Again, these are the relations which structure the holdings of wealth and capital, and social classes stemming from these.

This neo-Marxist view agrees with the functionalist view, that education contributes to the working of industrial society, and of contemporary economic organisation. It agrees with the second, compensatory, view in finding the characteristic account of these processes idealised. Education does serve the needs of society but these are for the production and reproduction of a labour force, largely domesticated by ideology (which includes versions of the functionalist account) into accepting its situation as just and appropriate. It accepts its relative 'failure' and lack of power and control.

The most influential theorist of this view is the French Marxist theorist Louis Althusser (1977). He argues that fundamental economic relations are both the input to and the output of social processes: they contribute to the structuring of what occurs, but essentially what occurs is structured so as to maintain, or reproduce, those relations themselves. The key to understanding capitalism is the classic Marxist account of it as a system of the production and exchange of commodities. The power of labour, what a worker can do, is a commodity, but one of a special kind: it produces value. The commodities produced by labour power will exchange for more than the costs of their production, which include the costs of the reproduction of what is used up in their production, which, in turn, includes labour power. Education is part of the system of the reproduction of labour power: in systemic (and ideal) terms, it must contribute to the reproduction, at minimal cost, of labour power. The state is responsible, within the system, for the control and reproduction of the commodity of labour power. It cannot depend on simple force to do this and creates an apparatus of organisations and ideas (such as schools) which work by persuasion and indoctrination. These 'ideological state apparatuses' work to ensure that those who are to do the work will do so co-operatively, out of the belief that the situation is just and reasonable.

Analysts of this persuasion can regard the fact that achievement is at a low level for many people not as a failing of the system but as a product of its inherent nature. If working-class children come to regard schools as compulsory, alien and unreasonable places with incomprehensible curricula taught by the incompetent and bewildered, within a mindless bureaucracy; if they find life outside the school more attractive and interesting and drop out, then the system is working successfully. If those who survive in it are recruited, with relief and gratitude, into the minor bureaucratic echelons required by industrial capitalism and its complex apparatuses, then the systems are doing what the theory claims they should do.

The idealism of the functionalist view is neatly reversed: the notion that education is a process developing human potential becomes the idea that education exists to prevent its realisation. The economic possibilities for individuals are limited and channelled into their provision of labour power. For societies, the economic possibilities of different forms of organisation (for example, socialism and communism) are denied by the reproduction of the forms of commodity exchange. Similarly, the cultural possibilities for fulfilment are inhibited by ideological repression, the school curriculum appearing absurd and meaningless, the systems of dicipline and examination seeming pointless and alienating, all this leading to withdrawal, dropping-out and exclusion.

Such a view is clearly capable of fitting the evidence on achievement patterns. It also gives a new emphasis to other phenomena such as the processes of negotiation and interpretation in the classroom which are opened to analysis as inculcating habits of obedience and the tolerance of unintelligibility and irrationality, and surrounded by an ideological ethic of concern, responsibility and caring. Similarly, the processes of construction of largely working-class anti-school ideologies, (cf. Corrigan, 1979) is only to be expected. A persistent theme in recent investigation has been the realistic nature of working-class attitudes to education. Some recognise that educational achievement will not serve as a path to effective social mobility, and will prove costly in terms of commitment and their connections to neighbourhood and community. They correctly appreciate that education offers them nothing in terms of real prospects of improvement. Hence the generation and acceptance of what for educational reformers is 'underachievement'.

## CRITICISMS OF 'EDUCATION SERVES THE NEEDS OF CAPITALISM'

Critics *could* argue that the neo-Marxist account is just as idealised as the functionalist one. Does education in the capitalist West really produce an ideologically dominated and quiescent workforce? One can try to strengthen the connection with empirical reality in this regard by emphasising that it is a theory of basic real structures, overlain by historical chances and variations. However, if the functionalist view is oversimplified, then so too is this Marxist one – the working class are not, at least in Britain, willing fodder for capitalist industry. They are the most obviously wised-up, cynical, politically and economically effective working class in the world, and their educational experiences contribute to this. Nor are the middle class products of the educational system obviously attuned to the needs of capitalist production. One can talk of the 'relative autonomy' of education from economic determination and appeal to special historical factors to explain the extremely persistent tendency of the educationally successful to despise industry, and to choose academic, professional and administrative careers. To represent British social structure as an ideologically misled working class, and a powerful ruling class based in profit-oriented economic enterprise, may not be wholly a myth, but certainly requires a great deal of discounting of counter-evidence to become plausible.

It can be argued that despite the profound changes in economic dominance, from private to state owned and controlled, and with large private industry profoundly dependent on expanded state activity, the basic economic relations remain capitalist in character. Those undertaking the administrative and organisational tasks which multiply in an apparently 'organic' state become, in so far as they dispose of wealth and power, not capitalists, but agents of capital. However, the original idealised analysis of capitalist relations is becoming strained here. Similarly, critics have argued (for example, Karabel and Halsey, 1977) that in the socialist countries the actual performance of the educational system is remarkably similar to that of the advanced West, with educational certification used to reproduce differences of status, children of officials and cadres becoming officials and cadres. In fact, it can be argued that markers of status replace those of overt wealth, with wealth such as it is in such societies, transmitted via the educational process, and control over it certainly so. Hence, the reproduction of patterns of inequality is not a question of an underlying set of capitalist relations, but of the protective measures of politically defined status groups. It is still possible for proponents of the view to argue that the so-called socialist societies of the East are state-capitalist, and converge with those of the West in their emergent institutional forms. Again, the strain on the theory is evident in the argument.

This neo-Marxist view treats ideologies as functioning parts of systems and thus regards 'functionalism' as itself a functioning part of the structure of contemporary capitalism. It is a 'lived' ideology, that is, built into institutions, believed and lived out by people, shaping their experience of the world. It is an ideology as opposed to a genuine science, which is how the neo-Marxist view presents itself. The similarities of functionalist and neo-Marxist views on education suggest that the separation is not so easily made. If the functionalist view is a moralising one, which tends to value positively and thus to justify the existing system, then this alternative to it is no less moralising; it simply substitutes a negative assessment for the functionalist's more favourable one. Otherwise it accepts many of the same facts and explains them in much the same way.

## (4)  Education Serves the Interests of Bureaucracy

Each of the three views considered has seen the relationship between the economy and education as central to an understanding of the latter. But our fourth interpretation rejects this idea, regarding it too as so much ideology. The primacy which the three previous views have given to economics is better given to politics, that is, the differing ways in which one particular section, educators, try to promote *their* interest in increasingly pervasive schooling. Neo-Marxists regard political position and control as dependent matters with, at best, relative autonomy from economic determination and thus are unable to understand why in practice, that is, in so-called socialist societies, Marxist views merely reproduce the stratification and inequalities of capitalist society. The reason is that the capacity of political power to determine things independently is greatly underestimated, and that the fact that possession of power *itself* creates definite interests is not appreciated.

Max Weber suggested throughout his work that political power was analytically independent of economic position (although the two are often connected in practice). Political authority can be of differing kinds, but that of the modern world is essentially derived from the application of scientific rationality to the organisation of institutions (see Chapter 6 below). This Weber called rational bureaucracy. It is, he insists, a form of power, legitimated by appeals to science and rationality, which is mandated to act to carry out tasks assigned to it by political authorities. Once established, bureaucracy can often become independent of its political directors and pursue its own interests instead of the tasks assigned to it. One of the bureaucracy's prime interests is its own expansion and this means that this form of power spreads, inevitably, to encompass new areas. Foucault (see Sheridan, 1980) has particularly developed the connection between rationality, bureaucratisation and the spread of 'legitimate' power throughout all areas of life and the effective creation of new 'sites' for administrative power. The educational system may thus be regarded as the bureaucratisation of socialisation, and the reorganisation of activities so that all kinds of teaching and learning that were previously scattered throughout the society and which were not then connected to one another, are brought into one unified system. The educational bureaucracy has been enabled to expand so comprehensively because it has been able to borrow the prestige that the idea of the 'educated man' has enjoyed through its association with high-status groups and their attractive life-style.

Arguments for the centrality of politics emphasise the expanding state of the mid-nineteenth century, the spread of its interference and control, and the rejection of classic liberalism as an obstacle to its further extension. Correction of the abuses of child labour in early industrialisation meant an existing interest in children who were thus unemployed. In factories, their assembly (for protective reasons) had taken over the early forms of schooling; its replacement by a bureaucractic and universal system of schooling was an obvious step and one in line with the prevailing tendency to bureaucratise everything. The popular ideology of an educated and industrious workforce was supplemented by a felt need for control over a potentially unruly population of young people. Once compulsory education was established, a variety of bureaucratic groups became concerned with and interested in its consolidation and expansion. Ironically, the expansion of the bureaucracy is something that justifies itself, for it creates a market for its own product and generations of upwardly mobile working class enter the lower middle class by the route of teaching and other bureaucratic employment. The ideology of the economic need for education began in a misreading of the economic success of those who had received a 'gentleman's' education, but who were not necessarily wealthy because of that, for, of course, they had started out as members of the economic and political elite. The growth of government itself required elements of common cultural skills, and the reforms of the civil service provided the basis for formal education in the public schools.

The argument is, then, that compulsory education created an education industry; it is a political creation, backed by the enforcement powers of the state. Its ideological resources include the claim that the needs of an economy can be met by schooling and that schools are the necessary modern form of 'socialisation'. Expansion of control appears as a praiseworthy and beneficial extension of the powers of particular farsighted bureaucratic reformers, and their existing staff-empires. Thereafter, the actual extension and supervision of the area provides indefinite numbers of stable careers for bureaucrats. They have continued interest and commitment to their site of control as a source of power and rationalised wealth.

As a set of institutions dedicated to rational ends, such a structure also provides the ground of immense differences of opinion as to what is best. It is in the inevitable quarrels that the ideological strength of such provinces of power and meaning thrive. Disputes can become institutionalised; there can be academic critics and their practitioner followers, all 'within' the parameters of the reality of the institutional system. 'Radical' change is a possible option. What is not 'thinkable' is the abolition of an entire province of rationality, meaning and organisational possibility, that is, the 'de-schooling' of society. It seems unthinkable to contemplate the abolition of the institution of education as a whole.

The education system grows by embracing ever-larger age-groups. Its bureaucratic tendency, and the only way in which its output can be rationally measured, is an increasingly monopolistic control of 'knowledge', and of gradations of certification. Where some knowledge is securely entrenched in rival provinces, the distinction between 'pure' or 'basic' and 'applied' will be rigorously utilised. Other provinces have adopted the mode of 'educational' rationality and used it as part of their own organisation. They develop their own educational practices, certificates, training staff and academics.

The growth of schooling is thus linked to the broader movement of 'professionalisation', and the utilisation of the academy within the stabilisation of bureaucratic professions and provinces is important. Requirements of certification for an ever-widening range of jobs has increased, with upward pressures on the standard. Minor clerical roles come to demand degrees for entry, with the ever-increasing output of graduates. Some reject the system, with bright students explicitly opting for early employment to distinguish themselves from what has become the mass, and employers beginning to react favourably to job experience rather than certification. The province responds with plans for indefinite extension: for 'continuing education', or education throughout life.

The bureaucratic monopoly of knowledge, and the imposition on it of organisational forms – departments, timetables, periods, preparations, examinations – characteristically produces bureaucratically unavoidable absurdities. Certainties, boundaries, rote-learning, simplification, arbitrary limits are bureaucratic impositions on 'knowledge', and an acceptance of them becomes a mark of the professional. The victory of skills of such kinds leads to the downgrading of some original skills and knowledge. The professionalisation of 'knowledge', and of practices around knowledge, can hence reduce the pleasures that knowledge can bring. In addition, the existence of professionalism, certificates and courses can themselves turn what was once pleasurable into something less attractive and can reduce its following among the non-professionals. The growth in the academic study of classical literature, for example, has been accompanied by a decline in its appeal to non-academics.

What counts as achievement and quality in bureaucratised education is a complex matter. The social creation of success is seen as the outcome of historical processes of conflict and negotiation between bureaucratic groups, with the specification of criteria for achievement being a non-rational collection of what is bequeathed by such conflicts. They are to be understood, as in the educational compensatory and Marxist theories, as created by the need to reproduce social groupings. Now, rather than those involved in a situation of clearly structured class dominance, they are reproducing such groups as happen to result from the complex struggle amongst a multiplicity of interests. Instead of Salter and Tapper's (1981) claim that the contemporary scene in Britain is the construction of a clearer and gloves-off correspondence between education and economy, an explicit making true of recent Marxist approaches, this view suggests that an unstable mix of free-market liberalism and invocations of a mythical educational golden age leads to an ideology of increased freedom and choice within the boundaries of bureaucratic education. The existence of education and its state licensing, supervision and backing is never questioned, despite the inheritance of a clear theory that control should be relinquished. Schemes for kinds of economic freedom within the province are often proposed with distorted reproduction of external arrangements, for example, the introduction or educational vouchers, a special form of money extracted from taxation but earmarked for spending only on the bureaucratically defined education, thus maintaining it. Within the province bureaucratic groups vie for power, by claiming it represents what people (that is, parents and industry) presently want. Whatever the virtue of particular analyses, the elaboration of a Weberian style emphasises the continuous transformation of the conditions under which institutions and individuals operate in politically created and transformed 'empires' and 'provinces'; the social, but unstable, frameworks for 'success', and consequently the continually reconstructed social input to educational success. 'Class' in the sense of economic relations is one, and one only, of the factors in the mix.

Illich (1971) has suggested that the system produces people who are transformed into 'consumers', passive receivers of irrationalised materials, varyingly and nonsensically certificated. Such consumers, not questioning their markets or menus, are the economic basis of the late industrial state. In part, this is a version of economic correspondence, with too much success and determinant power attributed to education. However, there is a growth of particular and unexpected forms of dependency and incompetence for which educational bureaucratisation is partially responsible, 'deskilling'. Traditional masteries over nature built into domestic skills, in working-class and other households, are replaced by consumerism. The corresponding skills are those of survival in clashing and confused bureaucratised worlds, whose characteristic form of conflict becomes moral appeals, with no rational means of resolution between individual, and institutional, claims to economic support. As well as the consumer, such worlds favour the pliable and the Machiavellian, rather than the puritan stabilities of middle capitalism.

## CRITICISMS OF 'EDUCATION SERVES THE INTERESTS OF BUREAUCRACY'

These are most easily constructed on the basis of the other three views. Functionalists would find it to be based in a romantic and deeply conservative anarchism, essentially seeking a return to an idealised pre-industrial age and its forms. The extraordinary value of technology, rational organisation and detailed division of labour require kinds of discipline, and kinds of skill, which can only be transmitted in schools. Advocates of the fourth view presume the continuation of the products of industrial society, without the conditions of their production. It is poor sociology because it neglects necessary social organisation rendering genuine forms of freedom and choice possible.

Theorists of compensation recognise some of the criticisms. If the system is over-bureaucratised, that can be corrected. If particular status-groups have gained a temporary dominance, that is either inevitable, and the struggles will continue, always yielding further successes and further problems, or they will simply have to be overcome. For the neo-Marxists, the advocates of deschooling are romantic critics, who fail to see the basic relationships that determine wider social structures, even if their criticisms anticipate possible social amelioration and reflect real abuses. The emphasis on the conflict of multiple and historically situated status-groups overlooks the fundamental process of the reproduction of labour power. It diverts attention from the continuing inequalities which in school as elsewhere reproduce a working class. Thus, objectively, its impact is a deeply conservative one. The other three would agree in finding notions of deschooling anachronistic, sociologically uncomprehending, and finally fantastic.

## Conclusion

The four views, and the distinctions made within them, are intended only to give the student an initial purchase on the area. Debates in this field, as elsewhere, are complicated, and do not fit tidily into classificatory schemes. No attempt has been made to hide or disguise the political and moral connections of views in the sociology of education. Rather, their continuing relevance to central and irreconcilable political debates has been emphasised. The student must use his own reactions to the arguments, for and against the positions he may wish to adopt, or may wish to investigate further. An introduction of this length can only be a sketch. The interest of the sociology of education lies in the detailed studies which illuminate the value-laden extremes presented here.

## References: Chapter 4

Althusser, L. (1977), 'Ideology and ideological state apparatus', in B. R. Cosin (ed.), *Education, Structure and Society* (Harmondsworth: Penguin), pp. 242–80.

Bernstein, B. (1971), *Class Codes and Control*, Vol. 1 (London: Routledge & Kegan Paul).

Blackstone, T. (1980), 'Falling short of meritocracy', *Times Higher Education Supplement*, 18 January, p. 14.

Corrigan, P. (1979), *Schooling the Smash Street Kids* (London: Macmillan).

Edwards, A. D. (1976), *Language in Culture and Class* (London: Heinemann).

Halsey, A. H. (1980), 'Education can compensate', *New Society*, 24 January, p. 17.

Illich, I. (1971), *Deschooling Society* (London: Calder & Boyars).

Jencks, C., *et al.* (1972), *Inequality: A Reassessment of the Effect of Family and Schooling in America* (New York: Basic Books).

Karabel, J., and Halsey, A. H. (eds), (1977), *Power and Ideology in Education* (New York: OUP).

Labov, W. (1973), 'The logic of nonstandard English', in N. Keddie (ed.), *Tinker, Tailor . . . The Myth of Cultural Deprivation* (Harmondsworth: Penguin), pp. 21–66.

Parsons, T. (1961), 'The school class as a social system', in A. H. Halsey, J. Floud and C. A. Anderson (eds), *Education, Economy and Society* (New York: The Free Press), pp. 434–55.

Rosenthal, R., and Jacobson, L. (1968), *Pygmalion in the Classroom* (New York: Holt, Rinehart & Winston).

Salter, B., and Tapper, T. (1981), *Education, Politics and the State* (London: Grant McIntyre).

Sheridan, A. (1980), *Michael Foucault: The Will to Truth* (London: Tavistock).

## Further Reading

Bowles, S., and Gintis, H. (1976), *Schooling in Capitalist America* (London: Routledge & Kegan Paul).

Cosin, B. R. (ed.) (1977), *Education, Structure and Society* (Harmondsworth: Penguin).

Halsey, A. H., Floud, J., and Anderson, C. A. (eds) (1961), *Education, Economy and Society* (New York: The Free Press).

Hammersley, M., and Woods, P. (eds) (1976), *The Process of Schooling* (London: Routledge & Kegan Paul).

Lister, I. (1974), *Deschooling* (Cambridge: CUP).

# Chapter 5

# The Social Realities of Deviance

## WES SHARROCK

## The Durkheimian Tradition of Social Pathology

One question that has often puzzled sociologists is whether they could ever hope to be the social equivalents of physicians, able to diagnose, understand, prescribe for and remedy pathologies of society. One of the main objections to this idea is that judgements of *social* pathology lack the sense of objectivity that many medical diagnoses possess. There is nothing like the same consensus on social well-being that there is on physical well-being. As to what might be good or bad for society, here there is deep and fundamental disagreement. Consider, for example, the issue of strikes. Are they harmful? Some people certainly think that they are, and that they ought to be prevented. Others think that the right to strike is a vital and basic freedom that must be preserved at all costs.

The existence of this kind of disagreement on all sorts of social issues might appear to stand in the way of any prospect of the sociologist ever creating standards of judgement analogous to those of the physician. Emile Durkheim (1950), however, thought that sociologists could develop some objective standards for the identification of pathological conditions of society. He suggested two main tests for the *normality* of a social phenomenon. The first was the extent to which it was widespread in many different societies. The second was the extent to which it was a non-malign product of society's nature.

Social conditions which failed to meet these tests would be counted as pathological. Judgements of normality and pathology could, therefore, be made, or so Durkheim thought, without expressing the sociologist's own feelings or involving his value judgements, for they would result from the 'mechanical' application of the criteria. The sociologist could make comparative studies of the extent to which conditions of a certain kind were present in societies *of the same type*, and could assume that if a condition was common to the great majority of societies of a certain type, then it was normal for societies of that kind. He could also conduct investigations into the structure of societies in which the condition seemed to be normal to see if that condition was integral to the organisation of such societies, and whether it played a benign role within them. Did it interfere with the functioning of such societies? If the research revealed (1) that the relevant condition appeared only in one or two societies of that type, and (2) that its role within them was to disrupt and disorganise the society, then the conclusion would be inevitable: the condition was pathological.

Though objections can be made to Durkheim's assumptions, these are of no concern to us now, for it is the *idea* that we are interested in, the suggestion that there can be a difference between our commonplace judgements of normality and pathology and those which would issue from objective sociological standards. This idea is of interest because Durkheim uses it to suggest that the usual assessment of 'crime' can be inverted. If they were asked to say if crime was pathological or not, a great many people would say that it was. Crime is a sign of, and a cause of, social decay and disorganisation. Durkheim aims to show that the consequences of applying his proposed criteria of pathology is to find crime to be a normal, and not a pathological, phenomenon. Crime is widespread in society and among societies, and hence passes the first test. Durkheim argues that it is not harmful to society but, in truth, makes a positive contribution to its continuance, thereby meeting the second test as well.

Crime seems to many to be harmful to society. Certainly the arguments which are offered about the need for policing and the treatment of offenders are premised in assumptions about the need to protect society from the harm that crime and criminals do. But, if such attitudes were indeed premised in considerations about the prevention and repair of damage to society, then it ought to follow that reactions to crime, detection, punishment and the rest should be of a calculating and rational kind. Thoughtful consideration would be given to deciding just what measures would be essential to the elimination of crime through preventative measures and the rehabilitation of offenders. It would also follow that the degree of punishment inflicted on offenders should be carefully graded. The most socially harmful offences would be the most severely punished, the least socially harmful being less severely treated. However, the reaction to crime does not appear to be of this cool and rational kind. It is, rather, emotional. The demand for punishment often expresses a desire to see the offender suffer pain, deprivation, humiliation, or degradation. The nature of the reaction to crime is readily enough visible in newspaper reports of trials and crimes which are replete with horrific, dramatic and *moralising* elements. Such reactions are not nicely calculated to correspond with the extent of social harm done by criminal activities, nor are punishments administered on the basis of a congruence with the damage done by an offence. The harm which is done to society by (say) an act of sexual interference with a small child may be slight indeed, especially when compared, for example, with the harm done by the violation of industrial safety laws. Yet the reaction against child-molesters will be much stronger than will that against the corporate offender. Durkheim thought that the different responses to crime were best understood if crime were to be seen as offence against strong, well-defined and widely shared sentiments. Many people have very strong feelings about the sexual inviolability of children. They also have feelings about the desirability of safety and health, but these are neither so strong nor so well defined. Hence, reaction to actions which break health and safety laws is much milder and lacks the element of horror that is felt towards the child-molester. The demand for punishment also corresponds to the extent of these feelings. Many feel that nothing could be bad enough for someone who interferes with a child. They are not even satisfied by long prison sentences, and, in some cases, even call for punishments such as castration. Reaction and punishment do not appear always to conform to the extent of social harm, but often express the strength of common sentiment. It is this which enables Durkheim to argue not merely that crime is normal, but that it is an *indispensable* phenomenon.

From Durkheim's point of view, the essence of society was its moral order, the set of ideas about right and wrong which is disseminated among the members of society. There was certainly a sense in which, for Durkheim, society existed in the minds of its members, for a society could not exist without (1) extensive agreement on morality among its members, and (2) some awareness on the part of these members of the fact of agreement between them. Without this common morality, a society could not possess a unity. However, the mere existence of agreement on morality is not enough to unify a society. Sentiments can and will become attenuated unless they are exercised. Durkheim tended to look upon human states of mind as somewhat akin to muscles: they tend to atrophy if they are not used. The same kind of thing is exhibited in the decline of feelings of friendship when we no longer see with the same regularity someone towards whom those feelings are directed. If we have feelings of friendship, their strength is often connected to the frequency of contact with the friend. If we are separated for some time, we subsequently find that the feelings have weakened. Durkheim treats many states of mind as analogous to this. We may feel strongly against murder. But if no one is ever murdered in our society, eventually we shall cease to feel so strongly against it. If our feelings *are* to be kept alive and strong, they must be provoked and stimulated, that is, *exercised*.

Durkheim also goes on to say that agreement on what is moral will only remain genuine if people are given the occasion to discriminate between the moral and the immoral, and if they are led to react to immorality. Crime serves to create just such reaction. Durkheim argues, therefore, not only that crime perpetuates strong feelings against itself, but that the occurrence of crime is *essential* to the continuation of society. If society is to exist as a unity, it *must* have a crime rate.

Durkheim's argument is then this. The strong reactions against crime are the product of the strong feelings that people have. These reactions reinforce the feelings and reinvigorate them at the same time. But it is not just a matter of exercising agreement. Such agreements have to be recognised by those who subscribe to them. One of the ways that this can be done is by selecting out and contrasting those who do not share the sentiments with those who do. It is through the common reaction to criminals that people can come to see that they do have something in common. What marks one society off from another is a moral boundary, not a physical one. Such a boundary determines who can be a member of a society and who cannot. Setting criminals apart serves to clarify the boundaries of society by separating those who are inside the boundaries of moral acceptability from those who are outside them.

It is worth pointing out here that Durkheim is not arguing that crime is *never* pathological. He does recognise that while it is necessary for a society to have a crime rate, none the less it must have the sort of crime rate which is appropriate to societies of its type, and not one which is too low or too high for the well-being of society.

The argument that crime is necessary to society raises the question of how society ensures that there will be crime. Though society might require crimes for its survival, why should people oblige it by commiting them? Can we not envisage a community of saints in which no one committed crimes? Would that not refute Durkheim's argument?

The way that Durkheim would respond to such questions follows, in a large part, from the terms in which he has set his argument. *If* society is a moral community, *then* it must have a sense of internal unity and external difference. It cannot exist without setting itself apart from outsiders. It cannot be a unity without points of contrast. Any *moral* community, therefore, must have those whom it regards as morally excluded, as defaulters, degenerates and deviants. The community of saints would be *unthinkable* as such in these terms. If there were to be a community within which people conducted themselves in what *we* would regard as impeccable and saintly ways, then, Durkheim's argument implies, *within that community* the lines between acceptable and unacceptable conduct would be drawn far more tightly than we draw them. Conduct that we might regard as trivial and conforming would there be regarded as heinous and the occasion for outrage and the imposition of sanctions.

It is important to see that the argument for the necessity and inevitability of crime, as Durkheim gives it, does not involve attempting to explain why some people are motivated to engage in criminal activities. The fact that there will be a crime rate is to be understood in terms of the nature of society as a moral community, and what is necessary if it is to define itself as such. This is very different from the view of many sociologists who are, however, only too willing to grant that society makes deviance such as crime. They suppose that such a proposition means that society creates the *conditions* (for example, poverty, poor housing, broken homes, slum neighbourhoods, and the like) which are thought to motivate people to crime. They steal out of financial necessity. They develop the kind of psychological predispositions which make them incapable or unwilling to keep the law. They join adolescent gangs and begin a pattern of association that leads to a life of crime (Sutherland and Cressey, 1955). Such an attitude, however, is closely connected to the 'pathology' conception of crime and is not, therefore, compatible with the sort of theory which Durkheim advances. The clear presumption of a 'pathology' view of crime is that if it were possible to eliminate poverty, marital disharmony, slums, or whatever unfavourable social conditions supposedly give rise to crime, then the motivation for crime, and hence crime itself, would be eliminated. The Durkheimian position is that crime *cannot* be eliminated for it is integral to society itself.

The question which Durkheim is tackling does not have to do with the causation of specific acts of deviance such as criminality, but with the nature and possibility of deviance such as crime. 'What sort of phenomenon is it and how is it possible?' are the questions, not 'Why do some people do such things and others not?'

One implication of Durkheim's views is that the agencies of social control, rather than seeking to eliminate deviance are likely to appear to promote it. Research that has been carried out into the organisation of agencies such as the police (Skolnick, 1966) shows that this is, indeed, the case. They do not attempt to eradicate deviance but behave in ways that are likely to ensure the persistence of deviance. These studies reveal that if the system of law enforcement was intended to eliminate crime then it is remarkably inefficient. The police spend very little of their time investigating crime and quite a lot directing traffic, helping out in problem situations, assisting the medical professions, doing clerical work, waiting in courtrooms, and the like. When they are out patrolling the streets, they are better thought of as engaged in 'keeping the peace' than 'enforcing the law'. There are many situations where a policeman might make an arrest but prefers not to, and thereby keeps things under control and restores order, as well as avoiding tedious paperwork.

The fact the police do so little in the way of law inforcement might be taken by some as signifying the corruption of police ideals. For Durkheim, it would be nothing of the sort. It would show the normality of crime, and with that the way that the police have adapted to its ineradicable nature. Rather than seeking to eliminate crime, the police seek to accommodate to it, and, therefore, to regulate and contain it. They establish what might be thought of as a 'working relationship' with criminals for they are dependent on criminals if they are to do their work. Very few cases are broken by brilliant detective work. Most are usually based on 'information received'. The police are willing to overlook many offences so that they can concentrate their efforts on those crimes that matter to them, for example, those that have gained public attention or might attract disapproval if left unresolved. Thus, they are willing to allow certain kinds of criminal activities to be carried on provided they are carried out within certain limits, do not intrude upon the public at large and allow the police to monitor them. Drug-dealing, for example, is often allowed to continue uninterrupted, providing it is carried out by small dealers who are known to the police and who do not attempt to take advantage of police tolerance. Allowing drug-dealing to continue in this way means that the police can keep a close eye on it.

A second important element in Durkheim's analysis of crime was that it provokes public, dramatic reaction. This can be seen in the fact that while the entry of someone into the status of 'criminal' is a public affair, there is no corresponding recognition of *exit* from that status and a return to normal life. The process of trial and conviction often makes the offender out to be a different *kind* of person from 'the rest of us', someone who is abhorrent, if not dangerous, and someone whose actions originate not in their circumstances but in something essential about them and their character. Conviction, therefore, involves a powerful stigmatisation of someone, and it will not be easy for other members of society to accept again as a fellow member a person who has been set apart in this dramatic way. The person who has been imprisoned will find it difficult to resume normal life. They will find that they remain, in the eyes of the police, someone who is constitutionally disposed to crime. They are likely to be sought out if suspects are wanted for the type of crime that they were known to have committed. The constant reappearance of the police in their lives is further disruptive of any efforts to resume a normal life. The difficulties of returning to normal society may be sufficiently great to mean that it will be easier and more practical to engage in crime as the basis of a livelihood (Erikson, 1964).

## Labelling Theory

The key feature of 'labelling theory' is the abandoning of the assumption that society is a moral community and hence the idea that it is possible to judge what kinds of actions are deviant from some neutral and objective standpoint. (This is not the same thing as saying that it is not possible to have a neutral and objective theory of deviance.) Here labelling theory is in agreement with Durkheim. Society makes deviance in the sense that it makes deviance *possible* by making rules. If we take deviance to be, more or less, the infraction of rules, then it is clear that without some rules to break there cannot be any deviance. To this, labelling theory adds a futher suggestion. Society makes *deviants* by setting up 'agencies of social control' for the enforcement of rules and the identification of rule-breakers. Actually, this is not precisely what labelling theory wants to say about the operation of social control agencies, but it will do as an initial starting-point.

### (1) RULES AND DEVIANCE

Having discussed Durkheim at some length, the idea that society makes deviance ought now to be plain enough. Though we have shown why it makes sense to say something like this and how it follows from and is defensible in terms of certain assumptions, it may still be very difficult to accept the argument when it is applied to cases. It seems to imply, for example, that if we were to abolish the laws against robbery and assault, then we should have abolished that form of deviance known colloquially as mugging. And yet this seems absurd. Surely we cannot imagine that changing the law will, somehow, stop burly youths from attacking and robbing old ladies?

We don't. By the way, we ought to emphasise that for our purposes here we will talk largely about deviance in terms of matters having to do with legality and crime, but we are far from identifying crime with deviance. Much that is talked of as 'deviance' concerns the violation of rules which are not enshrined in laws, but which are none the less of considerable consequence for social life. So, while for now, we may talk as if changing the law might be decisive in altering 'the rules' against some deviant activity, this would not always be true. Indeed, in some cases it would be importantly false. The argument that society makes deviance by making rules implies only that if the rules were abolished the *standing* of the activity would have changed. It does not imply that the activity itself would be stopped thereby. If the rules prohibiting the activity are removed and the standing of the activity is changed then *the way in which that activity is regarded and treated will also be changed*. And that may have all sorts of consequences, but one of them need not be the cessation of the activity previously judged to be deviant.

Consider the case of marijuana smoking. This is an illegal activity, which some people regard as a serious problem. Although not serious in its own right, marijuana is bad, in their eyes, because it can lead to the use of hard drugs. Marijuana is a social problem too. Since it is illegal, many people who want to use the drug do so in defiance of the law and, thereby, engage in criminal activity. The implication of the argument which labelling theory puts forward is clear. If people ceased to be concerned about marijuana, then the *problem* would disappear. Marijuana use would not cease: smoking it would stop being an illegal activity. One might speculate that the amount of marijuana use would also decline as a consequence of legalisation since some people might be smoking it now for the satisfaction to be obtained from a relatively harmless but illegal activity. The 'solution' to the marijuana problem is not the prevention of its use but a changing of attitudes towards it. Such a change could well have other consequences. If the cultivation, distribution and sale of cannabis were legalised, then one would do away with a lot of deviant activity. One would have put an end to the need to smuggle the drug and also the illegalities involved in the use of the profits from the trade. Whether marijuana is harmful is a complicated question, and whether it is more so than other drugs in widespread and legal use is debatable. As to the suggestion that 'soft' drugs lead to the use of 'hard' drugs, this too might be contested. If it is the case that they do, then part of the reason may be that it is in someone's *economic* interest to move people from 'soft' to 'hard' drug use, together with the fact that because of its illegality, the marijuana trade and the 'hard' drug trade are tied up with one another. Last but not least, one can point to the way that the treatment of narcotic use has given rise to the development of organised crime and the formation of criminal gangs which go on to break the law in a variety of ways above and beyond the dealing in drugs. In much the same way, the prohibition of alcohol in the USA led to murder and the formation of gangs through the development of bottlegging.

Starting from the assumption that society makes deviant acts possible by setting up prohibitions, the argument leads to the conclusion that by setting up such rules, society also provides people with the circumstances which will motivate them to perform further deviant acts, to develop life-styles and organisations around the needs of the prohibited activity. This will result in the formation of deviant groups. The effect of lifting the proscription on the original deviant act might not be the prevention of the act from occuring, but it would be the elimination of the possibility of and the need for many other illegalities arising from it (Lemert, 1967).

## (2)  RULES AND ENFORCEMENT

Thus far our discussion has been somewhat generalised. We have avoided any attempt to say just what deviance is or what kinds of persons and activities have been counted as deviant. All we have said is that deviance might have something to do with the violation of rules. To illustrate this we have pointed to one or two examples (child-molesting and marijuana use) which have the advantage of being pretty widely viewed in our society as deviant. We cannot continue in this vague way and we have to to recognise straightaway that any attempt to delimit the field of deviance is problematical. Any attempt to achieve a consistent definition is only too likely to drive us towards the conclusion that 'We are all deviants now'.

*In theory*, a Durkheimian position seems fine. Deviance is that activity which offends against the morality of society. We have, therefore, no difficulty in saying who the deviants are: they are those who have acted in violation of society's moral rules. But it is not so easy to say what the morality of a society is, nor to say which people have offended against it. It would be extremely difficult to spell out the agreed understandings of a society and to list the people, or even types of people, who deviated from those understandings. However, there is one group of people that we can identify, or so it seems. There are people in prison who are guilty of murder, rape, assault, and so on. These are deviants, are they not?

Let us look at this a little more closely. What are we saying about people such as these? Are we saying that they are deviants *because* they have broken one or other of society's rules? If we identify 'deviant' with 'someone who has broken society's rules', then, although people in prison may have broken society's rules, we cannot say that they are there because they have done so. The one thing we do know about society's rules is that there is no automatic connection between the breaking of a rule and punishment. There are many people who have broken the pro-hibition on murder and have not been imprisoned, just as there will be people imprisoned for murder who are innocent. There are murders which have been committed and have not been discovered, and murders which have never been solved. All we can say about the connection between prisons and societal rules is that there are in prison people who have been convicted of a crime – which, as we said, will do for our purposes as a designation for 'deviance'. But, those in prison are not necessarily those who committed the acts for which they were imprisoned, nor, if they are, are they the only ones to have done such things. If we want to talk about the various kinds of deviance, we could, perhaps, begin with the distinctions set out in a simple diagram (Figure 5.1).

|  | Obedient behaviour | Rule-breaking behaviour |
|---|---|---|
| perceived as deviant | falsely accused | pure deviant |
| not perceived as deviant | conforming | secret deviant |

**Figure 5.1**   Types of deviant behaviour.
*Source*: Becker, 1963.

The suggestion we are considering, then, is that we should consider deviants not in terms of the act that they have committed but whether or not they are known to have committed the act. The diagram is useful because it points out the important, we shall later argue inseparable, connection between being deviant and *being seen to be* deviant. We shall argue that, *for sociological purposes*, there is an identity between being deviant and being seen to be deviant.

Although the diagram is useful in this way, it also has a number of limitations. Consider the category 'conforming'. These are people who do not break rules, and are not seen as breaking rules. But, is there *anyone* who can be said not to have broken some social rule, or even some law. Even the most law-abiding of us will have done something like driving without fastening a seat-belt which is, technically, a crime. So, if we press it, the term 'conformist' is not all that well derived. Now consider the categories 'falsely accused' and 'secret deviant'. These are fine as *notional* categories because we can feel confident that there *must* be people who have been falsely accused, and even convicted, who did not do what they were charged with. Similarly, there must be people who have done things which are indisputably deviant but who have not been caught. But, how are we to identify these people? How are we to know which is which?

We can now see the direction that the complications involved in defining deviance are taking us. We have managed so far to avoid these complications by not addressing the ambiguity in talking about 'rules as products of society' and 'social rules'. Rules are products of society in the sense that it is only within the context of social life that rules can be made. But this is not quite the same thing as saying that rules are *produced by society* acting as a unity.

If we want to identify the kinds of *activities* which are taken to be deviant, the assumptions which Durkheim adopts might appear to be attractive. They do allow us to make some decisions. If society is a moral unity, and if the rules are products of society as a whole, then there will be one set of rules for society and the deviant activities will be those which the rules forbid. If, however, we admit that societies are much more complex entities quite often, with a more of a 'federated' structure than Durkheim allows, then we open up the possibility that within society there might be more than one morality. What might be deviant from the point of view of one group and its morality may not be from that of another. Indeed, there may even be conflicts between such groups as to what is and what is not deviant. We may even be forced to say, as we hinted earlier, that all activities are deviant since any activity might turn out to be forbidden under someone's rules.

But, what about laws? Are these not promulgated for society as a whole? Do these not apply to all of society's members and override all other rules? This is true enough, but the fact that a set of laws has provenance over a whole society does not entail that the society is a moral unity. To investigate the extent to which society was unified morally, we would have to look at the relationship between the imperatives expressed in the rules and the moral requirements current among the various groups in society. We would also have to look at the ways that the rules of society were created, and how they relate to the laws that are made and enforced.

Even a brief look at the law-making processes in *our own* society will tell us that often the laws that are made fail to express *anyone's* sentiments. They are produced through a complicated legislative process which involves bargaining, argument, compromises and threats. The result is that sometimes the actual laws which emerge satisfy hardly anyone. In that sense, laws are made through a political process. It is through such political institutions as that of law-making that the interests, power positions and relationships of groups and organisations which make up a society are mediated. The formal and informal activities which make up these institutions shape the laws which are made. Part of this political process will be the agreement on the procedures to be used to determine which rules should be enshrined in law. *Sometimes* it can be argued that a given set of political and legislative arrangements has, in fact, been imposed; one group may have come to dominate the institutions which make the rules and promulgate the laws. Thus, asking how rules get made leads one to investigate the ways that rule-making procedures come to be established, and how they relate to the distribution of power in society. Even where it appears that a dominant group does not press for the primacy of its interests and its definitions of rules, the fact that the political institutions were established by that group, that their membership was mainly drawn from its ranks, could well lead to a situation where the rules that were made actually did express that group's interests even though they were decided as if they were the views of all in society.

The existence of this possibility should not lead us to assume that we have discovered a simple formula for understanding the law-making system of any society. Nor can we say that laws always reflect the interests and conceptions of the ruling group. Such a formulaic interpretation is different from, but no better than, Durkheim's view that society is a moral unity. Rather such a possibility ought to lead us to the view that the relationship of laws to society is a complex one and that the structure of interests, power and political domination in a society is quite likely to involve a mixture of shared and divergent interests, of general and very restricted moral attitudes. Such a view would lead to the conclusion that there is need for specific studies to show just how specific processes produce the rules they do and just what connection they have to the social settings in which they originate and persist.

Pointing to the possibility that a given group may dominate society and its rule-making procedures to such an extent that it can impose its conception of morality upon society as a whole is an important idea, not because it gives us the key to understanding how power relationships must always be, but because the very existence of this possibility implies something important for a *general* conception of deviance. One of the primary assumptions of sociology is the diversity of outlooks and moralities to be found in differing societies. As sociologists, we seek to take account of that fact, describe it and examine its consequences. From our point of view, for our *sociological* purposes, we cannot treat different outlooks and moralities as other than equivalent. All are suitable candidates for the same kind of scrutiny. We cannot even take our own accepted attitudes as the yardstick for the study of other people's; such ethnocentrism is a real danger for sociological work. And, if we cannot take our own outlook as the measure for all things, we must certainly avoid adopting someone else's, or some group's, as the definitive standard. If there is genuine disagreement in a society about what is right and what is wrong (and we shall suggest in a moment that the very fact that there is deviance means that there is) then, even though one conception may be institutionalised in the law, and even though that conception might have widespread support, we cannot accept it as exclusively definitive of deviance in that society any more than we can when the conception so institutionalised is that of one highly sectionalised interest.

Why is this so? Well, for the very obvious reason that one category of person has not been heard from yet, namely, the population of alleged deviants. Though, from the point of view of the dominant and powerful groups, what such people do is wrong, they may not themselves agree. They may regard what they do as perfectly right and proper, and what those who denounce them do as bizarre and immoral. This leads us to think that it is the fact of the existence of deviance in a society which indicates that there is more than one point of view to be found there. Sometimes the deviants are perhaps those who do not conform to the prevailing morality; they have their own.

We are faced now with a problem. We have been speaking as though it is the minority of people who are the deviants, although earlier we suggsted that there are grave difficulties in picking any group out as *the* deviants. And in doing so we appear to have sided with the majority against the minority's definitions, even though we said at the outset that we wanted to maintain a *neutral* position. From our *sociological* standpoint, no morality can claim supremacy or superiority. The only way to avoid this problem would seem to be the giving up of the attempt to determine which sorts of activities and people are deviant. Notice, though, that this does not mean that we have to give up an interest in and the study of deviance. Rather, it means that we will have to set about pursuing that interest in an entirely different way. First of all, it means recognising that deviance is *quintessentially* a matter of competing and conflicting claims, and the study of deviance is the study of the way that *the claims are made, and made to stick*.

This brings us to the core arguments of labelling theory:

(a)   deviance is not an intrinsic property either of actors or activities;
(b)   deviance is whatever people in society say that it is. Deviant conduct and persons are those which are *labelled* as such – hence the name of the theory (Becker, 1963).

The first argument gives the reason why there is no point in seeking to say what deviance is by listing deviant activities, groups and persons, or by looking to see what characteristics mark such activities and people off from those which are not held to be deviant. Such a listing is doomed to failure simply because under some set of circumstances, any group and any activities could be called deviant. Deviance is, then, a highly circumstantial matter. We will only come to understand why an action is regarded (in some circles) as deviant by examining the circumstances in which it is so regarded. We will not find anything out by looking at the activity as such. It is not the nature of the activity which makes it deviant.

Just as, if one follows this view, the question 'What makes deviant acts deviant?' has to be replaced with 'What leads some activities to be regarded in some circles and on some occasions as deviant?', so the question 'What leads people to engage in deviant activity?' needs modification, even rejection. There cannot be specific kinds of motivation to engage in deviant activities if there are no categories of activities which are inherently deviant. The idea that deviant activities require a special type of explanation derives from the adoption of one specific point of view which, earlier, we said was undesirable. The suggestion that deviant activities require special sorts of explanations, perhaps the identification of special sorts of motives, derives from the attitude that since there is something disgraceful, disgusting, or immoral about the deviant activity, only someone who was different from the rest of us could possibly do that kind of thing. Something, that is, a special type of motive, must *make* a person engage in deviant activity.

However, the view which labelling theory adopts runs counter to this. It points out that *for those who engage in deviant activities*, there is often nothing repugnant about them. Such activities may be the most ordinary, natural, everyday things in the world, and require no different explanation from those which we give for our own everyday activities. We are brought up to do them; they are fun; there is an economic advantage in doing them; they are the way we have always behaved; they are how we make our living; and so on. Labelling theory might even take the point a little further, and invert it. What stops 'straight' people from engaging in deviant activities? Given that they can be gratifying and rewarding, and under some circumstances normal and acceptable, and given that even the most conforming of us can feel impulses towards some deviant activities, why do we not allow those impulses a greater freedom than we appear to? Not what *makes* deviants behave in that way, but what *stops* the rest of us from doing so? The line in which answers might be sought to this would be one which investigated the costs and hazards of engaging in activities which are viewed as deviant, the losses which identification as deviant could inflict upon us particularly in regards to the way of life which we may have built up and to which we may feel inextricably attached.

The second of labelling theory's core arguments was that deviant activity was that which people so labelled. It is this which provides the rationale of the corollary to the idea that society makes deviance by creating rules which we said earlier was the view that society makes deviants by setting up agencies of social control for the enforcement of rules and the identification of rule-breakers. This rationale can be brought out by thinking about the notional character of the types of deviant identity we discussed earlier. What the typology does is to forge a connection between 'being deviant' and 'being known' to be deviant. Even then, we pointed out that this was purely a notional connection which we would have difficulty in sustaining in actual cases. There is no way that one could separate the 'falsely accused but found guilty' from the 'true deviants' in the prison population. The difficulty with this typology might lead us to propose that the connection should be an identity. For our *sociological* purposes, being deviant *is the same as* being identified as such.

No doubt many people will object to this. Why do we think that we should obliterate the distinction between 'falsely accused' and 'true deviant' in this way? The point is that if we do not, the distinction will be an idle one *in our theory*. It could not be used in the study of actual cases of deviant activity since we would be in no position to be able to separate the two elements in the 'deviant population'. Sociology is not equipped to tell who is innocent of the charges against them and who guilty. From sociology's point of view, and for all its intents and purposes, being found guilty *is the same* as being guilty. And yet we may still want to insist that there is a real difference between a murderer and someone who has wrongfully been convicted of murder. But, even if we accept this, we cannot say that the difference has any effect on the way in which the two people are treated. The judge, the police, prison officers, and so on, treat them identically. Protestations of innocence will be treated as the kind of thing that everyone who is convicted makes. The police, the prison officers, the public at large cannot tell the difference between the 'guilty as charged' and those that are 'innocent of the charge but have been convicted', and so it is on the basis of the fact that *they have been convicted* that they react towards them. Being convicted is to be identified publicly as a deviant.

The consequence of this is that for understanding how people act towards one another, it does not make much difference in many important respects whether they did or did not do what they were charged with. Hence, the distinction between 'true deviant' and 'falsely accused' is not of much use to us. But, of course, we should expect that if someone is seen by others to have been wrongfully convicted, then they would be treated differently from those who are seen as rightfully convicted. In sum then, for the organisation of social activities *being found guilty is the same as really being guilty*. Hence 'being known to be a deviant' is the same as being one.

It is for this reason that labelling theory can say that the agencies of social control make people into deviants by making them publicly identified as guilty of criminal or other acts. This is a very different contention from the view discussed earlier that a system of social control can lead people to engage in rule-breaking conduct. All it says is that whatever it takes to single someone out and put him on display as 'deviant' is what makes him into a deviant. The important thing to notice here is how the study of deviance is reoriented. Attention is drawn away from the deviants and their activities towards those who deal with deviants. If we want to know what makes the difference between a convicted criminal and an ordinary law-abiding citizen then we will have to look at why the police choose to arrest the one rather than the other; what leads some to appear in court and others to be discharged; what leads some to be convicted and others to be found not guilty (Cicourel, 1976).

Once again the focus of interest is given to the police, lawyers, courts and the other agencies of social control. But this time emphasis is given to wholly different aspects of their work. We now would have to take up how it is that the police, judges, juries and lawyers tell differences between cases, make findings and establish facts. How do they come to see people as 'potentially engaged in criminal, activity', 'a candidate for arrest', 'someone against whom there is enough of the right sort of evidence to make it worth going to trial', 'someone who is visibly and indisputably guilty' and 'someone who is only tenuously connected to the charge by the evidence as far as we jurors can tell'.

In following this line of interest, attention has been paid to the ways that policemen operate as observers. How they *learn* to observe the public places which they frequent in the course of their work, as scenes in which criminal activity is visible; how they learn to recognise by dress, bodily stance, location, and so forth, those who are likely to be doing something which is against the law and hence worth investigating (Sacks, 1972).

One aspect that has been taken up and given particular attention is that of 'plea-bargaining' (Sudnow, 1978) because it has thrown light on crucial areas of how decisions to proceed are made. What studies of plea-bargaining show is how organisational considerations 'dictate' the connection between what someone might be said to have 'really' done and what they will be 'known' to have done by the general public. Plea-bargaining involves defence and prosecution lawyers in making arrangements to offer to charge the accused with a less serious offence if the accused will plead guilty to it. Lawyers who agree to such deals have an interest in not taking cases to trial. In particular, defence lawyers who are not very successful may depend on the goodwill of the prosecution to obtain cases through the Court's system of appointment. The defence lawyer as a professional colleague involved with many different cases at once may be under some pressure to encourage his client to accept the lesser charge and plead guilty to it rather than risk being convicted on the more serious one. So pleading guilty to 'loitering around a schoolyard' may be offered as an alternative to the more serious charge of 'child-molesting', and have attached to it a fine rather than a prison sentence.

One of the things that plea-bargaining illustrates is the difference between the *formal* presumptions of an institution and the *actual* presumptions of those who operate it. The formal presumption of the legal system is that the accused is innocent until proven guilty; the actual presumption of the police, lawyers and court officials is often that the accused did do what he was originally accused of doing and so pleading guilty to a less serious crime does not, in fact, do him any injustice at all. He is actually receiving a lighter punishment than he deserves for the more serious charge laid against him.

The practice of plea-bargaining is routine in American courts but is somewhat frowned upon in Great Britain, although it does still take place. What it highlights is the number of organisational steps between first coming to the notice of the agencies of social control, for example, being picked up by the police, and the eventual appearance in the court records and newspapers as a convicted criminal. Because of the number of steps involved, how one first came to the attention of the police, and what one was charged with initially, may bear little resemblance to what one is eventually charged with. An initial charge of 'child-molesting', say, may end up as one of 'loitering around a schoolyard', when the one thing the offender was not doing was loitering around a schoolyard. What makes the difference between someone who is convicted as a child-molester and someone who is not, even though the latter might actually be guilty of that crime, is (i) whether he is the sort of person who fits the idea that lawyers have of what a normal sex offender is like; (ii) whether he is willing to accept, if offered, a chance of pleading guilty to a reduced charge; and (iii) whether or not he is able to afford his own lawyer rather than relying on a court-appointed public defender.

Attention, then, is switched away from the predisposition of offenders to act in certain ways towards the *decision-making procedures and fact-finding methods* used by the officers of the social control agencies. A person's passage through the judicial system from first being noticed and apprehended to eventual disposition of his case is shaped by how that person is treated by others and how decisions are made as to the direction the case should take as it proceeds step by step through the organisation.

In studying the fact-finding and decision-making methods that are employed, it would be important to see that although 'organisational reasons' of the kind mentioned already are important, they do not have exclusive priority. A defender may press his client to accept a lesser charge and, thereby, reduce the inconvenience to himself and the prosecution of going to trial, but in doing so he will not necessarily see it as a matter of placing his own interests above those of the client. It is in his client's interest too to take this course. This is so because the defender 'knows' that the client is guilty. He 'knows' that the client is guilty because he shares with other court officials, lawyers, and so on, views about how the world is, what sorts of people typically commit what sorts of crimes, how those offences come about, what the circumstances were and what the motivations usually are. In examining a case, a lawyer may look at the details in a way that we might regard as too perfunctory to enable him to establish what really happened. But, from the point of view of the experienced courtroom practitioner, that inquiry is wholly adequate since the establishing of a few of the facts of the case may reveal the outlines of 'the classic case'. With such an outline, he may feel he knows all he needs to know and far more than can be established by any further investigation. He can say without any further inquiry just what happened and why, and how things went.

Because lawyers do develop ways of determining to their own satisfaction what happened, who is guilty, and so on, any description of their fact-finding methods would involve us in depictions of the ways that they gain familiarity with typical cases, how they obtain the sense of a normal crime, and how they develop 'old hand' confidence so that they can tell certain sorts of offenders virtually on sight. In addition to these fact-finding methods, we would also have to investigate those other methods used for the determination of guilt. These might be the methods used to reconstruct, under the rules of legal evidence, by using means that will be persuasive to a jury, just what did actually happen. This would involve considering the ways that lawyers show how some evidence and testimony indicate that only one possible course of events was possible, at least within the bounds of the ordinary world that the jury know about, and hence the examination of how court proceedings feature as means for establishing and deciding what is and what is not unequivocal fact.

It can be seen, then, that labelling theory does not say that all that is involved in making someone a deviant is to call him one. Labelling someone a deviant involves the demonstration by properly constituted courtroom methods, under the supervision of a judge, and through the presentation of evidence which may be contested, enough of a case to convince a jury. It is a complex and institutionalised process directed towards establishing that a person has done what he is found guilty of, with the fact-finding methods documenting that he did indeed do the action concerned and was responsible for the consequences which followed. Built into the fact-finding methods are notions that one is required to produce evidence which is satisfactory beyond all *reasonable* doubt to *ordinary* members of society, that the accused be tried by those not likely to be prejudiced against him, and that only certain kinds of evidence will count – evidence that he will have the opportunity to contest. The finding of 'guilty as charged' could, therefore, be explicated as 'guilty as charged, on the strength of the evidence adduced, to the satisfaction of the jury's understanding of what is ordinarily possible and reasonable'.

The establishing of the 'fact' of someone's guilt is, then, a complex and institutionalised matter. Though the courts do set higher standards than we ask of each other in daily life for the establishing that someone did do something, notice that they only aim for the elimination of reasonable doubt. By indicating what such an elimination involves and how difficult it is to achieve it, we want to argue that sociologists are *bound* to be parasitic on the institutionalised practices of society for the identification of deviants and criminals and for the determination of whether people actually did do the things that they are accused of.

## Conclusion

We have tried to show how far removed are many sociological arguments that 'society makes deviance' from the idea that society makes deviants by setting up the conditions of poverty, deprivation and disorganisation which induce people to become deviants. These latter views are often thought to be the standard views of sociology concerning deviance, but, as we have seen, this is not so. We argued first of all that society makes deviance possible by making rules. We then went on to argue that society makes deviants by setting up agencies of social control which achieve the public identification of people as deviant, and hence they create a *recognisable* deviant population. As we have tried to show neither of these arguments is silly or paradoxical. Together they make good defensible sense.

## References: Chapter 5

Becker, H. (1963), *Outsiders* (New York: The Free Press).
Cicourel, A. (1974), *The Social Organisation of Juvenile Justice* (London: Heinemann).
Durkheim, E. (1950), *The Rules of Sociological Method* (New York: The Free Press).
Erikson, K. (1964), 'Notes on the sociology of deviance', in H. Becker (ed.), *The Other Side* (New York: The Free Press), pp. 9–21.

Lemert, E. (1967), 'The concept of secondary deviation', in *Human Deviance, Social Problems and Social Control* (Englewood Cliffs, NJ: Prentice-Hall), pp. 40–61.

Sacks, H. (1972), 'Notes on police assessment of moral character', in D. Sudnow (ed), *Studies in Social Interaction* (New York: The Free Press), pp. 280–93.

Skolnick, J. (1966), *Justice without Trial* (New York: Wiley).

Sudnow, D. (1978), 'Normal crimes', in P. Worsley (ed.), *Problems of Modern Society* (Harmondsworth: Penguin), pp. 519–31.

Sutherland, E., and Cressey, D. (1955), *Principles of Criminology* (Chicago: University of Chicago Press).

# Further Reading

Bittner, E. (1974), 'Florence Nightingale in search of Willie Sutton', in H. Jacob (ed.), *The Potential for Reform of the Criminal Justice System* (Beverly Hills, Calif.: Sage), pp. 17–44.

Buckner, H. T. (ed.) (1971), *Deviance, Reality and Change* (New York: Random House).

Cohen, S. (1971), *Images of Deviance* (Harmondsworth: Penguin).

Cohen, S. (1972), *Folk Devils and Moral Panics* (London: MacGibbon & Kee).

Erikson, K. (1966), *Wayward Puritans* (New York: Wiley).

Lemert, E. (1952), *Social Pathology* (New York: McGraw-Hill)

Rubington, E., and Weinberg, M. (eds) (1978), *Deviance, the Interactionist Perspective*, 3rd edn (London: Macmillan).

Rubenstein, J. (1973), *City Police* (New York: Random House).

Scheff, T. (1966), *Being Mentally Ill* (London: Weidenfeld & Nicolson).

Taylor, I., and Taylor, L. (eds) (1973), *Politics and Deviance* (Harmondsworth: Penguin).

Taylor, I., Walton, P., and Young, J. (1973), *The New Criminology* (London: Routledge & Kegan Paul).

# Chapter 6

# Bureaucracy

## JOHN HUGHES

Living as we do in a society in which organisations, such as schools, business firms, trade unions, government agencies of various kinds, and more, are so visibly impinging on almost every facet of our lives, it is difficult to imagine how we could ever live without them no matter how much, at times, we wished we could. Filling in forms, paying income tax, renewing a subscription, enrolling in a college, visiting the doctor, going to school, switching on the television are all routinely bound up with the activities of one organisation or another: organisations whose task is to demand or require something of us, to provide us with a good or service of some kind, or simply to record who and what we are. In contrast to some social units as the family, neighbourhood and friendship groups, organisations are usually regarded as social units specifically established to achieve some stated task, whether it be manufacturing, education, entertainment, the treatment of illness, defending the nation, or whatever. In other words, the aims to be achieved, the structure of the organisation and the rules defining proper conduct for its members have not emerged spontaneously in the course of interaction but have been designed to produce activities which serve the goals of the organisation. Their distinctive characteristic is that they have been formally established for the purpose of achieving designated aims, hence the common term 'formal organisations' used to refer to them.

## Max Weber and the Bureaucratic Phenomenon

Sociological interest in formal organisations begins, in the main, with Max Weber (1864–1920) and his studies of bureaucracy. One of Weber's abiding interests in his unfinished political sociology was the question of why men obey and the social and historical conditions that shaped the forms in which this obedience was displayed.

In one form or another this issue had concerned social thinkers since the Enlightenment, a period in European history not only noted for major intellectual innovations in art, literature and philosophy but also marked by tremendous political and social upheavals. The predominant view, and one most clearly exemplified by Thomas Hobbes's *Leviathan*, was that political and social stability could only be ensured by the threat and use of force. For Weber this answer was unsatisfactory. To put the point in an economic idiom, force as a basis for social organisation is extremely inefficient, especially in the long run, since the costs of surveillance of a resentful and alienated populace are so high. Further, coercion rarely provides the motivations to do more than the avoidance of punishment, even death, requires. Force needs to be transmuted into something else, something that provides a social mechanism in which social actors obey because they think it *right* to do so. In other words, what Weber was looking for was a set of social arrangements in which the commands of a superior are obeyed by subordinates because the latter regard the commands as legitimate.

These kinds of arrangements Weber referred to as systems of domination: that is, systems in which there is a reciprocal relationship between rulers and ruled involving the claim by the rulers that they have legitimate authority to issue their commands and expect them to be obeyed. In Weber's view, beliefs in the legitimacy of a system of domination contributed to the stability of an authority or power relationship. Persons in power desire to see their position as rightfully theirs and the fate of the subordinated many as deserved. Accordingly, rulers are normally keen to develop, or at least contribute to, myths of their natural superiority; myths which, under stable conditions, are accepted by the majority but which can also be the target of intense hatred when the social order is in crisis.

Weber distinguished three 'pure types' of legitimate domination, each related to its own form of administrative apparatus. 'Traditional domination' is based on the legitimacy and 'sanctity of immemorial traditions' behind those exercising authority. Commands are legitimate because they accord with custom or because they issue from a ruler whose position is buttressed by traditions and to whom one owes personal and time-honoured loyalty. The administrative apparatus typical of this system of domination consists of the ruler's personal retinue of household officials, relations, favourites or vassals and loyal allies as in a feudal society. A different source of personal authority is that arising from the exercise by a leader of 'charisma' which may take the form of control over magical powers, heroism, the power of revelation, or other extraordinary gifts. 'Charismatic domination' is the very opposite to the authority of tradition. The followers or the disciples of such a charismatic leader believe in his extraordinary powers which, by their very nature, represent a break with custom and tradition. The administrative apparatus typical of this form of domination consists of persons selected by virtue of their personal devotion to the leader rather than on any other qualifications, status, or special expertise.

The final type of domination which Weber offers, and the one most pertinent to bureaucracy, is 'legal domination'. This is a system of legitimacy which rests on a belief in 'the legality of enacted rules and the right of those elevated to authority under such rules to issue commands'. In this system, superiors are typically appointed or selected by legally sanctioned procedures and are themselves oriented to and subject to this legal order. Obedience is owed not to the person of the superior, but to the office as defined by the legal order itself. Subordinates accept a ruling or a command as justified because it agrees with a set of more abstract rules which they consider legitimate and from which the ruling or command is derived. In this sense the system is rational. The organisational apparatus which is appropriate to the system of rational-legal domination is one in which the exercise of authority consists in the application of formal rules in bureaucratic administration.

Weber characterised bureaucracy as (1) an hierarchically arranged organisation of specialised administrative appointments, (2) occupied by those whose full-time occupation it is and whose income is derived solely from it, (3) who are themselves trained and specialised in administrative skills, (4) whose conduct is regulated by impersonal and written rules, and (5) whose relationships within the organisation are regulated in terms of super and subordination.

According to Weber, from a purely technical point of view bureaucratic organisation is capable of attaining the highest degree of organisational efficiency. Each of its highly skilled members, carrying out their duties with impersonal detachment, occupying official positions organised by a system of rules and regulations under a hierarchy of supervision, motivated by personal policies ensuring a high degree of loyalty to the organisation, all further the rational pursuit of the organisation's objectives, whether it be an army, a government ministry, a hospital, an industrial firm, or a political party.

## Bureaucracy's Other Face

While there is little doubt that Weber's work on bureaucracy constitutes the main inspiration for the sociological study of formal organisations, it is one that has been complemented by approaches deriving from rather different traditions. Perhaps the more important of these is that of the Human Relations school which, though itself diverse, encouraged the empirical examination of human behaviour within organisational settings, albeit within a managerial perspective, concerned with finding those factors most conducive to work efficiency. The first of these studies was, of course, the now famous Hawthorne Experiments. The study of bureaucracy has also spread itself, often in other guises, beyond the confines of political sociology where it first appeared in Weber's work. The sociologies of occupations, crime and deviance, law, health, education, and more, all produce material relevant to the understanding of bureaucracies. However, matters are complicated by the fact that not all studies of bureaucracy share the same assumptions or derive from similar perspectives, even within the investigation of one institutional sector. Often Weber's work tends to be not so much an integrating framework as a facilitating contrast that by its familiarity better delineates the alternative on offer. Yet, despite this burgeoning of perspectives and enlargement of the scope of organisation analysis, there are two areas which Weber identified and which have contemporary relevance, namely, the spread of bureaucratic power and its relationship to its wider social environment, and the interactions which sustain bureaucracy as a social form.

One of the key elements in Weber's characterisation of bureaucratic administration is its embodiment in rules defining, in the strictest possible terms, the rights and duties of officials, their range of authority, their relationship with other officials and the methods by which they should execute their official functions. It is these rules which constitute the formal organisational structure and are designed to maximise the efficiency of the organisation in meeting its overall goals. Thus, the official is seen as a social actor who acts according to stated policies and procedures designed to advance the organisation's formally defined goals.

One of the earliest amplifications of Weber's conception was the 'discovery' of bureaucracy's 'other face'. What this concept points to is the 'informal' patterns of behaviour which appear, as it were, behind the 'formal' official procedures as specified in the organisation's rules. Many of these patterns appear as unexceptional day-to-day activities, such as greeting a colleague, offering him a bit of a Twix bar, lamenting the sad performance of the local football team, and so on. However, in view of the 'spirit of impersonality' and the strict specification of duties, among others, that are supposed to govern official conduct, it was argued that many of these activities might not be as unexceptional as they might appear at first glance. Many studies have shown that bureaucracies in many settings, including the military and prisons which are particularly hierarchically organised and rule governed, display patterns of informal interaction not specified in the official rules and, sometimes, expressly forbidden by them. One interest the 'discovery' of such informal patterns has provoked is investigation of the effect they have on the functioning of the organisation itself. For Weber, the hierarchical co-ordination and control of officials by rules enhances the reliability and predictability of an organisation's functioning and produces the most rational and efficient form of human organisation. Accordingly, if Weber is correct, then any departure from this official pattern could jeopardise the overall efficiency of the system. Alternatively, under certain conditions, such informal patterns could increase organisational efficiency by providing channels for a more flexible response to issues than allowed for in the official rules. As Merton (1949) pointed out, the relationship between bureaucratic rules, behaviour and the efficient functioning or otherwise of the organisation is much more complex than Weber allowed for in his ideal type. Merton goes on to characterise some of the ways in which officials themselves subvert the aims of the organisation, often by following too closely its rules and procedures. Such ritualism represents for Merton a displacement of goals whereby the rules are no longer seen as measures designed for specific purposes but ends-in-themselves. Similarly, under certain changing conditions the official's expertise may be a form of trained incapacity and an overdevotion to the organisation's ways of doing things, a stifling of initiative which impairs the efficient realisation of the organisation's goals. By implication, the organisational 'deviant' may, again under certain conditions, be more functional for the organisation than the over-fastidious bureaucrat.

The general point here has major consequences for the way in which bureaucracy is pictured. Bureaucratic rules are applied by and affect human beings with personalities, goals and interests of their own. Despite the fact that bureaucracies, through security of position, regular salaries, the payment of increments, the provision of staff 'perks', and more, endeavour to provide more than adequate motivations for office-holders to perform their duties satisfactorily, there are no guarantees that they will do so. Officials may well have goals and aspirations of their own which do not always coincide with organisational ones. Indeed, organisational goals, be they defending the nation, making cars, building houses, educating the next generation, or whatever, may be, from the point of view of the individual, simply a means towards achieving more personal aims. Thus, we might expect, *contra* some interpretations offered of Weber, that bureaucracies, far from being impersonal organisational instruments devoted to the efficient realisation of whatever goals are set for them, are arenas of conflict constantly threatening the achievement of predefined schemes and objectives. It is this tension between the formal rules controlling official behaviour and the informal interpretation of these rules which give bureaucracy a dynamic aspect.

A now classic illustration of this is provided by Gouldner's (1954, 1957) study of a gypsum plant. Following the death of the previous manager, a new man was appointed to manage the wallboard factory and the gypsum mine. As a newcomer, the successor, though anxious to improve productivity, was unfamiliar with the customary ways of working, had no established informal relationships with his subordinates and had yet to secure the allegiance and loyalty of the workforce. Accordingly, he could only discharge his managerial responsibilities by resorting to formal bureaucratic procedures in contrast to his predecessor who had worked largely through informal relations relying on old and familiar bonds, developed over many years, with the workforce. This change to a more formal discipline alienated the workers which, in its turn, forced the new manager to rely even more on bureaucratic methods of administration. However, this process of formalisation failed in respect of the mine. The stronger informal bonds between the miners, their more pronounced group solidarity, due in no small part to the ever-present common dangers they faced in the mine, meant that they were able to develop a vital unofficial system of organisation and control more than capable of resisting the attempts of the new manager to introduce formal methods of disciplined administration.

On the basis of this case study of managerial succession, Gouldner offers some modifications of Weber's contention that the effectiveness of bureaucratic functioning depends upon officials' accepting the legitimacy of the rules. As his study shows, the manner in which rules are imposed, for example whether by agreement or by coercion, can have an influence upon the processes and effectiveness of bureaucracy. He identifies, on this basis, three types of bureaucracy, 'mock', 'representative' and 'punishment centred'. In the first of these the rules are imposed on the organisation by some external agency and neither management nor workers particularly support or identify with them. By contrast, in 'representative bureaucracy' both management and workers initiate the rules and regard them as their own, while in a 'punishment-centred' bureaucracy rules arise in response to the pressures of either workers or management but are not jointly initiated by them. In a not dissimilar vein, Etzioni (1961) has made the relationship between an organisational actor's response and orientation to a superior's power central to his comparative analysis of organisations. He argues that superiors can make use of three major means of power to secure compliance: coercion, remuneration and symbolic or normative rewards. The full typology of compliance relationships is achieved by associating the three kinds of power with three kinds of involvement, that is, the orientation of subordinated actors to the power exercised by superiors, namely, alienative, calculative and moral. Although the combination of each of the three types of power and involvement produces a nine-fold typology of compliance relationships, Etzioni expects to find only three congruent types with any frequency. Although organisations make use of all three kinds of power, they vary in the emphasis placed on each. Indeed, organisations will tend to specialise in one means of power since attempts to use more with any determination will, he argues, effectively neutralise each of them. For example, the use of coercive power usually creates such a high degree of alienative involvement from the organisation that it becomes difficult if not impossible to use symbolic or normative power with any hope of success. This he offers as one reason why rehabilitation is rarely achieved in traditionally organised prisons. Similarly, an over-enthusiastic use of remunerative power in a church is likely to undermine the power of the moral appeal. To refer to the traditionally organised prison once again, one can often find a conflict between the organisational need for containment, solved in the traditional case by highly structured, frequently coercive, relationships between staff and inmates, and the goals of rehabilitation which require rather different organisational arrangements involving more personalised contacts, a less strict regime and a less punitive atmosphere. It would be hard, to take another example, to reconcile the need for professional expertise in the modern military services with the traditional means of securing compliance in the nineteenth-century British army, namely, the lash and the cat.

This relationship between the formal structure of organisations and the informal, unintended, unprogrammed activities that also occur within them has been one of the abiding interests of modern organisation research. To a large extent the informal patterns have been seen as 'deviations', often unwelcome ones at that, from the formal programme. As the works of Gouldner, Etzioni and others illustrate, bureaucracies are not rigid, monolithic, or unchanging but full of conflicts, adjustments and changes that are only poorly reflected in Weber's typology. Selznick (1948) argued that formal administration design can never adequately or fully reflect the concrete organisation to which it refers. In his view, the formal administration represents a particular conception which management seek to explicate and, as such, is a source of tension and dilemma due, in large part, to the 'recalcitrance' of human beings and their profound inability to match actions to ideal plans and programmes. Formal organisations, for Selznick, are simply ideals: practically unattainable states of affairs which, none the less, are active ingredients in determining the patterns of behaviour which actually arise in organisations.

What this suggests is that bureaucratic rules, like all rules, are not so much disembodied standards as products which are used in the day-to-day conduct of organisational personnel, a feature amply illustrated by a study conducted by Strauss and colleagues (1978) into hospital organisation. They begin by making the point that in Michael Reese Hospital, a sizeable psychiatric establishment, hardly anyone knows all the rules pertaining to its organisation 'much less exactly what situations they apply to, for whom, and with what sanctions' (Strauss *et al.*, 1978, p. 394). Rules would be forgotten, fall into disuse, be ignored, be reiterated by the administration only to fall into disuse once again, even rules formulated and agreed by staff for their ward. The researchers also found, to no one's surprise, that all members of the hospital's organisation were adept at breaking or stretching the rules on occasion. It was found that the area of action covered by clearly enunciated rules was, in fact, very small. Indeed, these few rules which were clearly enunciated and generally followed, such as those obtaining for the placement of new patients within the hospital, were better regarded as shared understandings of some duration rather than explicit rules. In any event, such rules, again like all rules, required judgement on the part of the personnel concerning their applicability to a specific case and were often displayed to the researchers by the use of analogy rather than universal answers.

Although all the personnel working in the hospital agreed with the overarching goal of the organisation, that is, to improve the health of its patients, what this involved, 'on the ground' so to speak, was a source of considerable dispute and negotiation. The overall aim, though shared, was often used to justify and to reject courses of action designed to help a particular patient recover. Personnel disagreed over the proper placement of patients within the hospital, between psychiatric ideologies, even over what constituted 'getting better'. In other words, the 'generalised mandate', the overarching aim, of the hospital does not help handle specific issues relating to a particular patient and 'a complicated process of negotiation, of bargaining, of give-and-take necessarily begins' (ibid., p. 396). If negotiation arises because a generalised mandate requires implementation, it is reinforced by the differential motivations of each professional group working in the hospital and the fact that each patient, almost as an article of faith, is an 'individual case' involving a high degree of medical uncertainty so that few rules could be laid down in advance. This bargaining process is not only typical of the professionals working within the hospital; patients, too, played their part. Most visibly they could be seen bargaining with staff, not only for more privileges, such as more liberty to roam the grounds, but also seeking to affect treatment programmes. In short, patients are part of the social organisation of the hospital and not merely passive recipients of the treatments it metes out.

The model presented here pictures the hospital as a locale where personnel, mostly professionals but not exclusively, are 'enmeshed in a complex negotiative process in order both to accomplish their individual purposes and to work – in an established division of labour – toward clearly as well as vaguely phrased institutional objectives' (ibid., p. 404). It brings to the fore, which the authors argue the current preoccupation with formal organisation fails to do, the interactional features of organisations. In this example of a psychiatric hospital, the organisation can be pictured as a place where numerous agreements are continually being forged, terminated, revoked, forgotten, remade, revised, and so on. This *is* the social order of the hospital at any given moment, an order that is continually being reconstituted as a basis for concerted action.

This picture of bureaucratic organisation is, admittedly, derived from a study of a professional organisation which, it could be argued, makes it very different from the more typical kind of bureaucratic organisation as elaborated by Weber and others. For one thing, the exercise of professional knowledge is very much an exercise of individual judgement, and performance a matter of evaluation by fellow professional colleagues, not by superiors in some hierarchical authority structure. In other words, we might expect that in organisations staffed largely by professionals the extent of bureaucratisation and hierarchic control would be minimal. Indeed, as research shows, one of the areas of tensions in such organisations, and they include universities and schools as well as hospitals, arises from attempts to impose a bureaucratic, hierarchical principle of organisation upon the professional principle of colleague authority. However, Strauss's argument that rules are not 'disembodied standards' but the product of negotiation, often intensive, deserves further comment.

The distinction we noted earlier in this section between the 'formal' and the 'informal' organisation suggests that there is a clear and determinate distinction to be drawn between those patterns of behaviour within the organisation which fall under each heading. However, what Strauss's example suggests is that, in practice, it is difficult to draw this distinction without ambiguity. One could also suggest that the idea of the organisation as a negotiated order further implies that the distinction, and others like it, is very much a matter for the members of the organisation as well as for researchers. As Weber well knew though did not fully exploit, the members of society know what bureaucracy is, know what hierarchy looks like, know what officials are and do, know what impersonality is, what is 'red tape', and more. If they did not know these and other things it is hard to see how they could be regarded as organisational actors at all. But they know these things as part of their everyday lives, not as some disembodied normative idealisation. Another way of putting this is to say that members of any organisation, as part of their routine day-to-day life, have to interpret the rules, official or otherwise, make decisions about what to do in a particular case, rationalise what was done, determine the relevance of any instruction, any record, or any remark, and assemble these into some accountable form that consists of 'proper' and rational organisational practice. It is this perspective which informs Zimmerman's (1970, 1971) study of a public assistance office in the United States.

In this study of the everyday rationality of members of organisations, Zimmerman makes the point that what rules mean to, and how they are used by, personnel is determined on actual occasions of bureaucratic work. In this way it focuses upon the judgemental process concerning what it takes to warrant the application of any rule, whether formal or informal, in concrete situations and, in particular, how the formal plan of the organisation is used by personnel to deal with everyday work activities. The office concerned was responsible in its district for administering several programmes of federally financed assistance. Before aid can be given intake workers have to establish that the applicant is eligible and be able to justify that decision in terms of the official requirements of the programme in question. The first step of this process involves the applicant appearing before a receptionist to fill in the relevant form. The receptionist must then 'clear' the case by checking the form and assigning a caseworker to attend the applicant. It is at this point that documentation and investigation of the client's case begins.

A major responsibility of reception is to preprocess applicants and assign them to a caseworker in an orderly fashion. The rule governing this process was, in essence, 'first come, first served' and was operationalised in the use of an intake book in which the caseworkers on duty on a given day were listed in the order they were to receive assignments. Applicants were then allocated according to this listing. As a system of activities reception's task is to 'keep people moving' and for most of the time preprocessing proceeds in a routine fashion. However, the rule itself depends upon the dispatch with which caseworkers conduct their interviews with clients. In other words, the capacity of the rule to achieve an orderly and rapid flow of applicants is contingent upon the intake worker's dealings with an applicant. In one such case, where an interview was of longer than normal duration, the applicant was switched to another caseworker. The rule was, so to speak, 'suspended' – an act involving the alteration of various records.

As a general point, the implication here is that what a rule is to mean, what it is intended to provide for, is discovered in the course of employing it over a series of actual situations. Any modifications due to troubles a rule provokes can be subsequently invoked or assumed to be what the rule intended 'all along'. By deciding to suspend the rule in this instance of its potential application, the intent of the rule was not seen to be violated. The modification, instead, was regarded as 'reasonable', and in doing so, receptionists 'appear to provide for ways to ensure that the continuing accomplishment of the normal pacing and flow of work may be reconciled with their view of these tasks *as governed by* rules' (Zimmerman, 1970, p. 233). So, the notion of action-in-accord-with-a-rule is a matter not so much of compliance, or otherwise, but of the ways in which persons *satisfy* themselves and others concerning what is or is not 'reasonable' compliance in the circumstances. Instead of being 'disembodied' regulatory norms, rules and reference to them can be seen as a 'common sense method of accounting for and making available for talk the orderly features of everyday activities, thereby *making out* those activities as orderly in some fashion' (ibid., p. 233).

What Zimmerman has done, following the precepts of ethnomethodology, is to treat rationality, the notion central to Weber's analysis, as a practical accomplishment of the members of organisations. From this perspective the study of organisations consists in the investigation of the sense-making activities of members who, routinely and commonsensically, relying on their taken-for-granted knowledge of social structures, including organisations, accountably produce in the context of actual social scenes the observable and reportable phenomena of organisational life. As an approach it departs from traditional studies of organisations by deliberately refusing to treat, in this case organisations, as if they were objects and structures independent of the activities of those persons composing them. Instead, it seeks to study organisations, and the social relationships out of which they are built, as dependent upon the interpretative practices which provide for ways of attending to the world. Much of this interpretative work is understood to be tacit rather than explicit in its operation but, none the less, provides for and displays an actor's sense of an objective social structure.

It is from this stance that Bittner (1974) criticises Weber and others for taking the concept of organisation structure as unproblematic. He argues that it is a notion derived from the common-sense knowledge used by actors in situations to produce an accountable, and thereby orderly, state of affairs, masquerading as a scientific concept. In other words, the notion becomes a 'resource' for analysis when it should be a 'topic' of inquiry. The concept of bureaucracy, for example, builds upon the taken-for-granted, background, commonsensically understood knowledge that competent members of society use to render their activities sensibly accountable. Accordingly, what the theory of bureaucracy represents is a 'refinement and purification' of the actors' theorising and is, thereby, an incomplete version of it.

From this perspective, rules are seen as the ongoing practical accomplishments of organisational members, as are the other social features of bureaucracy, such as hierarchy, 'formalistic impersonality', official rights and duties, the objectivity of records, and more. Weber, according to Bittner, relied on everyday knowledge of 'bureaucracy' to produce his ideal type. Unfortunately, what Weber failed to do was investigate the methods by which members employ their everyday knowledge of bureaucracy to provide for the sensible and rational nature of their activities. Bittner's point is not that Weber was wrong to select this or that as characteristic of bureaucratic organisation, but that he, and his followers, failed to appreciate that 'formal organisational designs are schemes of interpretation that competent and entitled users can invoke in yet unknown ways whenever it suits their purposes'. It is these ways in which the scheme can be invoked for such things as information, direction, justification, and so on, which 'constitutes the scheme's methodical use' (Bittner, 1974, pp. 76–7). Thus, Weber's 'spirit of formalistic impersonality' can be treated as an organisation member's interpretative rule which may be used, by members, on occasions to display the sense of activities as bureaucratic. Bittner's own suggestions involve treating the concept of rational organisation as a 'gambit of compliance'; that is, as one way in which a member of an organisation, who is after all not a disinterested bystander, invokes certain rules by the concept of formal organisation and, accordingly, clarifies the meaning of some action by bringing it under the auspices, by letting it be seen as, complying with a formal rule. His two further suggestions of ways in which members' use of the concept of formal organisation may be looked at arise from the complexity and large scale of many enterprises. In such cases, there is always a tendency to fragmentation, with little sense of the overall pattern, and a difficulty in perceiving how well a part fits in with the whole. Bittner suggests that members may use the concept of formal organisation as a 'model of stylistic unity' acting as a principle of discipline allowing members to see and justify specific activities and instances as variations of a more general pattern and 'what properly goes with what'. Similarly, as 'corroborative reference' members can use the formal scheme to display the fact that what may appear to be isolated, fragmentary, even worthless activities are, within the overall scheme of things, significant within the whole field of the organisation's activities. On this approach, investigations into the bureaucratic phenomenon become inquiries into the methodical ways in which members construct the rational grounds of their own activities as an occasioned matter. It eschews treating bureaucracy and its features as phenomena independent of the ways in which they are displayed through the common-sense practices members use to impute meanings and construct a sense of social order.

One major consequence of taking this position seriously is that many of the products of much organisational activity, and these would include not only the records and statistics but also the criminals, the mentally ill, the dead, the cured, the educated, suicides, the unemployed, and so forth, as represented in the statistics and records, have to be looked at not merely as facts, as it were, but more as the members' accomplishment of facticity. As Cicourel shows in his *The Social Organisation of Juvenile Justice* (1976), the information contained in an official file on, say, a juvenile deliquent is not understandable as an organisational and organised matter without reference to the rules and theories utilised by police, probation and other officials in their day-to-day activities. These rules or theories have their roots in common-sense typifications which constitute law enforcement officials' stock of often taken-for-granted knowledge. It is this stock of knowledge about the district, what normally occurs there, about the type of people normally to be found in it, personality sketches of the people encountered, what is a 'good family', what is a 'bad attitude', and so on, which the policeman uses to make sense of the particular occurrences he comes across. In addition, these events and persons must be located within some legal context to justify and explain any further inference or action which might follow. 'Virtually every instance of categorization requires decisions that transform a truncated behavioural description of ''what happened'' into some precoded, but almost never unidimensional category that enables the police to invoke legal language' (Cicourel, 1976, p. 104). In their day-to-day encounters with the police, probation and other officials Cicourel shows how juvenile cases are filtered, retrospectively and prospectively, so that they assume typical 'delinquent' features, such as coming from broken homes, showing a 'bad attitude' towards authority, poor school performance, ethnic group membership, poor families, and so on. The official records mask this filtering process and exclude an understanding of how legal and other rules, along with common-sense knowledge and typifications, were invoked to interpret and justify a course of action. The records and the categories they contain become divorced from the social context in which the categorisations and the actors' routine activities occur.

The point about this categorisation work as illustrated by Cicourel's study is that many organisations are concerned to produce classifications of members of society as a way of producing types of social actors. In other words, the classifications are profoundly consequential matters not only for the persons intimately affected but also for the rest of us, if only because they tell us what kind of people exist in our society. Law enforcement organisations 'produce' criminals of various kinds, hospitals 'produce' ill and healthy people, coroners 'produce' accounts of how certain people met their deaths, social security organisations 'produce', amongst other things, the needy, and so on. The production of these categories is a routine occupational matter for the members of these organisations who must assemble the particularities of the events, activities and persons they encounter in the course of their own day-to-day activities, using their own practical reasoning and knowledge of the ordered world of society-at-large, into an organisationally proper form as an account of the factual order of some social domain. In this way, investigations of the bureaucratic phenomenon become inquiries into the methodical ways in which members construct the rational grounds of their own activities as an occasioned matter the outcome of which is the non-problematic production of an 'obvious' and non-problematic world.

I want now to turn to another theme arising from Weber's germinal work on bureaucracy, namely, the relationship between bureaucracy and the modern state.

## The Bureaucratic State

Although Weber recognised that bureaucratic organisations had appeared in earlier epochs, it was the advent of capitalism which gave bureaucracy its fullest expression. The development of large-scale production and mass democracy 'largely under capitalistic auspices, has created an urgent need for stable, strict, intensive, and calculable administration. It is this need which gives bureaucracy a crucial role in our society as the central element in any kind of large-scale administration' (Weber, 1964, p. 338). For Weber, the rise of the free enterprise economic system had the paradoxical effect of fostering, often in long complex chains of causation, the development of bureaucracy not only in private firms but also in government, political parties, trade unions, armies, churches, education systems, and more. Nor did he feel that socialism would fare any better in this regard. Far from inaugurating a new democratic era, socialism would require a still higher degree of formal bureaucratisation than capitalism. Indeed, for Weber one of the more enduring threats posed by the rise of bureaucracy is that its indispensability, technical and organisational knowledge, and tradition of secrecy could so easily, especially in the absence of effective political leadership, subvert the rule of law and political authority and turn itself into the kind of bureaucratic absolutism that characterised Imperial Germany under Bismark.

Whereas in Weber, and in the liberal tradition which he represents, the 'dictatorship of the bureaucrats' was an ever-present danger against which parliaments and politicians must always be on their guard, in some recent writings bureaucracy becomes an ineluctable feature of the state in monopoly capitalism. Such a 'corporatist state' rules through a variety of bureaucratic institutions which act as appendages of state power. In contrast to the pluralist view of the power structure of the modern state as fragmented, diffuse and, above all, a competitive process between various elite groups, theorists of the corporate state argue that this conceals the way in which a dominant economic class exercises its power through state institutions. Miliband (1973), for example, argues that the economic base of advanced capitalist societies is constituted by large corporations in whose interests the state administers. The state itself consists of the interrelationship between bureaucracies of the government, the military, the police, the judiciary and local government. These institutions, despite the occasional conflicts between them, generally act in support of a dominant ideology favourable to the economic interests of the large corporations. The so-called multiplicity of elites beloved of pluralist theorists is, according to Miliband, a sham. Personal ties, social background, shared values, and so on, serve to unite the members of the various elite groups into a 'dominant economic class'.

As far as the theory of organisations is concerned, it is Miliband's claim that such a theory cannot satisfactorily be developed until the role of the state is properly understood. In this respect at least, Miliband builds upon Weber who also developed his theory of bureaucracy in the context of an analysis of systems of domination. What this means is that to understand the ways in which the police, the judiciary, local government, the education system, in addition to economic and industrial enterprises, operate it is necessary to view them as more or less integral parts of the state apparatus. This is in stark contrast to the predominant view in organisation theory which regards organisations as distinct, self-regulating entities acting largely independently of the state. However, it can plausibly be argued, as Weber did, that the rise of the modern state and the development of bureaucratic forms of administration within other institutions are linked. And, within a Marxist framework, the state and other organisations, especially but not only industrial corporations, constitute a structure of domination in which not only does power reside within a small elite group but also acts as a repressive system for the exploitation of labour.

However, precisely what the relationship is between the state and other bureaucratic organisations is a moot point. Miliband, for example, relies considerably upon the common background and social experience between the leaders of organisations in the various institutional spheres and government to make his case that there is a 'dominant economic class', possessed of a high degree of cohesion and solidarity 'using the state apparatus in the interests of capital'. In this sense, he takes his analysis little further than C. W. Mills's pioneering work, *The Power Elite*, and is subject to much the same criticisms.

However, it has to be admitted that the debate on the state within Marxist political and social thought, and hence the relationship of bureaucracy and its various manifestations to it, is very much alive, often stridently so. Poulantzas (1973), for example, has criticised Miliband's work from an Althusserian structuralist perspective as being in the grip of the 'problematic of the subject' which seeks to explain patterns of social organisation and process ultimately in terms of the motivations of individual actors: a sin, incidentally, of which Weber is also guilty. For Poulantzas the role of the state within capitalism must be theoretically derived as an objective structure from a thorough analysis of the capitalist mode of production. In brief, he argues that the capitalist state must be understood as possessing a necessary and objective function in the reproduction of social cohesion. In this sense, the state includes all those political and ideological apparatuses, such as government, army, police, the church, political parties, trade unions, through which the cohesion necessary to capital accumulation is maintained. Specific juridico-political and ideological practices mediated through the state create an 'isolation effect' by sustaining the beliefs that 'agents of production' are individuals rather than members of antagonistic classes. Thus, economic agents do not experience capitalist relations as class relations but as relations of competition among mutually isolated individuals and/or fragmented groups of workers and capitalists. This 'isolation effect' extends over the entire field of economic relations in capitalist societies and is coupled with the cohesive function of the capitalist state. That is, the state presents itself as representative of the political unity, as a nation of free and legally equal citizens, and which through representative institutions and centralising bureaucracy is able to organise and regulate the relations among individuals and social categories. In other words, class relationships as such are absent from the organisation of the capitalist state and it can assume the form of rational-legal administration. The bureaucracy appears as impersonal and neutral enshrining the general interest and operating according to a hierarchically structured, centrally organised system of formal, unified, rational and legal rules. Yet, given the need to reproduce class domination, the capitalist state must secure the hegemony of the dominant class by making material concessions to the dominated classes and, perhaps more important, through transmission of a dominant ideology that is not the exclusive creation of the dominant class but includes petit-bourgeois and working-class elements, cement the social cohesion in a class-divided society. This permeation of the dominant ideology into the ideologies of subordinate classes comes to structure even the forms of popular resistance to the state through trade unions, democratic political parties, pressure groups, and so forth. In this sense, Poulantzas argues, the liberal democratic state is the best possible shell for securing the political domination of competitive capital.

Braverman, in his study *Labour and Monopoly Capital* (1974), offers an account which attempts to link bureaucratic organisation with the ideological and other needs of a capitalist state. Under later capitalism, it is argued, the typical economic unit becomes the large-scale enterprise able to produce a significant share of the output of an industry, rather than the small entrepreneurial firm. These large corporations, then, become the major vehicles for the accumulation of capital and profit maximisation, and the main users of the surplus they produce. Necessary to this process is the control of labour. Braverman's contention is that management, the agents, as it were, of the capital accumulation process, control labour by, first, replacing it by machines so the importance of skill declines and the worker sinks 'to the level of general and undifferentiated labour power, adaptable to a large range of simple tasks', and lessening the need for organisational and disciplinary control; and, secondly, by harnessing science, especially organisation science. This latter point constitutes a major attack by Braverman on the perspective of 'scientific management' which has dominated the theory of managerial practice for much of this century. Begun by F. W. Taylor, its aim was to place workshop management on a scientific basis by encouraging an empirical and experimental approach to the factors affecting productivity. Further, it provided a justification for management itself, in that it is management who must bear the main responsibility for applying this scientific knowledge to the problem of production: workers merely have to be trained in the ways decided by management as the most effective method of doing the particular job concerned. According to Braverman, this doctrine constituted yet another means of controlling labour and further contributes to its 'dehumanisation' under capitalism by treating it as simply some input within a socio-technical system. In other words, 'scientific management' views work and life through the 'eyes of the bourgeoisie' and in this respect is an ideological reflection of the economic base of monopoly capitalist society and the development of the labour process within it. As a theory of organisations, 'scientific management' both describes the labour process and actively ensures its viability. This internal control of the labour force within the industrial corporation serves a further important function. Braverman argues that the complexity of the division of labour under capitalism requires a prodigious degree of social control to a level beyond the ability of the official organs of the state to provide. Accordingly, as Burrell and Morgan (1979) argue, the internal control and co-ordination exercised by management within corporations becomes in effect 'social planning to fill in the existing large gaps in social control left by the state'.

The argument being advanced here is that the predominance of bureaucratic organisation within capitalist industrial society is not the result of a particular concatenation of events within European and American history, which is Weber's view, but a necessary result of the capitalists' need to control production. The essential feature of bureaucratic organisation is that it is highly stratified, each level being responsible for the levels below and accountable to the levels above. Although the organisation's rules allow each person in the hierarchy enough authority to perform assigned duties, it is the few at the top who have overall authority and the power to make decisions affecting the whole organisation. In addition, workers within the organisation must be motivated to perform the assigned tasks, hence they must internalise the values and goals of the organisation despite the fact that these reflect the capitalists' interests, not those of the workforce. Although bureaucratic organisation promotes efficiency and rationality, it does so only within the context of managerial control: its reliance on multiple levels of authority and supervision, and emphasis on discipline and predictability, is probably the only way of ensuring efficient production using alienated labour.

# References: Chapter 6

Bittner, E. (1974), 'The concept of organisation', in R. Turner (ed.), *Ethnomethodology* (Harmondsworth: Penguin), pp. 69–82.

Braverman, H. (1974), *Labour and Monopoly Capital* (New York: Monthly Review Press).

Burrell, G., and Morgan, G. (1979), *Sociological Paradigms and Organisational Analysis* (London: Heinemann).

Cicourel, A. (1976), *The Social Organisation of Juvenile Justice* (London: Heinemann).

Etzioni, A. (1961), *A Comparative Analysis of Complex Organisations* (New York: The Free Press).

Gouldner, A. (1954), *Patterns of Industrial Bureaucracy* (New York: The Free Press).

Gouldner, A. (1957), *Wildcat Strike* (London: Routledge & Kegan Paul).

Merton, R. K. (1949), 'Bureaucratic structure and personality', in *Social Theory and Social Structure* (New York: The Free Press), pp. 151–60.

Miliband, R. (1973), *The State and Capitalist Society* (London: Quartet Books).

Mills, C. W. (1956), *The Power Elite* (London: OUP).

Poulantzas, N. (1973), 'The problem of the capitalist state', in J. Urry and J. Wakeford (eds), *Power in Britain* (London: Heinemann), pp. 291–305.

Selznick, P. (1948), 'Foundations of the theory of organisations', *American Sociological Review*, vol. 13, pp. 25–35.

Strauss, A., *et al.* (1978), 'The hospital and its negotiated order', in P. Worsley *et al.* (eds), *Modern Sociology* (Harmondsworth: Penguin), pp. 394–405.

Weber, M. (1964), *The Theory of Social and Economic Organisation* (New York: The Free Press).

Zimmerman, D. (1970), 'Record keeping and the intake process in a public welfare organisation', in S. Wheeler (ed.), *On Record* (New York: Russell Sage Foundation), pp. 319–54.

Zimmerman, D. (1971), 'The practicalities of rule use', in J. Douglas (ed.), *Understanding Everyday Life* (London: Routledge & Kegan Paul), pp. 221–38.

# Further Reading

Albrow, M. (1970), *Bureaucracy* (London: Pall Mall Press).

Daniels, A. K. (1975), 'Professionalism in formal organisations', in J. R. McKinley (ed.), *Processing People* (New York: Holt, Rinehart & Winston), pp. 303–38.

Etzioni, A. (1964), *Modern Organisation* (Englewood Cliffs, NJ: Prentice-Hall).

Jessop, B. (1982), *The Capitalist State* (Oxford: Martin Robertson).

Mouzelis, N. (1975), *Organisation and Bureaucracy* (London: Routledge & Kegan Paul).

Vollmer, H. M., and Mills, D. C. (1966), *Professionalisation* (Englewood Cliffs, NJ: Prentice-Hall).

Chapter 7

# Occupation and Control

### JOEL RICHMAN AND JIM LORD

Many social science studies of work have been criticised for taking a notably 'one-sided' approach to their topic. They have been accused of an unreflective identification with the managerial outlook (Braverman, 1974). They have, that is, based themselves on the assumption that management's goals can be taken as representing those of the corporate entity as a whole and have, therefore, tended to take maximisation of organisational efficiency and output as the sole desirable objectives. Consideration of everything else has been subordinated to these goals. It has further been assumed that managers are possessed of technical expertise in the organisation of production and are sound judges of what needs to be done to realise their objectives. 'Problems of work' come, on such assumptions, to be understood as all those things which are seen as such by management, which bear upon its interests and obstruct its policies.

Viewed on the basis of such assumptions, the conduct of the workforce can become 'a problem', for often it does not fit in with the patterns that management regards as desirable and the issue for management (and, consequently, for many social science inquirers) has been to see how labour can be more effectively manipulated in the interests of management, how it can be rendered more co-operative, and so forth. In so far as workers are resistant to managerial policies, they are looked upon as irrational, for it is assumed that management's activities are meant to enhance the prosperity of the organisation as a whole and are to the benefit of everyone in it, including the workers. If workers obstruct or resist managerial demands they seem to be acting against their own interests, their own economic well-being – what could be more irrational than that? 'Restrictive practices' have provided the classic example of this kind of alleged irrationality, for in innumerable ways workers limit their effort and fail to use working practices and technology in ways which would make them as productive as they might be. Ethnographic studies of alien societies have done much to show that judgements of rationality are more complex and difficult than some of the more enthusiastic makers of such judgements are apt to think.

Whether or not something is judged irrational depends very much upon the point of view that is taken towards it. The supposedly irrational practices of other societies only seem so because they are being looked at from an unsympathetic, insensitive, or even ethnocentric point of view. Attempts to examine the ways of alien societies 'through the eyes' of their own inhabitants suggest that seen in that way, the doings of such societies are typically no less rational than those of our own.

Ethnographic studies of work have played a similar role, because problems of understanding exist not only between societies but between groups within the same society. If the conduct of workers is looked at not *through* the assumptions that managers make about what is in the workers' interest and to their benefit, but in a way which attends to the workers' attitudes and objectives, and which therefore sees the workers' activities in the light of their own perception of their circumstances, then such activities do not look anywhere near so irrational.

A more impartial view of the organisation of work begins by recognising that a social situation involving the coexistence of two quite differently situated groups (one in control, the other being controlled) is not best understood by assuming that the point of view of one of them can be taken as an adequate guide to the situation as a whole.

In order to achieve a more balanced assessment of the respective rationalities of management and workers it has been proposed that the work situation be viewed as being centred on an 'effort bargain' (Baldamus, 1957). The notion is intended to draw attention to the fact that employer –employee relations do not consist in a bare economic transaction, an exchange of wages for work. Management's role in production is not simply a technical one, for its activities are extensively devoted to regulating the worker's behaviour as a means of controlling the worker's level of effort. The employer–employee relationship is focused upon the issue of control.

Management seeks both to stabilise and intensify the level of the worker's effort, and if it is rational for management to do this by extending its control over the workforce, it does not follow that it is rational for the workers to comply with management's demands, *even if* this might prove economically beneficial to them. The wage *is* a central element in management–worker relations, but the very force of the idea of the effort bargain is to stress that it is not the only one. Payment arrangements are to be seen as *part* of the system of administrative control, but the extent to which they are effective will depend upon their relationship to other aspects of the effort bargain.

The theme of control over work activities achieves prominence as a result of such arguments, and in the first part of this chapter we will examine some examples of the ways in which the effort bargain is 'struck' from the worker's point of view, and of the ways in which workers react to managerial efforts to adjust its balance.

## Working on the Line: Technological Control

The production line is a developed form of technological regulation of effort. The mechanical character of the line means that effort levels can be stabilised, for the line moves at constant speed. Effort can also be intensified by variation, increase, in the speed of movement. If the worker is to 'keep up' with the line, then he cannot vary the speed with which he works, for the line moves without regard for his pace of work: 'Working in a car plant involves coming to terms with the assembly line! "The line never stops" you are told. Why not? '. . . don't ask. It *never* stops."' (Beynon, 1973, p. 109). Men either keep up with the line or they collect their cards. The workers are capable of working, some of the time at least, at a rate faster than is needed to keep up with the line, so that they can get ahead of it, and hence can work their way 'back up the line' until they are far enough ahead to take a brief few seconds' respite.

In Beynon's account of a Ford motor plant, the line dominates the worker's experience. The remorseless progress of the line, and the virtually total control it entails over the lives of those harnessed to it, colours everything. Life is regarded as a constant battle against the line. Escaping its imposed routines becomes the name of the game at all times. Even the speedy who can get ahead and 'make time', have a few words, a laugh, a joke, or half a cigarette with others similarly placed, find that the line intrudes even then. The noise is terrific. Sign language is necessary at all but point-blank range. For the rest of the time, the work provides a stultifying tedium borne in social isolation so that any relief from its pressure is welcomed.

It comes as no surprise, then, to learn that the line, particularly its speed, becomes the subject of an obsessive, almost paranoid, concern. It is starkly and obviously 'the frontier of job control', the mechanical incarnation of management, of 'Them' or (in Beynon's case and that of some of the shop stewards) of 'capitalism'.

Work speed-up was the main fear and horror stories about surreptitious increases in line speed circulated. Whether the stories were true or apocryphal is not clear. They were certainly firmly believed. The most obvious way to extract more work from the labour force was to increase the speed of the line gradually during a shift. Done slowly enough, this speed-up would be virtually undetectable. The temptation would be too great for management, who were thought to have succumbed and exploited the possibility. The first intimation that this was happening came as making time became progressively more difficult and finally impossible. What was to be done? This was the stuff of last stands. Critical sections of the workforce just walked off the job and refused to return until normal speeds were resumed. Others indulged in acts of 'sabotage'. Some simply and repeatedly pulled the safety wire that stopped the line. Some deliberately did bad work so that prominent faults appeared in finished vehicles. By these means management were prompted to slow or stop the line to find out what was happening. As a result, it was agreed that the first man on some sections of the track had a time allowance for monitoring line speed and the stewards were given the right to stop the line if the speed exceeded agreed levels.

Regardless of substance, the tales about disruption were seen as examples to follow whenever the occasion arose. Where management had negotiated procedures with the union, the procedural arrangements could always be swamped with unresolved grievances. So management trod warily, avoiding anything which might provoke more open forms of confrontation.

This account of the assembly line shows that even in a situation where workers are prepared to accept far-reaching control of their effort, there are limits to this. They might have forgone much autonomy at work in return for relatively high rates of pay but they are not prepared to lose it all. Retaining some last vestige of control assumes a great importance which might seem wholly exaggerated to those who are not in that situation, but which – for those who are – provides a 'sanity-saver', a necessary relief from the intense, scarcely bearable monotony, futility and tedium of the work itself. Industrial confrontation becomes almost a form of therapy.

## The Lorry-Driver: Regulations and Control

An occupation which is at the opposite extreme in many ways from auto-mobile manufacturing is the road haulage business. The 'technology' of lorry-driving makes the driver's daily work independent of direct managerial supervision (or, at least, until quite recently it did). When asked, most drivers stressed the virtually complete freedom from direct supervision and the correspondingly large amount of discretion which could be exercised on the job, the fact that it was the next best thing to being your own boss, as its advantages and contrasted these virtues with the indoor, intensively supervised employment that was their alternative. These virtues were regarded as making up for the disadvantages of a job which was not particularly well paid, was physically demanding and involved working 'unsocial hours'. However, in this occupation the struggle over effort has been a prominent feature of its recent history.

Twenty years ago, most of the drivers working in the industry were paid a flat weekly wage with enhanced rates and payments for overtime working where this became necessary. Drivers' hours, in so far as they were involved in driving, not in loading, queueing, or unloading, were controlled by law, both in total and distribution over the working day. The law was enforced through an obligation on drivers to fill in log-sheets recording their activities on a daily basis. The Ministry of Transport policed this system through ministry inspectors who could make random checks on vehicles, anywhere at any time, and whose findings would be matched with the log-sheets. Major discrepancies between inspectors' sightings and declarations in drivers' logs were automatically grounds for prosecution for falsification of documents. Penalties were usually in the form of heavy fines. As far as intimate levels of job control were concerned, the construction of the log and the potential ministry check were the only serious problem and these had become accepted by the drivers as reasonable risks of the occupation (Hollowell, 1968).

The situation was a relatively stabilised one that was unsettled by the incomes policies of the later 1960s, when pay rises were severely restricted unless they were related to productivity increases (though it was, through the exploitation of technicalities, possible to give pay rises that were not linked to genuine productivity increases in many industries). There were not many possibilities in the road haulage business for increasing productivity without an extension of illicit and dangerous practices. The drivers had, furthermore, already made considerable use of these to make their work more congenial – by speeding, working excessive hours at a stretch, unsafe but fast loading. The introduction of incentive payments would encourage further use of such practices and mean increasingly hazardous working conditions. However, the need to find ways around incomes policy restrictions meant that productivity deals were made, though neither side was keen on having them. The deals were made by tying rates of pay to mileage, but such deals were differentially beneficial to different kinds of drivers, favouring those with long hauls (involving large amounts of motorway and rural mileage and with little loading and unloading time) over those involved in short hauls and work in congested areas (involving urban mileage, queueing, waiting and slow loading.)

Those who handed out work were now in a critical position to be able to influence the drivers' wages and allegations of favouritism and discriminatory practices ('blue eyed boys') were rife. Moreover, as had been feared, and despite modifications of the payments system, attempts to 'pull back' or 'make up' list time did lead to speeding and more regular infractions of the laws relating to drivers' hours. Many of the more elderly vehicles in the fleet proved totally inadequate to the strains which were being placed upon them and maintainance crises became almost commonplace. Among the less reputable operators such incentive schemes became a device that enabled management to secure all manner of illegal and undesirable performances from the drivers whilst keeping their own hands formally and officially 'clean'. The extent to which drivers were prepared to co-operate in such practices can easily be underestimated: such 'cowboys', often regarded in the classic 'odd bad apple' style, were in fact quite numerous.

The haulage business is one in which the effort bargain is struck in a way which trades the drawbacks of the job (low pay and poor conditions) off against not only the corresponding advantages of freedom from supervision, but also against the opportunities that lack of supervision opens up for side benefits (for example, for concentrating a week's driving into three days and using the extra time for moonlighting). That drivers engage in surreptitious, even illegal, practices is something that is often known, tolerated – perhaps even expected – by employers. The employer's capacity for supervision and control over the driver out on the road is limited by the nature of the business, but drivers' work is also constrained by state intervention and regulation. Employers can therefore find their incapacity to stabilise and intensify effort being compensated for by the fact that they have to pay relatively little, provide relatively few facilities and benefits and yet have a fairly docile workforce which has reconciled itself to these shortcomings of the job by exploiting the side benefits. Management can, further, shift the responsibility for hazardous and illegal practices on to the empoyee: whilst being aware of and tolerant to these, it can remain formally ignorant of them but reaping an indirect benefit from them.

Of course, of late the situation has been further changed by state intervention and the imposition of mechanical regulation of drivers' hours through the introduction of the black box regulation of the tachograph. Evasion of the law now requires more active collaboration between employer and employee, something which recent newspaper reports have indicated is not beyond the bounds of possibility.

## The Bread Roundsman: Accounting and Control

An occupation with many similarities to that of lorry-driver but with somewhat different circumstances, particularly those pertaining to the degree of frequency and regularity of contact with customers, is that of bread roundsman. This, too, is an occupation where the working day lacks direct managerial supervision, but where the opportunities for speeding, fast loading, and so forth are restricted in comparison with those open to the lorry-driver. The occupation exhibits an extensive range of illicit practices, quite different from those of the lorry-driver, involving 'the fiddle'.

Ditton (1977) details some of the ways in which the working situation of the roundsman makes deviant solutions to his organisational problems particularly attractive.

In this case, the centre of difficulty relates to 'balancing the books'. Each day the roundsman orders from the bakery the quantity of bread and cakes that he thinks will be needed to meet his customers' requirements. One of the first tasks of the day is to collect this order and the bill for the whole consignment. Most of the day's work consists of distributing the goods to individual customers. At the end of the day, the takings must be totalled up and this, with the value of any unsold returns, must be reconciled with the bill.

This may sound straightforward but, for a variety of reasons, this reconciliation is virtually impossible to achieve. Mismatches between the goods supplied from the bakery and the bill are not easily detected and late payers and bad debtors among the customers, together with ordinary mistakes in charging and/or supplying, ensures that legitimate balancing of the books presents a permanent and insoluble problem.

The impossibility of performing this task is matched by the urgency of doing so. If, as is most likely, the take is less than the amount shown on the bill, the bakery deducts the deficit from the driver's wages.

Bit by bit, then, the novice roundsman is introduced to the idea of 'adding a bit on' to customers' bills so that the threat of deductions is eliminated. Indeed, the introduction to this 'solution' will be provided by the training foreman and will be made at a ripe psychological moment.

Once the roundsman has moved on to the fiddle, however, further problems ensue. Most have (however slightly) permanent problems in reconciling themselves to the fact that they are robbing their customers. And once fiddling has started, where does it stop? Is the fiddling to be restricted to that necessary to 'come over' every day, or can it go further and provide a regular income supplement? Are the customers the only legitimate target, or should the employer be one too (as by stealing bread from the bakery)?

Roundsmen have ways of coming to terms with their dishonesty: not least, of course, by talking of the activity as 'fiddling', something which suggests that the goings on are trivial and of no real account and that it is, in any case, what *everyone* is doing in one way or another. Sensitivities are also eased by the acknowledgement of conventions in the selection of victims. The old and infirm, for example, are not regarded as fair game, only those who deserve the treatment are given it. This is backed up by the occupational tales (again possibly apocryphal) of scheming customers who cultivate the roundsman and deliberately build up debts without ever intending to pay them off.

The limits of the fiddle are variable, though there are tacit but vague understandings about the upper limits to customer fiddling, about who can thieve from the employer and how much. Thieving from fellow roundsmen was frowned upon but acknowledged to go on.

If all this were not enough, there are other problems too: tailoring the order to the demands of the round to avoid the problem of 'stales', handling problem customers, keeping up an adequate front of cleanliness and smartness for the customers and, again, the problem of boredom. Fiddles again provide ways of dealing with these matters and some of the more flagrant instances of fiddling, such as the outrageous marketing of stales by crushing them in order to make them feel fresh through the wrapper, were often indulged in, as much as anything else for the fun that they offered and because they provided a release from boredom.


## The Policeman: Discretion and Control

The worker, then, has to cope with the exigencies of the occupation and to establish ways of meeting its familiar and recurrent demands and problems. In many cases, economic improvement on his present condition must be 'bought' through the loss of other valued ends. Thus, on the production line increased productivity and higher pay does not just mean working harder, it means working in such a way that all control over one's work may be lost, along with the possibility of *any* kind of relief from an utterly oppressive tedium. In the case of the lorry-driver it is clear that what governmental bureaucrats count as improvements may be deprivations for those whom they affect. From the point of view of management it *may* be an improvement to reorganise work in ways that will eliminate opportunities for 'fiddling' (or more serious illegalities) but this will not be so welcome among those who regard such opportunities as their *legitimate* compensation for other deprivations that the work imposes upon them. Attempts to regulate the haulage business in ways which are meant to provide for the safety of drivers and to inhibit the capacity of employers to exploit them, may in fact eliminate the opportunities for drivers to exploit their employers.

The case of the lorry-drivers should, further, remind us that we are talking here as though the effort bargain always involved opposition of management and workers but we must avoid any oversimplified conception of employer–employee interests which implies that they are invariably or necessarily opposed. When faced with the operation of state agencies, drivers and bosses find that they have much in common and can collaborate in resisting and evading 'external' controls. It must always be an empirical matter as to how far interests coincide and diverge, it cannot be a case for *a priori* stipulation.

The worker–management relationship is not conducted solely in instrumental terms. Workers are not concerned with the *minimisation* of the effort they invest in work, for they are much concerned with 'fairness' and are governed by their own ideas of what a fair day's work for a fair day's pay may be and, thus, of what may fairly be asked of them. Work, like all other areas of social life, has its moral aspect. Workers are involved with considerations of what they *ought* to do, of what they owe to their employers, customers, victims, the public, the state as well as to themselves, their own pride and dignity, their standing in the community and in the eyes of those with whom they must deal on a day-to-day basis. Even the thieving of the bread roundsman is regulated by a code and by rationalisations which make it a fair and legitimate response: studies of fiddling more generally show that it is widely regarded as something which is hardly immoral, which is normal and acceptable and reasonable.

Even the work of the police is as much controlled by ideas of a fair day's work as any other occupation. Studies of police work repeatedly stress that the patrolman is concerned to balance the satisfaction of his own and his superior's conception of what doing the job properly involves. Policemen too engage in restriction of effort, refraining from making arrests where they could do so, avoiding that work which they think is uncalled for, not legitimately asked of them, or excessively demanding of their time and attention. They will, thus, substitute a caution for an arrest to avoid overtime paperwork arising from the latter, they will ignore situations which they regard as properly some other police officer's business, turn a blind eye to things that are not in their area of interest (cf Chapter 5 above). They will, however, make sure that they do the work that will be seen by their superiors as evidence that they are hardworking and effective officers, making the 'right' number and kind of arrests which are seen as 'normal' for the sort of neighbourhood, shift and assignment they are working. This attitude is exemplified in Taylor Buckner's report (quoted in Turner, n.d.) of the patrolmen's maxim 'A traffic ticket a day keeps the Sergeant away' and Turner's (n.d.) overheard (from officers in the juvenile detail) 'Let's get a couple of curfew kids and then go have dinner', which show officers' orienting to a tacit 'quota' for their day's work.

Studies of the police further emphasise the extent to which police decisions are shaped by the officers' sense of dignity, by their image of themselves as people acting in the name of the community. Police–public relations show an extensive interest, on the part of the police, in being the recipient of 'respect', the officer's attitude to the citizen being much tempered by that person's willingness to evince the right degree of regard (Westley, 1970). The police further show a marked reluctance to involve themselves in situations which require them to take an undignified posture or to do things incommensurate with their self-esteem: they are often called upon, but loath to act in situations which are demeaning and unpleasant – the forcible handling of candidate mental patients being one such.

These studies go to show that 'rationality' is not the prerogative of either side in the effort bargain, that both management and workers can be viewed as equivalently rational in the light of their respective circumstances, objectives and resources. Management is often concerned to regulate the workers' effort by such means as

- reducing the area of discretion and decision-making involved and by organising the work so that it can be standardised and expedited;
- depersonalising work, organising it so that it can be done by a standard and mechanical procedure if not by an actual machine;
- introducing technology which will set the pace of work and take the initiative for doing this from the worker;
- controlling the level of effort by making it visible through supervision, documentation and recording.

Such measures, from management's point of view, may well be

technical steps that enhance productivity, that increase the amount of worker's effort but which will be adequately compensated for by an increase in economic reward, but, we have suggested, these innovations have an impact upon situations which are, from the workers' point of view, more complicated than that. Matters of supervision, inspection and control are not simple technical matters, for they have consequences for such things as dignity, pride, independence and privacy which may be valued for themselves, and for the room that they provide to invest work with some satisfaction or to compensate for its deprivations by contriving some side benefit. Being away from the overlook of a superior, possessing some power to control one's own activities, having room for some autonomy in decision-making, these are things that can be as much valued by the lower participants in an organisation as by those further up the hierarchy.

## Professionalisation and Control

The classic studies of restriction of effort have concentrated on manual employees, but it is often pointed out that in modern society manual work is of declining significance. The nature of work is changing and one important aspect of that has been the expansion of 'middle class' (that is, non-manual) tasks, a growth which has involved a substantial increase in the number of professional (or would-be professional) occupations, a growth so marked that it has led at least one sociologist to anticipate 'the professionalisation of everyone' (Wilensky, 1964).

The practice of professional occupations has itself come under close scrutiny, and the topic of 'control' has turned out to be a prominent one there too, though taking a rather different form from that which it assumes in studies of industrial employment.

The professional occupation is often conceived in terms of a set of stereotypical features which are intended to contrast it with other kinds of occupations (cf. Carr-Saunders and Wilson, 1933), but careful study suggests that many of these supposedly identifying features are not all that distinctive (cf. Becker, 1970).

The professional is conceived as one who deals with people (clients) whilst the manual worker is one who deals with things (as does the assembly line worker), but we may easily note that the bread roundsman deals with people (customers) and that the police patrolman's work involves dealing with people (citizens) also. The professional is also conceived as one who is self-employed, an independent practitioner, but it is increasingly the case that the professional is an employee, a member of an organisation and part of an hierarchical arrangement.

Setting aside, then, the objections that can be made to oversimplified ideas about the distinctiveness of professional work, we can still notice that studies of professional work have placed primary emphasis on its interactive character, giving a central place to the analysis of the organisation of the face-to-face encounter between professional and client. The theme of control shows up here as an issue: who is in control, and how do they achieve and maintain it?

Though the professional is in the service of the client (or nominally so) it is often the client who is in the situation of dependency, for the professional is (or is assumed to be) possessed of an expertise that is not available to the client and who will demand complete compliance from the client in whatever steps the professional deems necessary for the solution of the client's problems. In addition to the discrepancy of outlook resulting from the differential access to technical knowledge, there is another factor which distinguishes the outlook of the two parties, for the business which brings them together is typically a personal problem for the client, but only a routine piece of technical business for the professional. The presence of the client in the professional's office is often the sign that the trouble has developed into something out of the ordinary, something which is important and pressing and which calls for instant solution, but which is for the professional just another case, a matter of everyday and routine familiarity, many such cases having been seen before. The professional will, further, often be aware that even if a solution can be forthcoming, it will not be provided instantly, and that treatment of the problem is likely to be a protracted and inconclusive matter.

Since medicine is taken as the paradigm of professional work we shall take our examples here from that field and our specific instances will be drawn from the specialised work of gynaecological consultation.

Time is a central matter in the organisation of the medical encounter. An encounter between doctor and patient will often be only the current one in a series, one step in a continuing relationship between the patient and medical practitioners. The importance of the present encounter will extend both forwards and back in time.

The patient's complaint has a history prior to the visit to the doctor, and that history will be reconstructed: questions about prior symptoms will be asked – was the pain first felt on rising in the mornings, did it move when bending down, standing up, and so forth? The interest in the past is connected with an interest in the future: the reconstruction is undertaken to enable some diagnosis or provisional assessment to be made of the nature of the trouble and to provide an answer to the question, what next? Will further treatment be called for? If the woman has fibroids, then different courses of action are possible: hysterectomy is one possibility, 'picking off' the fibroids is another. What will they mean? Will they, for example, mean that the woman's childbearing capacities will be curtailed or will they offer the prospect of further medical complications at a later time? Picking off the fibroids leaves scar tissue on the womb and has unpredictable consequences. These prospects are not viewed neutrally by the patient for they provoke varying degrees of anxiety, and explanation of their significance will be accompanied by attempts at reassurance.

Time enters as a strong constraint on the organisation of the occasions: the work of reconstructing the case, making physical examinations, discussing diagnoses and providing reassurance all has to be carried through in the course of a brief encounter, for the consultant is scheduled to see a fixed number of patients at the clinic and needs to get through the list.

The practitioner will want to set the pace of the encounter; dealing with the individual patient will have to be managed with an eye on the overall workload of which she is a part, the number of patients to be dealt with in a session, the time required to deal with their problems, the prospect of unexpected developments, and so forth. The practitioner will, therefore, typically be concerned to take and retain the initiative, to move the business on at an appropriate pace, and this will be greatly facilitated if the patient is under control. In hospital the capacity to dominate the encounter is greatly enhanced by the fact that the patient has been placed in a generally subordinate status.

Entry into hospital involves a symbolic transition in the standing of the patient, one which divests her of much of the independence and dignity she would normally possess as an adult member of the society. Admission involves, for example, the replacement of one's normal clothing by pyjamas, one's shoes by slippers. Pregnant women entering the maternity unit have their pubic hair shaved, something which is not medically necessary but which shows them clearly that their body is now in the hands of others. The patient is subject to all kinds of rules and restrictions on quite ordinary things: smoking may not be permitted, one has to ask permission to go to the toilet, and so forth. One is no longer allowed to do things for oneself: one cannot even cover oneself up when lying down but must be tucked in by someone else. In dealing with other people the lying down position puts one at a disadvantage: it is difficult, from there, to carry on an ordinary conversation and it is a disquieting experience to be looked down upon by others. People are, further, doing things to one and which affect one, but they are not forthcoming with information about it – even if one can see what they are doing, one cannot tell what it is exactly, but they will often conceal things and, when one is clearly the subject of a conversation, they will carry this on at sufficient distance to make it inaudible.

Another important respect in which the patient will be made to feel that the situation is quite out of her control is by being kept waiting. The extent to which people can keep each other waiting can typically be taken as a sign of their relative social significance and worth, and patients will be kept waiting for a long and indefinite time by the doctor but must themselves be immediately available to the latter's demands, a clear indication of whose time and activities are counted as having the overwhelming significance. All this is reinforced by the very setting in which it takes place, for it is *their* (the medical personnels') territory into which the patient comes, they own that setting. The equipment, its significance and right of use is theirs as is control of access to places and freedom of movement.

Finally, but not least, the patient may be physically restrained, sometimes by physical force, at others by being given drugs of various sorts, even against her wishes. In some labour wards, for example, the women are 'encouraged' to have pain-relieving drugs even though they do not want them and are sometimes given so much that the babies are born 'doped' and may have to be resuscitated.

We must beware of the suggestion that all these things are done for purposes of control alone, for they are often done for what the staff regard as good reason and their efforts at control are often regarded as being made on behalf of the patient's own interests. Thus the attempt to persuade women in the labour wards to have drugs will be associated with the staff's beliefs about levels of pain and the need to cater for them. Other practices *are*, however, undertaken more out of staff interests: the 'daylight baby' syndrome involves the use of medically unnecessary induction practices to speed up delivery and to ensure that babies will be born at other than inconvenient times such as nights, weekends and public holidays.

One other element of control is, of course, that over information. The question of what the doctor knows and can/will tell the patient is always a sensitive one, and the reasons for complication over the giving of information to the patient are numerous: doctors often do not know what is wrong but feel that to let this show will undermine the trust that the patient must put in them; they have bad news for the patient but fear that revealing this may make the management of treatment even more problematic, adding the problems of dealing with an anxious, even distraught, patient to those of treating a technically difficult case; they want to use the patient's case for their own technical interests and to do things which are not strictly necessary in medical terms.

## Language and Professional Control

The 'rites of passage' transforming the patient into a medical 'object' are reinforced by the distinctiveness of the language used.

The talk within the medical encounter is typically directed by the physician, who takes the initiative in deciding what shall be talked about and how it shall be talked of. As noted above, the patient's history needs to be reconstructed but the way in which that is to be done is not for the patient to say: letting patients tell their stories in their own way is something doctors see as being too time-consuming, for one thing. The patients usually get to give their account in a question and answer exchange, with the doctor asking most of the questions.

These features are clear from this example:

(1) Gynaecologist: Mrs X.
(2) Patient: Yes.
(3) Gyn: Trouble with discharge, is it?
(4) P: Mmh. (nods)
(5) Gyn: How long has this been going on for? It is six months, isn't it?
(6) P: Yes.
(7) Gyn: You are not on the pill? Ah, you are on the pill.
(8) P: Yes.
(9) Gyn: Two children.
(10) P: Yes.
(11) Gyn: You have had a miscarriage as well.
(12) P: Had two.
(13) Gyn: Well, let's have a look at you then shall we? (examination)
(14) Gyn: Cervical erosion at the neck of the womb . . . Fine. That's fine. All finished for the moment. Legs down

The way that the condition is to be talked about is strictly limited by medical relevance. The patient is not asked to elaborate her own theories, in fact she is presented with a statement of her condition (3) and committed to it in the opening sequences. The gynaecologist 'asks' and answers his own question (5) to reinforce the prior medical history she has 'given'. The questions are so phrased as to elicit predictable 'yes' responses. A content analysis of consultation shows that 'yes' (and its equivalents) is one of the commonest words used by patients. Once one is grooved into agreeing, it becomes difficult to switch topics. *Furthermore*, the obstetric history is paramount; no details are requested about the patient's children, their interests, or doings. In routine consultation, the patient has no 'time out' from the business in hand.

The talk in the medical encounter also emphasises the physician's control by the way in which it dissociates the patient's body from the patient, tending to 'dehumanise' that body and treat is as though it were a thing rather than a part of a person.

For example, in gynaecological consultation the body is redefined, with certain anatomical parts being treated as if they were detached. The body is portrayed as two major segments. Before commencing the vaginal examination (VE) the gynaecologist will say, 'I'm going to examine you *down below*'. The gynaecologist never personalises the word 'vagina' (although he will do that for breast), it is always 'I'm going to do *a* vaginal examination'. 'Baby talk' is also used as in 'let your tail go loose'. The body is further dehumanised, for the 'lower half' is presented as having two parallel points of entry in the gynaecologist–patient speech: a 'front' and 'back' passage. The 'disuniting' of the vagina maintains its 'sacredness', according to Henslin and Biggs (1971), during the transaction in which many other everyday things are reversed or drastically modified. Until the Second World War it was hospital practice for the woman's recumbent body to be bisected by a hanging curtain. The gynaecologist was allowed access to both 'parts' but medical students were confined to the lower torso.

There is, then, a neutralising of the physician–patient relation, talk being organised in such a way as to eliminate many of the sensitivities and delicacies that would be prominent in an ordinary encounter between adults. This is particularly noticeable in the case of the VE, where the business of (typically) a male making a close inspection of and contact with a woman's genitals would be intense with sexual significance, but in the VE the talk is such as to render it a coldly impersonal transaction, divested of any such meaning (Emerson, 1970).

## Teamwork in Professional Control

The patient is, furthermore, an individual playing against a team. The medical staff are very much united against the patient when it might be an issue of competing for control. The discussion so far has been carried on as if the doctor–patient situation involved only those two parties and was solely controlled by the doctor. In this respect it has overlooked the fact that (in hospital at least) the nurse often plays a crucial role, though a 'silent' and invisible one, never initiating dialogue with the patient, but buttressing the doctor's prestige and authority when that is threatened (Stein, 1978).

The nurse plays an important role in enabling the doctor to project an impression of competent, confident and effective performance. The doctor relies on the nurse's judgement, for example, in selecting the right size of speculum to be used in the VE. He would look less authoritative if he had to rummage about in the box for one or if he in fact chose the wrong one himself.

The nurse also plays an important part in managing the tensions that the occasion creates. When the nurse does address the patient, it is inevitably at times when the doctor has problems. In the gynaecological consultation the usual speech pattern is for the nurse to repeat or rephrase the consultant's instructions and to forge a link with the patient through which his message is relayed.

The nurse is often used as a 'prop', another medical expert, for confirming the gynaecologist's finding. Patients with atypical smears discovered by the family planning clinics are usually rushed to the gynaecologist's clinic. They are obviously anxious, fearing that they may have cancer. During the VE the nurse will be invited to inspect and 'confirm' the gynaecologist's findings. He will announce 'first' to the nurse: 'Look, a perfectly healthy cervix nurse', with the patient of course hearing this simultaneously. Gynaecologists very much exploit the woman-to-woman aura between nurse and patient to achieve client compliance.

The gynaecologist hives off what Hughes (1971) called the 'dirty work' (not that which involves physical dirt, necessarily, but that which is distasteful or difficult) to the nurse. Thus, low-level staff who are given no individual significance in the bureaucratic hierarchy – unlike the consultant gynaecologist whose clinic is known by his name – are used in ways that facilitate the exercise of higher authority and expertise over women.

When the doctor leaves the consulting room after each patient to complete case notes and letters next door, the nurse is momentarily left in change of the setting and it is often the case that a 'secondary consultation' takes place: although women have agreed with the gynaecologist and expressed understanding of what he has said, they will often raise the issues again with the nurse, and the nurse will give her version of the proceedings and may offer additional advice.

## Compliance and Control

Just as it is possible to adopt an unwittingly and illegitimately 'managerial' outlook on industrial work, so it is possible to do something similar in the examination of professional work, to make the mistake of going along with 'the line' that the professional is taking.

The professional projects to the client an image of the client's situation, a co-operative pursuit of the client's interest, best effected through the client's acknowledgement of and compliance with the professional's unquestionable and unrivalled expertise. The client's part in this is to take an 'accepting' attitude, believing what he is told, doing as he is asked and putting complete faith in the person who is looking after his interests, *assuming even when everything appears to contradict this* that the professional knows what he is doing and that it is all for the best.

Attempts on the part of the patient to do anything other than play out the part assigned will be met with stiff resistance: questioning what one has been told, expressing doubts about the efficacy of the things that are being done, seeking to introduce considerations other than those that the professional clearly considers relevant will not be responded to by reactions from the professionals which take these things seriously. They will be met with evasion and patronising treatment: for example, if patients want more information than the doctor is initially prepared to give, request for that will not produce it but will, instead, give rise to explanations as to why such information is not needed or irritated suggestions that the patient is not showing suitable trust in professional judgement. If it is given, it may be given in a 'blinding with science' manner which will ensure that it is unintelligible and unhelpful. More dramatically, patients who are loath to take the quiescent position that they are being invited to adopt may find that they are 'disciplined' into it, that they are treated in punitive ways: the professionals will, themselves, no longer offer anything above the minimum required of them, and they will allow things to be more uncomfortable, painful and protracted than they need have been.

If, however, we are to avoid the fallacy of the professional line, so we must avoid the alternative mistake of regarding the professional as the villain of the piece, concerned solely with asserting and maintaining control over the patient. We have been discussing these matters in a generalised way and must recognise that the actual character of the specific doctor—patient encounter must be 'worked out' between the parties to it, and that they do not follow a rigid format.

The same gynaecologist will vary his style of consultation according to, for example, his research interest and the interest or novelty of the symptoms involved. Long-term infertility cases will be taken out of the more 'regimental' clinic list and special arrangements made. Mutual 'colleagueship' between doctor and patient may develop and the gynaecologist will switch his role to that of tutor and friend.

Gynaecologists may believe that they all work in the same way, but they do not. They rarely, if ever, see their colleagues' consultations. However, it is still possible to recognise a 'routine' consultation, where all goes predictably for the gynaecologist and the patient may be satisfied with it, as when the condition complained of is very common and not at all serious. These cases are referred to as 'cold' or, less politely, as 'rubbish'. It is possible to diagnose these without the necessity for any talk, but talk is used to fulfil the client's expectations that she will be asked things. A clinic list composed only of such routine cases would create the same numbing monotony as is found on the shop floor at Fords.

Although we have been stressing the control devices which routinise the consultation there are patients who do not 'fit in'. Generally, these are allowed time out from the consultation, their personal status is acknowledged, they are given latitude to supply information from their experience, to shape the telling of their history. Such 'special patients' are often those who have some prior connection with the hospital – they are perhaps nursing staff from other departments.

Patients can also *emerge* as special during consultation. A woman referred for irregular periods can be found to be pregnant. This rare occurence fragments the tight scheduling, for the equipment – such as sonic aids for hearing the foetal heart-beat and which is kept only in the antenatal clinic – must be sent for. Some women can be tagged, unbeknown to themselves, with information of interest to the gynaecologist. He might notice a scar whose handiwork he admires, and a 'detached' interlude occurs in the consultation as he extracts information about one of his peers. This happens, too, when he sees a patient who has been referred for the first time by a new GP in the area. She is encouraged to 'evaluate' the unknown doctor. All consultants must keep their referral networks in good working order (that is, be able to assess the competence of the GP's preliminary screening).

'Professional patients' are ones who must be handled with exceptional care. They have spent a long time circulating through other medical specialisms and are readily recognised by their bulky case notes. Such patients must often be indulged when giving their meticulous accounts of their past history for if they are 'cut off' the doctor will have forfeited their co-operation and this is much wanted, for their present symptoms may be a product of past treatment, of the drug regimes they have been subjected to, for example, and there may be something in this for the doctor to learn that is of real interest to him.

The aim of this chapter has been the indication of a 'rationality' to the many 'irrational' practices to be found in workplaces. We have done this by relating such activities to the occupational context in which they are to be found and, thus, by seeing them as manifestations of the management and negotiation of structures of control. Finally, and most importantly, we have shown that this same negotiation is to be seen in that classic professional locale – the doctor's consulting room.

## References: Chapter 7

Baldamus, W. (1957), *Efficiency and Effort* (London: Tavistock).

Becker, H. (1970), 'The nature of a profession', in *Sociological Work* (Chicago: Aldine), pp. 87–103.

Beynon, H. (1973), *Working for Fords* (Harmondsworth: Penguin).

Braverman, H. (1974), *Labour and Monopoly Capital* (New York: Monthly Review Press).

Carr-Saunders, A., and Wilson, P. (1933), *The Professions* (London: OUP).

Ditton, J. (1977), 'Alibis and aliases; some notes on the "motives" of fiddling bread salesmen', *Sociology*, vol. 11, pp. 223–33.

Emerson, J. (1970), 'Behavior in private places: maintaining definitions of reality in gynaecological examinations', in H. Dreitzel (ed.), *Recent Sociology No. 2* (London: Macmillan), pp. 74–95.

Henslin, J., and Biggs, M. (1971), 'Dramaturgical desexualisation: the sociology of the vaginal examination', in J. Henslin (ed.), *Studies in the Sociology of Sex* (New York: Appleton-Century-Crofts), pp. 243–73.

Hollowell, P. (1968), *The Lorry Driver* (London: Routledge & Kegan Paul).

Hughes, E. (1971), *The Sociological Eye* (Chicago: Aldine).

Richman, J., and Goldthorp, W. (1977), 'Becoming special: gynaecological ideology, gift exchange and hospital structure', *Social Science and Medicine*, vol. 11, pp. 265–76.

Stein, L. (1978), 'The doctor-nurse game', in R. Dingwall and J. McIntosh (eds), *Readings in the Sociology of Nursing* (Edinburgh: Churchill Livingstone), pp. 107–18.

Turner, R. (n.d.), 'Occupational routines and the demand characteristics of police work', unpublished paper.

Westley, W. (1970), *Violence and the Police* (Cambridge, Mass.: MIT).

Wilensky, H. (1964), 'The professionalisation of everyone', *American Journal of Sociology*, vol. 70, pp. 137–58.

## Further Reading

Atkinson, P., and Heath, C. (eds) (1981), *Medical Work* (Epping: Gower).

Brown, G. (1977), *Sabotage, a Study in Industrial Conflict* (London: Spokesman Books).

Clegg, S., and Dunkerley, D. (1980), *Organisation, Class and Control* (London: Routledge & Kegan Paul).

Clockars, G. (1975), *The Professional Fence* (London: Tavistock).

Dingwall, R., Heath, C., and Stacey, M. (1976), *Health Care and Health Knowledge* (London: Croom Helm).

Holmstrom, M. (1978), *South Indian Factory Workers* (Cambridge: CUP).

Offe, C. (1977), *Industry and Inequality* (London: Edward Arnold).

Raffel, S. (1979), *Matters of Fact* (London: Routledge & Kegan Paul).

Richman, J. (1983), *Traffic Wardens: An Ethnography of Street Administration* (Manchester: Manchester University Press).

Spradley, J., and Mann, B. (1975), *The Cocktail Waitress: Women's Work in a Man's World* (New York: Wiley).

Van Mannen, J. (1974), 'Working the street: a developmental view of police behaviour', in H. Jacob (ed.), *The Potential for Reforming Criminal Justice* (Beverly Hills, Calif.: Sage), pp. 83–91.

Wood, S. (1982), *The Degradation of Work: Skill, Deskilling and the Labour Process* (London: Hutchinson).

Chapter 8

# Theories of Urbanisation

ROSEMARY MELLOR

Sociological studies of towns and cities have tended to fall into two categories: first, those stressing the distinctiveness of an 'urban way of life' (urbanism) and concentrating on social and political adaptation to population concentration; secondly, those setting urbanisation within the context of an overarching set of institutionalised structures. On this view, the city is better understood if seen within the boundaries of political and economic struggles. In this chapter we will set out the major features of these two viewpoints. We will start with the sociologies which concentrate on the urban way of life partly because they were historically prior to the others and partly because the contemporary class analysis of the city developed as a critique of them.

## Urbanism as a Way of Life

The first thing to be said here is that urbanism and urbanisation should not be conceived as a uni-directional, evolutionary, continuum-like progress. Indeed, it may well have a cyclical nature in which concentration of the labour force and the means of production in the initial stages of industrialisation is succeeded by 'de-urbanisation' and investment in peripheral regions and rural settlement zones. If the experience of Western Europe is any guide, the dislocations of urbanisation as labour migrates to the towns may well be associated with the invasion of the countryside as the urban populace and its industrial base take up rural sites. In England and Wales, between 1971 and 1981 the areas showing the greatest rates of population change were the large cities (London, Birmingham, Leeds, Liverpool, Manchester, Newcastle and Sheffield) with *losses* averaging 10 per cent (1.3 m.) in the decade, and the areas classified as 'remoter, largely rural' where the rate of *increase* was 10.3 per cent. There was also a resurgence in rural manufacturing employment. (Between 1959 and 1975 there was an increase of 77.2 per cent in manufacturing employment in the rural areas of Britain.) It is therefore possible to talk of the *ruralisation* of production, management and residence.

Migration remains a fact of modern society. Economic and social change generate new demands for labour in different locations. Industrial rationalisation means new working conditions and requires a less demanding labour force; expansion of an economy creates different categories of jobs; social mobility leaves some jobs 'uncovered', devalued as more amenable employment situations are generated; affluence is translated into improved living conditions – a better house, garden, pleasant surroundings, the car. Accordingly, the urban map takes on a new profile as the once rural population caught up in international labour markets moves to the towns, and the already urban population moves away from the city regions. An ever-widening swathe of countryside is vulnerable to development pressure while the newly urbanised population is abandoned in the inner city districts.

These cycles of urbanisation and de-urbanisation will interact in different ways in different societies. Both will involve (*a*) the movement of populations; (*b*) the transformation of the economy; and (*c*) political and social changes. For the most part, the sociologists of 'urbanism' have concentrated on the last of these, namely, social and cultural adaptations and the implications of these for the conduct of politics.

The initial explanation of urbanisation is to be found in the writings of Tonnies (1887), Simmel (1903) and Weber (1912). Their writings are best regarded as a critique of the social and political effects of the transformation of Western Europe. As societies developed from agrarian to industrial, rural to urban, there was a change in the conditions of association so that interaction was governed by principles of self-interest, individual gain and rational calculation. Democratic politics was prejudiced by this individualism and lack of mutual regard. The large cities, as centres of modern culture, failed as social and political entities because they could not provide a sense of common purpose in a world of 'a multitude of natural and artificial individuals . . . devoid of all mutual familiar relationships' (Tonnies, 1887, p. 77).

The position of Simmel and Tonnies on community life is best summarised in diagrammatic form:

| *Village/small town* | *Large city/metropolis* |
|---|---|
| Neighbourhoods | Cosmopolitanism |
| Family | Interest groups |

Consensus                                  Will of the state/public opinion
Common social life (community)             Individualism

Urbanisation meant an inescapable change in the nature of social life. From a situation in which there is a 'positive relation' to everyone, in the town the self is exposed to 'continuous external contacts with innumerable people' (Simmel, 1903, p. 53) to which there is adjustment with personal reserve, and a blasé attitude; that is, a lack of reaction to the passage, association and troubles of others. A city is a world of 'human beings who . . . accept and play this "role", each one assuming the "character" of a person like a mask before his face' (Tonnies, 1887, p. 179). Urbanisation signified avoidance, a disengagement from social and political life.

For most of those who live in towns such a portrait may seem laughable. Across the industrialised world, in the most affluent suburbs of the North American cities, as in the deprived inner city tenements of Paris, or New York, or Manchester, neighbours acknowledge and help one another; families, including those of the affluent, potentially mobile middle class, live in proximity; many jobs are recruited on the basis of family and neighbourhood connections; local business and politics is served by networks of friends, clients and contacts. And, while apathy towards political institutions is normal, neighbourhood life is vigorous. And there is no evidence to suggest that urban life was more individuated at the turn of the century than it is now. And yet, to the victim of a city centre mugging or a rape attack in a densely built-up neighbourhood where no assistance comes, the blasé attitude that for Simmel typified urban culture would be only too accurate a prediction.

The ideas in these writings were gathered together and extended by Wirth, in a short essay originally published in 1938 – 'Urbanism as a Way of Life'. He argued that certain social and political characteristics were inherent to the city as 'a relatively large, dense and permanent settlement of socially heterogeneous individuals' (Wirth, 1938, p. 148). The argument is this: the aggregation of population, and to a lesser extent its density, leads to the multiplication of interactive ties. Therefore, full engagement of one personality with another is not possible, secondary relationships (that is, those which are impersonal and rationally conducted) predominate, and individuals encounter one another in 'fractionalised' roles. Contacts are superficial, leading to indifference and the immunisation of the self against others. Divested of family and neighbourhood ties, free to associate in the range of urban activities, the urban resident is brought to a deregulated state. Finally, as there is breakdown of the traditional mechanisms of social control aggravated by the newly refined division of labour in an expanding industrial economy, so there is a movement towards communication through the mass media, 'the agencies of mass suggestion', and towards bureaucratic institutions.

Wirth's indebtedness to Simmel and Tonnies is clear, and to some extent this essay can be regarded as popularising their statements. He differs, however, both in that for him it is the city type of community that will bring about these social and political conditions, as well as in his assessment of their political implications.

Wirth was a key figure in a group known as the Chicago school which dominated American sociology in the 1920s and 1930s. The group also included Park and Burgess, the latter best known for the zonal model in which the city's expansion outwards from the central business district and consequent deterioration of inner city neighbourhoods was correlated with aspects of human behaviour such as divorce and juvenile delinquency. As a group, they were strongly influenced by the twin ideas of America as the land of opportunity, and the image of the city as a melting-pot in which old cultures would be mixed together in the ferment of city life. Burgess's model of the zones, and Wirth's definition of the city, are both premissed on an analogy of the city as a plant community in which different species contend for an optimal habitat. The approach is known as *human ecology*. The principal assumption was that settlements are organisms whose structure and functioning is to be understood in terms of laws differing from those governing society.

The weaknesses of Burgess's model are perhaps easier to detect than those of Wirth's statement. The zonal model is premissed on the conditions of urbanisation then apparent in Chicago – rapid growth from a single centre still heavily dependent on mass transport, segregation of immigrants in the inner city districts, unfettered private initiative in the development of land (that is, no government controls on land use and housing policies comparable with those of Britain), and a situation in which non-urban residence was highly valued by the dominant social classes. If one were to compare cities such as Paris, or Athens, or Johannesburg, where access to central city locations for the mass of the population is restricted, its limitation to America/Chicago 1925 would be more clear still. The abstraction of urban environment from social context led Burgess to take the circumstances of social disorganisation in inner Chicago as the cause of that disorganisation. And exactly the same criticisms can be levelled at Wirth. He takes the conditions of Chicago – a densely built-up, ethnic city racked by crime and corrupt in its government – as the cause of the characteristics of urbanism, rather than as indicators of the particular features of US society.

### THE REFUTATION OF 'URBANISM AS A WAY OF LIFE'

The empirical refutation of Wirth's statement has come from two directions — research in the developed societies, and that in under-developed societies, principally Latin America and Africa. In general research has pointed to:

(1)   the significance of family;
(2)   the pervasiveness of neighbourhood affiliation;
(3)   the association of class, life-style and gender with the characteristics of urbanism;
(4)   the resilience of ethnic identification;
(5)   the absence of 'mass' politics.

Each of these will be considered in turn.

#### (1)   The significance of family

The legend of Dick Whittington, an orphan with no dependants, belies the normal migration situation. Across the world urban migration is a family affair — the initial move to the city is primed by family savings and contacts, the income beyond subsistence needs being returned to the family of origin, whether from the dormitories of Southern Africa, the *hotels meublés* of Paris, or the Asian communities of Britain. Those moving to the city have, in effect, been sponsored by their family as an invest-ment. Co-residence and sharing of income opportunities between kin members is usual, therefore, among recent migrants. The migrant will be encapsulated in such version of the culture of origin as the urban context permits. And the evidence from both Britain and the United States is of stabilisation of family networks after the first phases of migration and settlement. In British towns the picture was of localisation, continuity in occupations followed, and everydayness in family contacts, at least until the disruptions of redevelopment, housing mobility and industrial restructuring in the postwar period. Despite the average mobility of American households, family ties remain strong, as this incident shows:

> On Long Island 35 policemen had to use tear gas to disperse a violent family feud. A member of the Trent family who live in and around Riverhead was blasted by a shot-gun, and his relatives ran into the street armed with baseball bats and other weapons intent on grabbing a member of the Childress family who live further up the street. The police moved in and took Mr. Ray Childress in for questioning but then two dozen of his relatives charged into the open and started hand-to-hand fighting with the Trents. (*The Times*, 20 July 1982)

## (2) The pervasiveness of the neighbourhood

Urban areas must be conceptualised as a series of neighbourhoods, each with a distinct social reference for their residents. While not always as visible to the outsider as the *barrio* or *favela* of the Latin American cities, perched on the edge of the 'official' city, or the black townships of South Africa isolated in the veld, nevertheless the neighbourhood remains the basis of everyday life in the city. Even in the most affluent cities of the world, each tract can be marked out in terms of class, ethnicity and stage of household in the life-cycle. And, according to these variations in their occupance there is also predictable variation in the extent of affiliation to the neighbourhood. For the young and single, there is a strictly utilitarian relationship; for the family household, the neighbourhood affiliation has been termed that of 'limited liability' (Janowitz, 1952) as parents are drawn into local life through their children. For the city poor throughout the world, the neighbourhood is a means to survival as they make out in a mesh of petty transactions – preparing food, caring for others' children, providing lodgings, servicing those with an income from the city's wage economy. For the not-so-employable, the city is in everyday life an economy, and a society, a few blocks in extent.

## (3) Characteristics of class, life-style and gender

The main wave of American community research, between about 1950 and 1967, amply demonstrated that the characteristics that had been denoted as 'urbanism' were better related to class position and life-style. The new suburban tracts were found to be sharply segregated in terms of both occupational status and ethnicity, blue collar workers did not adopt a middle-class, 'suburban' life-style, nor did the lower middle class modify their aspirations as to family and community life. (Much of the research is summarised by Greer, 1962, pp. 67–106.) Urbanisation did not mean attenuation of the categories of family, occupation and ethnicity. And in the inner districts of the American cities, as in the British, evidence pointed to parochialism ('urban villagers'), the sharpening of ethnic identity, as in the black ghetto, and the elaboration of local style. The conclusion had to be that the patterns of interaction and political association identified by Wirth were attributes of class and life-style.

In Britain, the distinctions between the conditions, the patterns of community association and the life-styles of middle and working classes have been taken for granted. Accordingly, research was directed to differentiation within these class cultures. One distinction was that between the traditional and non-traditional working class; another between the 'spiralists' and 'burgesses' in the middle class. In the Banbury study

(1960), Stacey and her colleagues argued for categories of 'local' and 'cosmopolitan' cutting across the more orthodox social class distinctions. And the studies by Pahl of commuter villages confirmed the salience of this local–cosmopolitan axis as well as class status in delineating village interaction and politics (Pahl, 1970, pp. 19–83).

Such studies were of households and only touched on the differences in the experience of men and women. Women by reason of restriction to domestic and familial roles and relegation to low-grade local employment (see Chapter 1 above) are more likely to be bound by the confines of the neighbourhood. The town, which offers greater opportunity in an equivalent radius, may, therefore, be a preferable location for women. But, even within the range of the neighbourhood, women are restricted in their use of public and semi-public space by the sanctions on 'inappropriate' behaviour. In movement through the city streets, association within the local community, gender distinctions are as determinant of life-styles as those of class or localism.

### (4) The resilience of ethnic identification

Comparatively speaking, British urbanisation may be unusual in that those drawn to the towns were not sharply distinguished in terms of ethnicity. Irish migrants were segregated in the slums of every mainland town, but the flow from the countryside of Scotland and Wales was largely contained within those regions or diverted in emigration. Neither does there seem to have been local identification as strong as those that marked peasant Europe. In Britain local or regional identities did not divide the urban population, and class, not ethnicity, became the medium of political association. Elsewhere in Europe, North and South America, Africa and Asia, movement to the cities has been followed by new idioms of ethnicity. With urbanisation and the bringing together of diverse populations, ethnic boundaries are highlighted, and ethnicity becomes the demarcator of political as well as social life (cf. Chapters 3 and 10 in this volume).

Recent urbanisation in Britain has brought ethnicity, and definitions of race and ethnicity, into the legal and political arenas. The Sikhs, for example, numbering some 500,000 in 1982, come from a small group of villages and towns of the Punjab and are distinguished from other Asian migrants by religion rather than language or physical traits. The general indication of research is that settlement in Britain had been followed by a greater articulation of the values of being Sikh. And, of course, observance of the prescriptions on clothing has brought recurrent controversy with public institutions and the law which in turn has intensified the need to fall back on ethnic ties. In the reaction to the state culture, ethnic identity is sharpened. Similarly, there is an evolving definition of difference among Afro-Caribbeans in which a religious movement has been a conspicuous element. It is not a question of the migrant carrying a culture, an ethnic identity, from one society to another, but of it being remade in the urban context.

### (5) Urban politics

Wirth's prediction was unqualified. The large city would become a society in which 'the masses of men in the city are subject to manipulation by symbols and stereotypes managed by individuals . . . through their control of the instruments of communication' (1938, p. 163). That is, the city becomes a 'mass' society as urbanisation detaches individuals from old loyalties and renders them vulnerable to the unmediated direction of elites. However, ethnicity has remained crucial to the conduct of American city politics; across much of Europe, church, political party and trade union intermesh to confer a basic identity. In Britain, party organisation and entrenched voting allegiances have ensured political continuity in many localities throughout the century. It can be argued, even, that the policies of the national state are mediated by the strength of local class structures, thereby restricting the creation of a mass political clientele.

The empirical exceptions to any general statement on urbanisation are easy to establish. Less clear are the relationships between the concepts adopted (city, urban, urbanisation), the definitions constructed (city equals dense land-use; urbanisation equals social and political interaction), and the hypotheses which are derived from them. The description of urbanisation as individualising, that is, placing society in a state of *anomie*, was contingent on the definition of 'city' adopted. If size and complexity of the aggregate are adopted as the criteria for 'city', then a mass analysis of urbanisation follows. Others have been wary of using size as a criterion. Weber was forthright: 'both in terms of what it would include and what it would exclude, size alone can hardly be sufficient to define the city' (1912, p. 23). A given magnitude of population may represent so many situations: 20,000 in the UK could be a mining township, a market town, a dormitory suburb, or a local authority housing estate. Similarly, 6 million might represent London, Lagos, or Lima – the first a world city (with children in its inner city schools having 134 home languages), the second riven by ethnicity, the last with all the problems of high rates of population growth and shanty town development that have characterised Latin American development. The range of opportunities, the nature of each as a place to live, its social and political dimensions, have no direct relationship to size.

Although there were several critical studies of the position of the Chicago school from the standpoint of structural functionalism, the systematic theoretical indictment of the statements on urbanisation came from French Marxist sociologists. In their discussion, there was outright objection to the abstraction of the city from its context of society. Once again the use of size as demarcator of 'urban' is dismissed sharply: 'Now, it only needs a few moments' reflection to realize the absurdity of a theory of social change based on the growing complexity of human association in terms of demographic growth alone . . . All evolution in size and differentiation of a social group is itself product and expression of a social structure and its laws of transformation' (Castells, 1977, p. 113). As we shall see in the second part of this chapter, taking the city as both the context of research and the explanatory framework obscures the class dynamics that underlie the 'problems' of urbanisation. The American sociologists had presented the problems of the city as those of community, not class; in their view the social control mechanisms of family and neighbourhood had broken down and a democratic political system was inoperable. To the Marxists such a position was ideological, one-sided, supportive of the position of the dominant class; the social problems and the corruption of the democratic system in the cities of the capitalist world, both developed and underdeveloped, are not the result of urbanisation as such, but of the exploitation and oppressive relationships of capitalism.

The general conclusion to be drawn, then, is that one must always be cautious. While it may be possible to pick out some features of urban life in particular places and attribute them to the conditions of urbanisation, much of urban experience does not fit the bleak picture painted by Wirth. Poverty and deprivation may be aggravated by the absence of a strong neighbourhood network in some areas of some cities, political life may be marked by blatant manipulation of an apathetic electorate. But both have to be analysed in their local context with due attention being paid to individual sets of circumstances. We should be very wary indeed of assuming that urbanisation alone explains impersonality, deprivation, or anything else today, or that it ever did so.

In fact, a case could be made for a description of urbanisation diametrically opposed to the conventional sociological portrait outlined above. If we look at the British experience in the period before 1851, we would find that the urban migrants formed their own friendly societies and benefit clubs as insurance against sickness and death, building societies, trade combinations and political societies; they built their chapels, ran the streetcorner shops and drinking clubs, and created a community life. This is a description of Merthyr as it was at the time of the 'Rising' of 1830:

> These people brought with them the *cwrw bach*: the little beer, bid-ales, communal festivals, marriages, celebrations, really collective exercises in self-help and mutual petty loans wreathed in fellowship and liquor . . . The eisteddfodau in the Merthyr pubs, over a score of which are on record in the 1820s, for the town was a leader in the Welsh revival, were as vigorous as the races and the boxing matches. So was the burgeoning world of music and poetry in the chapels with the fiercely competitive choirs and even more combative working-class conductors. (Williams, 1978, p. 29)

Note the ambivalence of emphasis – these activities were 'brought with' the young migrants from rural Wales, and yet there was a 'burgeoning out' and a 'revival'. The activities had rural antecedents, and yet they became something more in the towns. In Merthyr, as in other towns, there was a sense of vitality and opportunity as the urban working class, well paid if insecurely employed (by rural standards), step by step created the associations that would bring security, self-esteem and community stability. Urbanisation here meant a regeneration of community, and political mobilisation.

To this one case study could be added many more. Black migration to Harlem in the first three decades of this century saw the ghetto become 'the cultural capital' of black America, the base for a black political movement headed by Marcus Garvey and the focus of a 'literary Renaissance'. In the same way, African towns were the basis of new forms of political association as well as a reconstruction of traditional culture. For such societies, urbanisation would seem to have been associated with:

the consolidation of the kin-group;
the stabilisation of the community;
the reassertion of ethnic identification;
the revival of religion;
the resistance to state culture;
the formation of trade unions and political parties.

The conclusion is, then, that although urbanisation, defined demographically, may have had social and political consequences, the predictions made about the nature of urban life are unwarranted. The dimensions to 'knowing and being known' are more fluid in the city than in the small-scale society, but there is no lack of structure to the primary group association in the city. Nor are the political outcomes those which were predicted.

To summarise:

(a)  Evident in the urbanised societies is a double cycle of urban development, in which population continues to move from the world's underdeveloped regions to the cities, and yet there are strong indications of a disaggregation of population and economic activity.

(b)  A dominant sociological portrait of urbanisation emphasised the individualistic and rational-associative features of urban life, and pointed to a mass society analysis of the city.

(c)  In empirical terms there is little support for the urbanism thesis: historical evidence indicates a reverse portrait in the direction of pluralism.

(d)  Theoretically, the environment/social interaction model of urbanisation has been subject to criticism from structural functionalists, Marxists and political sociologists.


## City, Class and State

An alternative conceptualisation of urbanisation, deriving from Weber, and to some extent Marx, is to view residence in a city as a politically defined situation, that is, being urbanised confers political attributes. In this view, aggregation into cities historically represented the exercise of class power, whether to organise the movement of goods, command the labour of others, or determine the terms of trade so that resources from a dominated hinterland accrued to the benefit of the town population. Alternatively, the city is seen as a 'coliseum for political struggle' (Elliott and McCrone, 1982, p. 37) for historically there has been in the towns a juxtaposition of the institutions of control in the society and a concentration of those whom the ruling elites must suppress to ensure the stability of the state. It is therefore argued that there is a social dynamic to urbanisation as populations are freed from the traditional patterns of interdependence of the countryside and brought into the domain of urban politics.

Urbanisation, in the sense of migration from country to town, is seen as creating a new profile to the class hierarchy in that there will be a politically mobilised working class; secondly, a transfer of economic activity from country to town will entail a radical alteration in class relationships as the conditions of subsistence change; thirdly, there will be changes in the social association and culture of the townspeople. But the most pressing effect of urbanisation will be the redefinition of politics. The urban working class is brought into direct confrontation with the agencies of the state, and the political order has to widen in order to take account of new wants and new powers. If urbanisation is set in the context of class interests and state power, then the conventional constructions of urbanisation may be rephrased as:

(*a*) migration to (*a*) redefinition of class structure
(*b*) development to (*b*) relations of class and state
(*c*) social change to (*c*) politics.

## URBAN POLITICS

Since 1968 a political economy of urbanisation using the theoretical concepts and political concerns of Marxism has developed. For the English-speaking world, the most stimulating exponent of the new approaches has been Castells (1977, 1978). One starting-point for his model of urbanisation was the concept of 'urban problematic', that is, a series of actions and situations in daily life, ranging from housing, congested transport, motorways severing a town, the dispersal of ethnic minorities with comprehensive redevelopment, to the relocation of shopping facilities. All these aspects of urban development he terms a 'structured social process' to be related to the political economy of state monopoly capitalist societies. He argues that urban politics would take on new directions and new force as the contradictions between the society's capacities for production and its social capacity to use that productive capacity deepened. Accordingly social protest groups, termed 'urban social movements', would increasingly challenge the established order on aspects of this 'urban problematic'.

The key features of state monopoly capitalism are first, the accelerating concentration of the means of production and finance capital; and secondly, the increasing penetration of state agencies into all aspects of economic, social and cultural life, with an intensification of class antagonisms which the monopoly organisation of capitalist production creates and which state agencies in the long term cannot contain. On this basis, certain general assumptions as to the direction of urbanisation and the possibilities of urban politics are made:

(1) In spatial terms, monopoly organisation means centralisation so that development is gathered into the major metropolitan regions.
(2) Migration to these regions will therefore accelerate.
(3) There will be a concentration of demand for the 'means of repro-

duction', for example, housing, schools, leisure facilities, in these high-cost regions.

(4) The means of reproduction will increasingly be state provided. That is, the management of urbanisation hinges on the management of 'collective consumption', that is, the services which either by their nature, or by reason of cost, cannot be provided by individuals for their own consumption. Roads and transport provision are an example of the first category; education and health provision of the second.

(5) Urbanisation and state provision go together: the more complex the level of urban development, the more intense the demands placed on the infrastructure of the urban region, then the more the state must intervene to regulate the ensuing conflicts.

(6) As state management and provision is crucial to the well-being of the urban population, any inadequacy in collective provision must bring political confrontation.

(7) Urbanisation under conditions of monopoly capital must be seen as politically unstable, open to social protest movements, since, while it requires collective provision for consumption needs, the incidence of such provision is dominated by the interests of private capital.

(8) Increasingly the basis of urban change will be social movements triggered off by this urban problematic, and not the planning institutions. Thus the argument would be that community action groups and the riots of July 1981 in districts such as Toxteth, Liverpool and Moss Side, Manchester, were of greater power in changing investment strategies for these cities than the designated planning agencies. It could be argued that the general logic of investment (which had been to divest these areas of wealth) will have been modified by the people 'speaking of themselves'.

Empirically this model of urban change presents problems. Monopoly organisation has not meant spatial concentration of population in the metropolitan regions but the reverse – the location of specialised plant in remote regions where production costs are lower. Similarly, these congested regions show net losses of population. The difficulties of daily life have been resolved by 'de-urbanisation' rather than urban protest. And in Britain, as in much of Western Europe and North America, there is *dis*-investment by the state in the basic elements of collective consumption – housing, transport, health, education, all are subject to cuts. Urbanisation does not have to be accompanied by state provision for consumption needs as the history of the United States shows, and in Western Europe, inadequacies in collective services, with the possible exception of transport, do not bear heavily on all classes.

Theoretically this approach proved stimulating. Castells adopts the hypothesis that 'cities are made by men, i.e. by social classes' (1973, p. 17) in a polemic against the assumption that urbanisation is to be considered as a natural process logically implicated by economic development and industrialisation. So, whether considering the planning of the British new towns, the design of the '*grandes ensembles*' (system-built neighbourhoods) ringing Paris, or the preservation of central Paris for the elite of France and the international business community, it is class interests to which reference must be made. The language of planning with its emphasis on technically efficient solutions to conflicting interests is mystificatory since no balance is possible in a situation of irresolvable antagonisms. The most systematic exposition of Castells's understanding of the social construction of space is in the Afterword to the *Urban Question* in which he presents 'space, like time [as] a conjuncture, that is to say the articulation of modes of production' (1977, p. 443). The urban environment, local issues, however immediately experienced, however hotly fought over by local community groups, are in that respect neither local nor urban.

The most strongly criticised element in this model has been the definition of 'urban' in terms of the arrangements for 'collective consumption', which depends on the state for its production, distribution and management. As has already been indicated, this does not fit the experience of many developed societies, and in theoretical terms it directs analysis away from production and the contradictions inherent therein. However, Castells claims that the urban cannot be defined in terms of production (this more properly befits the region) but 'in terms of residence, in terms of everydayness. An urban unit is the everyday space of a delimited fraction of the labour force' (1977, p. 445). With the concept of 'collective consumption', everyday life, the mundane round of repetitive chores and social interaction, is linked with 'institutionalised class domination', that is, the state. The reality of urbanisation is that the global movements of capital, the militarism of the world power system and the impersonality of state institutions bring the people into political life as they impinge on the locality. Closure of a steel plant, construction of a NATO headquarters, planning of an airport, all bring the apathetic into political awareness.

Here one of the weaknesses of the model becomes apparent, for only in that they have a location are these *local* social protests. Nor are they of equal concern to all in a locality. The peace movement, for instance, is an international movement; protests about plant closure and unemployment draw on limited sections of a town, and such incidents as street riots indicate the marginalisation of a section of the population – the young, black, unskilled, unemployed – and its position as an understratum, and not the reaction of a community against the 'urban problematic'.

It would seem, then, that Castells, like Wirth, has mistaken context for cause; that 'urban' in an urbanised society is too vague a term to be of scientific use (as Castells himself has argued most fluently). Perhaps it is a question of terminology – much of what he puts under the heading 'urban' would have been termed 'community action' in Britain. Nevertheless, the model's attractiveness would seem to be two-fold: (i) it is a model of social change which is 'multiclass'; and (ii) urban social movements imply mass politicisation as they are (given the analysis of the urbanisation process) against the state.

One of the difficulties for orthodox Marxism is that in the advanced capitalist societies there has been a contraction and fragmentation of the labour force; references to the decomposition of the working class are now frequent. A minority of the population of working age are in the productive labour force, despite the movement of women into part-time jobs. The share of employment in manufacturing industry is contracting rapidly, a tendency not just confined to Britain. Further, unemployment also forces workers out of the labour force. Organisation on the basis of production, that is, class organisation, is therefore open only to a small section of the once-working-classes. If there is to be mass mobilisation against dominant interests, it will have to be 'multi-class'. Urban social movements, or community action, allow a broad-based resistance to class domination.

To appreciate the force of the second argument something of the Marxist position on the nature of the capitalist state must be understood. Although there are differences of opinion and emphasis, it is generally agreed that:

(a)  The capitalist state is a democratic one, and hence claims to a series of basic rights – a living income, housing, health, education, and so on – have to be admitted.

(b)  The operation of state power is regulated by statute law, formulated by an elected legislature and enforced by an independent judiciary.

(c)  The state governs by consensus rather than coercion. The domination of capitalist interest requires the willing agreement of the mass in the exercise of power on their behalf.

(d)  State actions may be justified in terms of technical rationality. That is, the use of resources is ordered by expert opinion – the professional intermediaries through which state policies are articulated.

The net outcome is the masking of the class nature of the state, for the state is presented as an impartial advocate of the most efficient policies which resources allow. If situations then arise such as a new airport, or a meeting resulting in death or injury from police action as a result of which the non-political come to question the state's actions, this image of the state as egalitarian, efficient and peaceful will be broken. The growing interest in urbanisation by Marxist writers is, in part, a response to the possibilities the contradictions in urban development open up for the exposure of the democratic state as class power.

Some of the emphasis of the French school was echoed in developments in British studies: Rex, in *Race Community Conflict* (1967), and Pahl, in *Whose City?* (1970), brought into discussion the allocation of urban resources such as housing, or neighbourhood space, by professional groups such as planners, architects, housing managers, and so on. For Rex, the central process of the city was defined as a class struggle over the use of housing; for Pahl, the city was considered as a 'socio-ecological system' in which professional groups managed the allocation of resources. Subsequently, the interest shifted to more broadly considered issues of political economy such as state spending on housing, and the 'managers' came to be seen as intermediaries in class domination rather than as agents of social reform. So, in studies such as that by Lambert *et al.* (1978), designed to explore housing management policies in an inner area of Birmingham, the analysis moved to the constraints on the local authority's housing investment, the difficulties over land availability and the unwillingness of the major construction companies to give priority to work in the inner city districts, and, overall, the shortage of good housing in the city. Within these parameters, their conclusion was that it was 'the style of urban managerialism that had potent ideological force' and that 'its tendency to competency and technicality . . . were mystifications' (1978, p. 169).

Recent research has concentrated on issues of representation and class interest as expressed in local politics. For example, Cockburn in *The Local State* (1977) reported on Lambeth's innovation of neighbourhood councils set up to stimulate participation in the investment strategy for areas like much of inner London apathetic in official politics. There was considerable hostility from professional officers and the political impact of the councils was muffled administratively. Local government is represented as an agency of the state in which professional groups further the interest of dominant classes by their defence of established administrative practice as well as by their advocacy of new policy. Also at issue was the engagement of groups not represented in the party–trade union–town hall alliances. The suggested theoretical resolution is that of 'organisation at the point of reproduction', to mobilise in the neighbourhood, as users of state services and employees of state agencies, to secure control over the conditions for living. Saunders's study *Urban Politics* (1980) from a less definite theoretical standpoint looked at the postwar redevelopment of Croydon, in particular the town centre, in which a political elite of businessmen and professionals promoted a 'Manhattan strategy' only terminated by tight planning controls over office development instigated by central government. For this elite, public and business interests were complementary: there was a partnership between the local influentials concerned for the standing of the town and the interests of the construction and property companies rather than a direct ordering of capitalist interests by the local authority.

In these, as in all discussions of the politics of urbanisation, there is unresolved debate as to the relation of local politics, urban or rural, to that of the national state. As we have seen, in Wirth's presentation urban community life governed national politics. In contrast, for Britain, the independence of local politics in an increasingly centralised state system has to be argued out. It is possible to demonstrate the relative autonomy of local authorities in the great variation in spending levels on essential services such as education, or refuse collection, or public transport, and the differing policy responses to similar needs. Equally, one can point to the locally derived initiatives of socialist authorities such as South Yorkshire or the Greater London Council, which place them in confrontation with national government, yet in line with local business interests. Such actions cannot be explained by the 'local state derives from national state derives from dominant class interests' formula. The current argument is that local state institutions index local class relations in reaction to the national state. Therefore urban politics, the urban community itself, may intervene to block subordination to the state.

To those unfamiliar with the inner districts of the large British towns, the riots of 1980 and 1981 were wholly shocking. They were generally represented as a turning-point in British social history, and a desperate protest against the radical economic policies of the government. To social scientists, however, they were unsurprising, a predictable outcome of the cities in which inner neighbourhoods have been deprived of investment, and incoming workers and their families, many black, have been unable to join the movement away from the city, either because they were trapped in the poverty housing market, or had been consigned to the surplus labour force. A series of community studies had detailed the antagonisms exacerbated by the shortage of decent housing, the resentment by black workers at the consignment to 'shit work' (Pryce, 1979), the stigma attached to inner city living, the scapegoating of black minorities, the war of attrition between youth and police, the sense of identity gained in community association, and the apathy towards institutionalised politics. The riots therefore confirmed the findings of studies conducted over the previous fifteen years. De-urbanisation is not just the engulfment of the countryside by houses, roads, factories: it also signifies a polarisation in society in which the not-so-employable – the elderly, poorly educated, disabled, ill, and/or unsupported parents – are excluded from the not-so-urban world of suburbs, small towns and villages. The resulting situation for the urban poor is set out in *Slump City* (Friend and Metcalfe, 1981). And it is the harsh, 'deviant' world of the inner city neighbourhood rather than the 'normality' of the small town or suburb on which community research publications have focused.

There has been a consistent denial that 'community' existed in such neighbourhoods. From Rex and Moore's (1967) declaration in Sparkbrook, Birmingham, that if this were a community, then it was one like no other, to Pryce's delineation of eight sub-groups within a West Indian population scattered across the city of Bristol, the picture emerges of extreme segmentation. The neighbourhood population may be viewed as a series of quite discrete groups defined by ascribed characteristics of age, sex, household status and race as well as the self-declared nuances of style. Even in the Liverpool housing estate described by Parker (1974) as long-established, cohesive and interrelated, the young men of the gangs with which he associated had an everyday routine with its own trajectory intersecting with that of their parents or girl-friends only at defined intervals. So any local activities, even stealing from cars, or fighting with the police, as well as the running of a tenants' association or a youth club, are not those of a community at large, but of one segment of a population with its own interests in the neighbourhood. Community studies have recognised this, and hence discussion has focused on one segment rather than the 'overall picture'. It is not surprising that the tendency has been to concentrate on those with high visibility in the neighbourhood – the youth, black and white, whose territory is the public or semi-public domain of street, cafe, club, bar and betting shop.

In the absence of associational activity which characterises the rural district or small town, the most visible community is the street community. It is the streets and the covered shopping precincts that the neighbourhood young attempt to claim as their own, and it is this public domain that police or security guards declare as 'open' territory from which 'undesirable' groups must be driven out. Playing on the pavement, football in the street, hanging out on streetcorners or shopping malls, are all seen as 'anti-community' activities. Clashes between police and youth, accusations of police harassment, are therefore endemic. None of this is peculiar to inner city neighbourhoods, but high concentrations of the 'not-so-employable' and the tightness of housing space drive the young on to the public domain and confrontations with the police are the reality of everyday life. Just getting by means recognising the coercive power of the state and the legal system which the inarticulate cannot manage, and thus expresses the failure of the basic guarantees of equality of livelihood. But without cohesion in the community, it was sporadic, random violence rather than the protest movements envisaged by the radical writers discussed above which was the predictable outcome.

The description of the neighbourhood as lacking in cohesion and identity should not be taken to mean that communities do not exist in urban areas. Communities exist in the sense of neighbourliness and are expressed in such institutional activities as tenants' associations or sports clubs, as vigilante groups, black or white, which seek to protect the neighbourhood against burglary, violent theft, personal attacks and arson. However, each of these aspects of community life draws on a different segment of the population within and outside the neighbourhood, and the interactive links between each are more attenuated than in the small-scale settlement. In that respect, the ecological definition of the city is vindicated, as size, density and heterogeneity have ascertainable effects. But 'community' is not just a matter of activity in the neighbourhood, but a question of identity and identification. Members of black minority groups would argue that the British state culture is racist, that political discourse, law and administrative practice set aside the black population so that minorities redefine their ethnicity and close off as a group in the neighbourhoods of the inner cities. 'The notion of community is also important for the way it can be used to re-establish the unity of black people in answer to the divisions which state policy . . . and common-sense racism have visited on their experience of domination' (Gilroy, 1981, p. 213). It is the neighbourhood community as a social entity to which state agencies must address the policies of decline. Low rates of residential and job mobility, and the denial of the 'guaranteed benefits' of an industrial economy, will mean that the urban poor will be marked off; political identity may then take shape within the locality as community. It follows that if it wishes to prevent this process happening, the state will have to direct its policies to the local community as an entity.

In contrast, then, to Wirth and the theory of urbanism, this view calls attention to the political and economic dimensions of urban life. Its general outlines may be summarised as:

(i)    Urbanisation must be viewed as a politically defined situation.
(ii)   The study of urban politics has become the key issue in urban studies.
(iii)  A recurrent difficulty in the study of local politics is the relationship of the local to the configuration of class interests and state power. This is apparent in the discussions of urban social movements and the policies of local authorities.
(iv)   The question of the 'urban' and 'urbanisation' has become that of the 'state' and 'state policies'. The theoretical concern has shifted from environment/social interaction to that of state/'politics in general'.
(v)    Marginalised inner city populations, left out of the mainstream of economic and social activity, but which have a base in the ethnically segmented neighbourhood, can be seen as the gathering ground for an urban politics in opposition to state culture.

# References: Chapter 8

Castells, M. (1973), *Luttes urbaines et pouvoir politique* (Paris: Maspero).
Castells, M. (1977), *The Urban Question* (London: Edward Arnold).
Castells, M. (1978), *City, Class and Power* (London: Macmillan).
Cockburn, C. (1977), *The Local State* (London: Pluto Press).
Elliott, B., and McCrone, D. (1982), *The City* (London: Macmillan).
Friend, A., and Metcalfe, A. (1981), *Slump City: The Politics of Mass Unemployment* (London: Pluto Press).
Gilroy, P. (1981), 'You can't fool the youths . . . race and class formation in the 1980s', *Race and Class*, vol. XXVII, nos 2 and 3, pp. 207–22.
Greer, S. (1962), *The Emerging City* (New York: The Free Press).
Janowitz, M. (1952), *The Community Press in an Urban Setting* (New York: The Free Press).
Lambert, J., *et al.* (1978), *Housing Policy and the State* (London: Macmillan).
Pahl, R. (1970), *Whose City?* (London: Longman).
Parker, H. (1974), *View from the Boys* (Newton Abbott: David & Charles).
Pryce, K. (1979), *Endless Pressure* (Harmondsworth: Penguin).
Rex, J., and Moore, R. (1967), *Race Community Conflict* (London: OUP).
Saunders, P. (1980), *Urban Politics* (Harmondsworth: Penguin).
Sennett, R. (1979), *Classic Essays on the Culture of Cities* (New York: Appleton-Century-Crofts).
Simmel, G. (1903), 'Metropolis and mental life', in Sennett (1979), pp. 47–60.
Stacey, M. (1960), *Tradition and Change* (London: OUP).

Tonnies, F. (1887, 1963), *Community and Society* (New York: Harper & Row).
Weber, M. (1912), *The City*, in Sennett (1979), pp. 23–46.
Williams, G. A. (1978), *The Merthyr Rising* (London: Croom Helm).
Wirth, L. (1938), 'Urbanism as a way of life', in Sennett (1979), pp. 143–64.

## Further Reading

Mellor, R. (1977), *Urban Sociology in an Urbanized Society* (London: Routledge & Kegan Paul).
Roberts, B. (1978), *Cities of Peasants* (London: Edward Arnold).
Williams, R. (1973), *The Country and the City* (London: Chatto & Windus).

# Chapter 9

# The Empirical Study of Power

BOB ANDERSON

## Introduction

It is more than a little curious that although we have had competing explanations of the distribution of power for a long time, we appear to be no closer to giving an empirical answer to Robert Dahl's question 'Who Governs?' than when he asked it twenty years ago (Dahl, 1961). We know *that* there are inequalities in the distribution of power, and we can offer different accounts of *why* these inequalities exist and persist. What we seem, so far, to have been unable to do is to show in actual cases *how* they operate. In this chapter we shall look at a number of attempts to make such empirical studies to see why this should be. Our conclusion will be that it is the way that investigators have defined power and the empirical tasks that they have set themselves which have brought this situation about. Drawing the moral from this, we shall end with a very brief sketch of an alternative way of carrying out empirical studies of political life.

The fact that inequalities of power exist is hardly to be designated a sociological finding. We all know from our everyday experience that we are not entirely free to do as we might wish. Occasionally other people can and will exercise control over what we do. This commonsense connection between power and control is at the heart of most of sociology's investigations of political life. By demonstrating the degree of control that some individuals, or groups of individuals, have over the lives of others through the domination of political decision-making, investigators have sought to spell out precisely how inequalities in the distribution of power are realised. Hence inequality is an axiom, not a finding. But, despite this universal agreement upon the fact of political inequality, there are very deep differences of opinion over how this fact is to be explained. This is the reason that empirical studies are so common. If it were possible to settle upon a procedure for measuring exactly the extent of inequalities in power, there might follow from that some criteria for determining the significance of those inequalities. We might then be in a position to decide whether inequalities in power were only a marginal but inevitable concomitant of the need to ensure efficient decision-making, or whether they were the outcome and expression of deep, structural rifts in the fabric of society itself. Both explanations have been offered by politicans and sociologists alike. Indeed, it often seems that the point of obtaining the measurement of power is simply so that sociologists can arbitrate upon the claims made by the proponents of various forms of political organisation. To be sure, the weight of sociological evidence is not the only test which political programmes may be subjected to. But, for many, it is a crucial one.

This interconnection between political practice and sociology can be brought out in another way. Most contemporary political theories are about the acceptability or otherwise of 'democratic institutions'. How democratic are they, in fact? On the one hand there are those (let us call them the Athenian Idealists) who have made it a point of principle to deny the term 'democratic' to any system of government which does not allow each and every member of the society in question the opportunity for full participation in all aspects of decision-making. Anything less than the full incorporation of all individuals is deemed likely to lead to the domination of politics by groups which will tend to rule in their own sectional interest. Opposed to the Athenian Idealists are a group which we might call the Pragmatic Elitists who define democracy in terms of the availability of effective procedures for the representation of views, opinions and interests. For these Pragmatists it is of no matter that a great number of people take no real part in decision-making just as long as they have their interests and views represented. Central to this judgement of the nature of democracy is the possibility of representative revocability. Any individual must have the right to seek to have his representative changed if he feels that the representative has failed. Such a pragmatic case rests on what might be thought of as an argument from large numbers. Full participation in modern conditions would be unworkable. The idealist case rests upon an argument from human nature. Unless there is a way of preventing the concentration of power, the groups which dominate will inevitably turn their power to their own ends. It is at this point that the connection with sociology is made, for both sides turn to the measurement of actual instances of the distribution of power to support their case. The Idealists wish to show not only that power is solidifying in particular groups or strata, but also that this process is continuing apace. The Pragmatists wish to show that such inequalities are minimal, non-cumulative and, in the end, balance themselves out. As we said at the outset, that sociology has continually failed to be able to give

either side definitive support has not led to any serious reflection about
the nature of the question being put. This is a thought that we will return
to.

We begin in some very familiar territory, with the debate over the
alleged existence of a 'power elite'. The two leading studies which we
will discuss are those of C. Wright Mills (1956) and Robert Dahl (1961).
The most important reason for starting with these two is that they are
classics. They are still taken as the departure points for modern investigations. A second and related reason is that they have become definitive.
The kinds of data which Mills and Dahl assembled have been taken as
determining whether or not there is an aggregation of power. This data is
taken to be quantification of types of individuals in types of 'power
position'. As we will see, Mills and Dahl differ quite extensively in what
they think will be required to show that some individual in a 'power
position' does indeed wield power. None the less, Mills and Dahl
circumscribed the range of investigative strategies that is still in use today.
As we move from the initial debate over the existence of a power elite to
more recent studies, we will see that the various attempts to preserve
Dahl and Mills's programme, while amending and rectifying it, have
caused it to behave more and more erratically, so much so that we will
offer the suggestion that it might now be time to start all over again and
look at political practice in an entirely different way.

## Does the Power Elite Exist?

What were the circumstances within which the issue of the existence or
otherwise of the power elite came to the fore? Apart from any contribution which a resolution of the debate might have made to the determination of the validity of the various claims about democratic institutions,
the central importance of the debate is to be found in its place within the
framework of conventional sociological thinking about political institutions at that time. In summary form, this conventional wisdom consisted
of three sets of interlinked propositions.

(1)  Underpinning the rapid social and economic changes taking place in
     the industrialised and industrialising world was the dissemination of
     an ethic of rational efficiency. All activities in every sphere of life
     were being subjected to organisation in terms of the effective
     achievement of goals, allocation of delimited responsibilities, hier-
     archical structures of power and decision-making, and the centralisa-
     tion of control. On this view, all aspects of social life were

increasingly conforming to the bureaucratic ideal. (cf. Chapter 6.)

(2) The asymmetric distribution of power and rewards which all societies display is a reflection of the need to distribute effectively the reservoir of natural talent within any society. Hence the distribution of talent necessitates an unequal distribution of power and rewards. Modern societies have sought to make the mechanisms of distribution more efficient.

(3) Part of the social transformation that is going on is a movement from a collectivist to an individualist basis for society. Unless properly controlled, this could lead to the atomising of society and the breakdown of all of the major intermediary groupings. Individuals would then stand in a direct and unconstrained relationship to the rest of the mass of society. Because of this, they would be more likely to be swayed by charismatic leaders and succumb to authoritarian and non-rational propaganda. This would be likely to lead to a continual vacillation of the masses between the political extremes. On this pessimistic view, the rationalist ethic was likely to end in the triumph of irrationalism.

Taking these three together what we have is a fear that the rationalisation of activities and ideas, rather than leading to tolerance, pluralism and the end of ideology, would result in the concentration of power and ultimately totalitarianism. That these processes were in train was attested to by a whole range of studies of local community life and of political parties, movements and systems.

Against this background, Mills's choice to study the occupants of what he terms the 'command posts' of society becomes understandable. Part of the argument about the fit between the distribution of talent and rewards was a suggestion that there were psychological differences between people, and that some were more predisposed, as well as fitted, to occupy power positions than others. Mills set out to see if the occupants of power positions have such a predisposition or unity of motivation. The way that he chose to do this was to turn the whole question around. If the occupants of power positions all came from the same kinds of social backgrounds, if they went to the same kinds of schools and universities, if they had much the same kinds of pre-political experiences, *then* it might be plausible to suppose that they share the same psychology. Further, if there was a tendency to apply a rationalistic ethic to all social life, there ought to be a tendency to concentrate power in the topmost echelons of society. Do such command posts in fact exist? And, if they exist, are they largely self-recruiting, based on the ownership of wealth and property, or professional expertise, or what? *The Power Elite* set out to answer all of these questions. It comes to the conclusion that there is psychological uniformity, there is a concentration at the highest levels, and there has been, and continues to be, a degree of integration and co-ordination between these highest levels. In particular, the members of the political elite tend to be drawn from the members of the other elites. As an effective unity, these 'command posts' form a power elite.

It has to be said that although the evidence which Mills offers is voluminous and much of it is quantified, none of it is really conclusive. The statistics which are cited are nearly all descriptive in nature and have not been subjected to any kind of testing. Mills's argument, if it convinces, does so because of the weight of the material brought to bear, the welter of examples offered, and not because of the systematicity of its collection nor the rigour of his analytic methods. He distinguishes three major administrative blocs which he claims dominate contemporary American life: the military; the industrial/economic; and the political/administrative structures. From lists of shared group memberships, interlocking directorships, committee memberships, and the like, he proposes that there are indeed command posts within each structure and that these are in the hands of an elite. This sifting of the data is bolstered by subsidiary arguments based on Mills's assessment of the trend towards centralisation of decision-making and the growth of conglomerate power in all three structures. Secondly, he shows that all three elites display a remarkable similarity in social background and educational experience, numerous intermarriages, and so on; so much so that it is perfectly plausible to assume that they share a common set of attitudes and orientations. Finally, and this is the key point, he suggests that from the list of Cabinet officers in the Eisenhower Administration of 1953–4, it can be seen that the political elite is being recruited from the other elites, particularly the economic one. America's political life is increasingly being subordinated, or so it seems, to a military-industrial complex. This can be seen in the form of legislation that is drafted, the systems of taxation inaugurated, the shape of the budget and the growth of presidential powers.

More recent studies claim to be able to document these trends even further. In a survey of all Cabinet members from 1952 to 1972, Freitag (1975) found that as many as 60 per cent were drawn from the business elite. This elite consisted of the wealthiest businessmen, the directors of the 200 largest companies and corporate lawyers. Likewise, 41 per cent of all of the Permanent Secretaries of the Cabinet were drawn from the business elite and returned to business after their period in office. Following Mills's lead, no one claims that this business elite is, in fact, a ruling class in the standard Marxist sense. This is the case because the group is

non-heraditary and is not based solely on the ownership of private property. It is an elite, *not* merely an economic category. Naturally enough,
Marxist commentators such as Miliband (1969) have found this use of the
concept of class somewhat strained, and have appropriated Mills's data to
support their own thesis that the USA is really dominated by a ruling
class, the owners of capital. Unfortunately we do not have the space to
pursue this particular aspect of the debate here; neither can we take up the
political implications which the elitists drew from their studies.

The concept of a power elite proved immediately to be an attractive
one. Part of its popularity resided in the fact that it was felt, with minor
modifications, to be generalisable to most of the Western democracies.
Studies of the British political elite, for example, showed a similar
tendency towards a concentration of particular types of individuals.
Johnson's survey (Johnson, 1973), for example, points to the increasingly
youthful recruitment of Members of Parliament together with the
emergence of a cohort of 'professional politicians' as a consequence. Both
of the major parties appear to select their candidates predominantly from
the middle classes and this has led to a decline in the representation of
what might be thought of as the traditional bases of their support,
namely, the manual working classes for Labour, and the law and landed
interests for the Tories. Fewer than 25 per cent of Labour MPs were in
manual occupations before their candidature, while 66 per cent of Tories
held company directorships. This latter diminution of traditional representation has been carried even further in Cabinets. Not one 'manual
worker' remained in any Labour Cabinet throughout its lifetime. In
Conservative Cabinets, there has been a marked decline in the representation of the dynastic aristocracies. Interestingly, the Labour Party
seems to be developing its own form of kinship network with several
families providing prominent members over two generations. The one
factor that does still appear to distinguish the parliamentary membership
of the Labour and Conservative parties is the possession of a public school
education. However, there are signs that this too may be weakening. The
overall pattern indicated by Johnson's study of the central government is
replicated at the local level. In local authorities, governmental agencies
such as the publicly owned mass media and the public corporations, and
elsewhere, distinctive elites are seen to be in operation, elites which display a remarkable similarity of background and outlook.

There can be no doubt that as regards the possession of offices, the
proponents of the power elite position appear to have the argument so far.
There is a centralisation of responsibility and control and there is a continuity of background and outlook among those who exercise this
responsibility and control. But although the evidence so far offered is

leading, it is not, of itself, conclusive. What remains at issue is the central question of whether the power elite can and does exercise its power in its own sectional interest. Neither Mills nor any of his followers offers any evidence that this is indeed the case. Instead they draw the common-sensical conclusion that since such powerful people are only human we must expect them to do so. In that sense, then, the power elite case rests wholly upon a version of the argument from human nature. And, of course, it assumes that such office-holders can exercise the power which it is presumed they hold. As such the power elite case is a reputationalist one (it is based upon beliefs concerning who occupies positions of power and not observations of what they actually do). Events such as the Water-gate Affair and the Crossman *Diaries* publication might lead us to be a little more circumspect about the obvious validity of such reputational-ism. It may be that it is the very conception of the necessity of someone exercising overall control that has to be questioned. But this is a topic to which we will return. Finally, the suggestion that the uniformity of elite psychology can be substantiated by evidence of social background homo-geneity remains unsecured. Although we can attribute a motivation to a group of people on the basis of what we think is plausible to say about them, such an attribution remains a speculation unless we can show that they do, in fact, possess the motivation and seek to realise it. As one reviewer remarked (Polsby, 1979), the power elite case has great simi-larities with the suggestion that since taxi-drivers presumably benefit when it rains, they must both want it to rain and be instrumental in making it rain.

These reservations about the power elite case are similar to the ones which Robert Dahl makes in his classic paper 'A Critique of the Ruling Elite Model' (1971). What Dahl is after is not suspicion and allegation, but clear demonstration that the elite exists and enforces its decisions. Dahl lists the following as the central propositions of the power elite case:

(i)   power is accumulated across the range of policy formation;
(ii)  the elite acts as a cohesive group against the interests of the majority;
(iii) crucial control of decision-making is in the hands of the elite.

To show that this is the case, the power elite proponents would have to show that these three were true in actual instances of decision-making. Dahl proposes, then, that the only rigorous test of the power elite case is the examination of the behaviour of the elite in policy decision-making. Only when it can be shown that the elite exists, acts as a unity, exercises control over decisions and enforces them in the teeth of opposition from the majority, can we say that the power elite case is undeniable. His study of New Haven (Dahl, 1961), he felt, provided just such a test.

The New Haven study took three broad areas of decision-making – education, urban renewal and party nomination – and sought, by following through the course of particular issues to their outcomes, to see if the elitist case could be supported. Notice Dahl has wrested the argument away from the degree of public participation in decision-making. He is, in our earlier terminology, a Pragmatist. It is the disposition and availability of political resources that is of interest. He accepts, right at the outset, one of the major planks in the elitist case. There are different levels of incorporation into political life and these do reflect differences in psychological predisposition. But, although there is a requirement of political apathy on behalf of the majority if democracy is to function, what Dahl wishes to see is the degree of openness and access which pervades the decision-making system.

To begin with Dahl rules out the possibility of a unification of the social and economic hierarchies. The social notables, as he calls them, largely live outside the city and take very little interest in its politics. Only 5 per cent of them have held office. In very large measure, they are opposed to the economic elite and suspicious of the policies which are identified with them. Such policies might be changes in the nature and structure of local taxation to discriminate in favour of local business, the importance of the urban renewal programme and the 'commercialisation' of relationships between the city authorities and the local university with regard to land sales and the provision of local facilities. The economic elite, on the other hand, were much more likely to be involved in politics, but most of them held office in just one agency, the Urban Renewal Agency. Dahl infers from this that individuals take up the political issues which are most relevant to their own interests. In much the same way, the control of decisions in the field of education appeared to be in the hands of teachers, educationalists and parents. The fact that different groups hold power in the various areas is taken by Dahl to mean that power is non-cumulative. No one group exercises control right across the spectrum. The economic elite certainly has the reservoir of administrative skills to be able to do this. It also has the opportunity. But what it lacks is the willingness. It has the potentiality for power and that is all. Like others, businessmen only become involved in those spheres of politics which are of direct relevance to them. Furthermore, within the business elite and all of the other elites, there are great divergencies of opinion as to which policies ought to be followed. New Haven politics, Dahl concludes, is a system of *dispersed inequalities*. Its form of government is *polyarchic*. In each sector, small groups do indeed dominate decision-making. But these groups do not form a unified, cohesive body. And, while the electorate does not have very much direct influence over decision-making, the fact that the decision-makers are elected means that it has a great deal of indirect influence. Policies are formulated by the decision-makers to be in line with what are felt to be the preferences of the electoral majority. Further, if individuals do not like the policies being pursued, mechanisms exist by which they can seek to have their opinions raised and, as a last resort, they can seek election themselves.

Dahl opts, then, for a modified, or democratic, form of elitism. In doing so he expresses a view of political life which is, we may say, demand-centred. If the suppliers of policies do not give the demanders the policies required, demanders will switch allegiances and such suppliers will be bankrupted. Such a demand-centred, market model seems to take little or no cognisance of the view that New Haven might equally well be described from within a different model in which the suppliers seek to convince demanders that the policies offered are the only ones available, and that there are no realistic alternatives. One has only to switch to a supply-centred viewpoint to see that Dahl's conclusions, resting as they do on the importance of indirect influence via the ballot box, may be less than compelling. We may grant Dahl all of his evidence and say that, none the less, he has missed the most important point. How do policy preferences get formulated in the first place? Whose policies become the ones that are decided upon? To answer this question we would have to look at the processes by which the 'political agenda' is drawn up.

But before we do that, let us spend a couple of moments reflecting on the nature of the task which Dahl has set himself. It will be remembered that Dahl faults the power elite argument over its most crucial aspect. No actual cases of elite control are cited. But what kind of a demand is this? Presumably in order to see the elite in action, any investigator would require access to the inner counsels of the policy-making groups. Without such access, if the investigator failed to find evidence of the elite in action, he could never be sure that central control was not being exercised away from the limelight and behind closed doors. But, if an elite was exercising control of the kind the power elite argument requires, it would, given the rhetoric of democratic systems, have to be pretty politically inept to allow such an investigator to see it exercising centralised control. And, if it were so inept it could hardly pose the political threat to the interests of the majority that Mills and his followers suppose. Of course, it might be thought that the elite would allow the investigator access simply to turn him into its cat's paw. It would feed the investigator the required propaganda of openness, consultation, and so on. So, if the investigator were to be allowed access to the elite, he could never be sure that his investigation was not being turned to political use. The only way that such a possibility could be countered would be to assume that this was, in fact, the case: to assume, that is, that what was happening in meetings was all decided in advance, that consultations were a charade, and so on; to look for significant omissions from agendas, inconsistencies of claims and policies, and so forth. But, if any investigator were to proceed on this basis as a fieldwork strategy, he could hardly claim that his findings were incontrovertible proof of the existence of a power elite. Rather his observations, having been collected via the theory, will turn out not to be inconsistent with it. As a consequence, no matter what Dahl had done, and no matter how he had formulated his investigative strategy, his conclusions were always likely to be open to the allegation either that he had failed to find the real centre of power or that he could not hope to offer an unequivocal demonstration of its existence. His study would be condemned either for reactionary apologetics or for muddleheadedness.

In order to measure the power which individuals have, Dahl sought to determine the amount of influence which they exercise over decision-making. This is not an impossible way of approaching the task, but it can only lead to a very crude measurement of power. Influence is the ability to bring about certain kinds of results; power is the ability to do so despite direct opposition. Influence may be utilised in a variety of ways, as we all know. Further, it does not rely on the ultimate use of force; power does. Hence power and influence, although closely associated, are not identical and the one should not be taken as an appropriate measure of the other without a fair degree of argument and clear-cut evidence. This Dahl does not provide. The study of 'non-decision-making' was designed to show just how influence and power are related and to indicate what kinds of evidence might be required to measure power. It saw itself as both remedying Dahl and going beyond him, and so it is to it that we ought now to turn.

## Non-Decision-Making and the Mobilisation of Bias

The commonest observation made about both sides in the power elite debate is that they take the framework of politics for granted. Neither side asks why it is that some issues are taken up and others not. They show no interest in what has come to be known as the drawing up of the political agenda. Neither Dahl nor Mills looked behind the overt processes of decision-making at the ways that campaigns are formulated, themes decided, legislation promoted and policy proposals defined. This is because the issue at stake in the power elite debate was the type of personnel involved in making the overt decisions, their commonality of outlook and the tendency to concentration and control. We have seen that the debate was inconclusive. One way of clinching it for either side would be to look beyond the formal decision-making processes to the procedures by which issues are brought to the forefront of debate. If there were to prove to be elite control over these *informal* procedures then there could be no gainsaying the elitist case, particularly if we could thereby show that influence was but one of the bases of the exercise of power. It is just such an investigation that Bachrach and Baratz attempt in their book *Power and Poverty* (1970).

The most immediate difference between Bachrach and Baratz's proposals and those of their predecessors is that they are framed within a clearly articulated model of political decision-making. Dahl, we have suggested, had some vague demand-centred model at the root of his investigation, while Mills's evinces an uncomfortable mixture of a rather restricted Marxism and classical elitism. The Bachrach and Baratz model is most easily summarised in diagrammatic form (see Figure 9.1). The two major phases of decision-making are marked by the four barriers to the processing of policy proposals. Barriers I and II constitute the covert phases and barriers III and IV the overt ones. For simplicity's sake, policy proponents are divided into those who would wish to confirm existing community values and those who would wish to change them. The two covert barriers entail the mobilising of community values and the bringing of some issue within the procedural framework. In order to get some innovative policy proposal on to the political agenda (and hence even considered at barrier II) the bias inherent in traditional community values has to be overcome. New, radical and provocative proposals are not deliberately excluded from the overt decision-making processes but fall

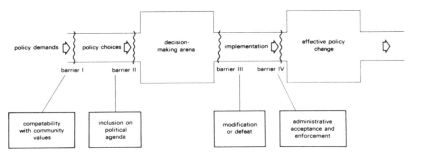

**Figure 9.1** Bachrach and Baratz model of decision-making.
*Source:* Bachrach and Baratz, 1970 (slightly amended).

prey to non-decision-making whereby they fail to counter the bias that is mobilised against them by their opponents, and hence fail even to be considered feasible political objectives. What is important about this set of proposals is that it makes a clear attempt to break with the personalised conception of power and of its expression in influence over decision-making. Instead power is to be looked at as just one of the resources that are available to groups of individuals who seek to exercise control over decision-making. Alongside it are ranged authority, influence and force. All of these are treated as both the means by which control is sought and the reasons for which others comply with an individual or group's wishes. At each of the barriers any one of the resources may be deployed or, indeed, any mixture of them. Thus appeals to community values may be used to support claims for the authority to act in particular ways (as, for example, through an electoral mandate) or to seek to influence pro-grammes of policies (as, for example, with nuclear disarmament). Such attempts to invoke authority, influence, power and force may all end in success and form part of the strategic reasons why those involved with decision-making complied with the demands made upon them.

The essential connection between non-decisions and decisions is made via the notion of *disjointed incrementalism*. Once a line of policy action has been initiated, the very fact of that initiative having been taken may well constrain further choices that can be made. It may no longer be possible to review the original decision because of the political costs which that might entail. A classic recent example of just this process was the develop-ment of Concorde. Once the original commitment had been made, the local, national and international costs of rescinding that decision gradually escalated until, although everyone knew that the aircraft could never be commercially viable, none the less the introduction of a supersonic service went ahead. The project picked up momentum, so to speak, which made it impossible to stop. The extent to which bias had been mobilised and the political agenda pre-formulated can be assessed by the failure of anyone to make serious and sustained attempts to have the whole project scrapped. Concorde is a dead political issue. Its continued existence is testimony to the nature of 'decisionless' decisions.

Bachrach and Baratz have clearly put their finger on something here, but it will pay us to be very careful about what we want to say about non-decision-making. In moving away from a personalised, conspiracy theory of political decision-making, there is a danger that we will overrationalise political processes. In describing everything in terms of the assessment of means and ends, the calculation of the effects of particular lines of action and the utilisation of a vocabulary of decision-making, we are likely to overemphasise the cognitive aspects of politics. Certainly diplomacy, negotiation, duplicity, alliance formation and the rest are the stuff of politics, but not everything politicians do is 'politicking' in a conscious sense at all, nor is it wise to assume that all political activity can be subsumed within a rational, perfectly planned scheme. The extension of the concept of decision beyond those instances where conscious choices are made to cases where no individual or group wills a particular end is surely an overburdening of it? The making of decisions is an active process; it is something that individuals do. It is not something that simply comes about. Robbed of this motivational vocabulary, Bachrach and Baratz's attempt to move beyond a conspiracy theory does no more than reiterate the cliché about the importance of political inertia and the truism that what people believe to be possible determines the range of the possibilities they choose between.

So, although there may be some problems with the way that Bachrach and Baratz wish to pursue decision-making, none the less there are some important if not very original points in their programme. What they refer to as 'the mobilising of bias' is no more than the way that the established rules of practice, the usual routines and procedures, the commonly accepted definitions and limitations, seem to work systematically to exclude innovative policy-making from all but peripheral areas. It is presumed that such innovation will always work against the interests of those who control decision-making. We are left, therefore, with the inference that it must be those who have such control who seek to establish the conditions under which bias will be mobilised. Being unwilling to put this process down to elite conspiracy, graft, or class oppression, Bachrach and Baratz are left with the conclusion that since the criteria of selection and implementation of policies is likely to be administrative feasibility and practicality, then the system serves to reproduce itself. And, where changes do occur, they appear on the margins. But that is hardly a novel observation to make.

If the conclusions which can be drawn from the operation of their model are not all that surprising, perhaps the real cutting edge of the proposal is to be found in the possibility of descriptions of actual practical politics? After all, it might not matter all that much if the model was a little sloppy and unimaginative if it enabled us to get closer to solving the descriptive problems we face. But a quick look at the 'empirical' studies contained in *Power and Poverty* shows that this is not the case. They are all concerned with the problem of poverty in Baltimore and the failure of the local authorities to involve the ethnic minorities which were also the poorest groups, in policy-making. One of the difficulties is that, in order to do this, the investigators have read this non-involvement of the ethnic groups as a *failure*, that is, as a significant omission, on the part of the authorities. The failure to take up the relationship between ethnicity and poverty, the failure to invite strategic groups into the decision-making processes is deemed from the outset to indicate non-decision-making. But in doing so, the investigators have pushed together two crucially different types of action, deliberate omission and selection based upon normal relevances. Let us take up a different example to show what we mean. If a television producer were to make a programme on narcotic addiction, we would expect there to be coverage of nature and consequences of the use of heroin, cocaine and perhaps barbiturates and marijuana. If the programme does not deal with addiction to alcohol and tobacco we would not normally find that to be a significant omission. For most of us cigarettes and alcohol are not in the same category as 'hard drugs'. In not looking at these things, the producer may be seen to be treating things in the usual way. Indeed for him to include them would be for him to be making a very particular point. They would be a significant inclusion. If we allow the concept of non-decision-making to specify who and what we are going to look at, then, in the end, we are forced to accept that any individual or group which finds that they have not had their views taken heed of can claim to have been the victim of non-decision-making. This would lead to the proliferation of non-decisions beyond all control.

Faced with this possibility, the investigators returned to the actual events which they could observe. They focused on decisions and ignored, to a large extent, non-decisions. They did this because it proved to be impossible to specify what exact courses of action were open to decision-makers at any time, and what were the precise reasons whereby one line was chosen rather than another. They could not attribute to anyone a failure to act and find in that failure a set of political reasons to do with the disposition of political resources without themselves becoming embroiled in the arguments that were going on.

## Power and the Social Structure

One feature that all of the proposals we have discussed so far have in common is that they are not particularly or even overtly sociological. None of them espouses a clear-cut sociological conception of the nature of political life. The usual suggestion for why this is so is that they were much too concerned with the need to get on with making investigations to worry about theoretical niceties overmuch and that, anyway, the sociology of politics is in such a shambles that it would be of little use to them. This may well be so. Certainly Steven Lukes seems to think so, because his book *Power* (1974) is deliberately designed to fashion a strong connection between investigative strategies and theoretical proposals, thereby indicating what the sociology of politics might aspire to and what empirical studies ought to be initiated. The theoretical component Lukes extracts from standard sociology; the empirical exemplification is taken from Matthew Crenson's study *The Unpolitics of Air Pollution* (1971). Because Lukes has such broad ambitions for his book, we will spend quite some time examining it.

In essence what Lukes wants to do is to broaden the concept of power beyond the one- and two-dimensional approaches of Dahl and Bachrach and Baratz. What he is taking issue with is what he considers to be their over-concentration on the measurable aspects of power. The non-measurable elements are, for him, just as important as the measurable ones. If power is experienced by means of both measurable and non-measurable components, then the taking of simple *control* over decision-making will be nowhere near an adequate measure of the distribution of power. For Lukes, power involves more than power behaviour. But how then might we go about studying these non-observable, non-measurable aspects of power? To gain some insight into this, let us look at what he has to say about political behaviour.

To recap, the failure of previous studies was their fascination with actual behaviour. They should have seen that 'behaviour (action and inaction, conscious and unconscious, potential and actual) provides evidence (direct and indirect) for the attribution of the exercise of power' (Lukes, 1974, p. 24, n. 4). It would appear that in order to be able to assess the power which an individual or group has, we have to be able to list what they could and could not do, what they might and might not have done, what they failed to do and what they neglected to do, since all of these are just as important as what they actually did do. But, as we have seen, it is by no means an easy task to find out what someone has refrained from doing, let alone why it was that they did so. The Falklands crisis provides an excellent example of the problems. The British government faced a range of choices between seeking to retain sovereignty of the islands and ceding sovereignty to Argentina and repatriating the islanders. The choice it made could have been followed by a policy ranging from armed confrontation to negotiation to unconditional withdrawal. Any consequent decisions were dependent upon the earlier ones that were made. To see who exercises power over these decisions, Lukes wants a ranking of all of the possible alternative choices and an indication of the basis of that ranking. To achieve this we would have to discount the 'political' reasons that we might be offered, the politically framed justifications and claims, in order to be able to get to the underlying (that is, 'real') reasons why the decisions that are made were made. What this would require, surely, would be a spectacular feat of mind-reading and yet Lukes both requires it and gives no hint as to how we might go about doing it.

The difficulty lies in the determination of 'unconscious' and 'potential' actions. Such things as blinking, coughing, sleepwalking and other unintentional actions may count as unconscious; but of course Lukes does not mean these. Rather, he wants to discriminate actions according to the actors' awareness or otherwise of their real motives. People may say that they are doing one thing but underneath it all they are really trying to do something else. The distinction between conscious and unconscious motives has been put to some good effect in psychiatry where therapy often consists in confronting patients with the possibility of unconscious motivation in order to cure them of the condition they suffer from. The analyst may ask patients to admit that their symptoms derive from un-recognised and unacknowledged motivations. But Lukes can claim no such therapeutic warrant. There are those who allege that the internal dissension in the Labour Party over the past few years is part of an un-conscious, or barely conscious attempt to purify the party by expulsion and emigration so that the 'militants' will be left as the leaders of the rump. But what would we expect Mr Benn and his supporters to say if we asked them whether this was true? Would the reasons we would be offered for Mr Benn's campaign give us what we would accept as the 'real' reasons? And if not, what other basis are we going to have for determining these 'real' reasons, other than the common or garden guesses and suspicions that we all have about politicians and political life? The same line of reasoning applies to potential actions as well. Either Lukes is going to have to ask politicians what was potential for them and when he receives political answers discount them by reference to what we all know about politicians, or he will have to speculate like the rest of us. His guesses and speculations might be more informed and plausible than ours, but guesses and speculations they would remain. None of which would matter at all, of course, but for the fact that Lukes's book is supposed to provide investigations with a firm foundation.

Lukes's contention that previous studies have been too individualistic in their view of power is a harkening back to a long-running dispute in sociology. Lukes holds to what is usually termed the 'holist' viewpoint. The actions which individuals take are best understood *sociologically* by looking at them from the point of view of the social structure. Such actions are expressions of structural relationships. The opponents of this view claim that the only entities which have any reality and which can take actions are individuals. In the end, all talk about collectivities, groups and institutions decomposes into talk about what individual people do. We do not want to join in this debate here. Suffice it to say that Lukes feels that the sociological understanding of political actions has to make reference to some overarching social framework which has a reality *sui generis*. Individual actions are elements within these collective actions. He makes his point quite clearly: 'collectivities and organisations are made up of individuals – but the power which they exercise cannot simply be conceptualised in terms of individual's decisions and behaviour' (Lukes, 1974, p. 22). As usual, the problem is not with the intelligibility of the assertion. We all recognise that on occasion we say that society expects us to do things, or that the surrounding community forces us to act in certain ways. But when British Steel decides to close another steel plant or the National Union of Mineworkers puts in a pay claim, who is taking the action? British Steel and the National Union of Mineworkers are corporate identities and are made up of individuals some of whom take decisions and make proposals on behalf of others. The utilisation of the corporate identity is often no more than a way of claiming legitimacy for the decisions which have been reached. 'The arguments are over and we all agree that . . .' We must be very careful to distinguish this rhetorical use of corporate identities from the 'objective' and 'scientific' designation of who can take actions.

The important point which Lukes wants to get across is that conflict and conflict management may not always be strictly observable. Culturally accepted norms and values may express and channel latent conflicts. As with Bachrach and Baratz, the point is a fair one. Politicians do make decisions within a climate of opinion which they try, in part, to shape and manipulate. But, if such climates are collective, and presumably they must be, then they must also be determining the politician's outlook as well. Can we have a collective entity being created by a group and at the same time determining that group? How much of the determination is collective and how much individual? Yet again, this would not matter at all if the point of the proposal was to warn us to beware of the disingenuousness of politicians, nor if it aspired to provide yet another exemplification of the underlying forces motivating history. But, presumably, neither of these is the case.

The notion of underlying or *latent* conflicts, while making a very neat theoretical point, provides the investigator with endless troubles. Latent conflicts may exist even though the participants do not recognise them. Indeed, it is their lack of recognisability which makes them latent. But in that case, how is the investigator to identify them and to weight them? If they cannot be seen 'on the ground', so to speak, then we have to presume that they must be present simply because our theory requires them to be. No doubt we will have little difficulty in finding latent conflicts, but what status will our discoveries have? To take a very familiar example: For many people in Ulster, the 'troubles' are about the political consequence of religious differences. For many sociologists the same events express underlying economic polarisations which are not recognised by the participants, and which are, in Lukes's terms anyway, latent. What we are faced with here is a dispute between two theories of politics, with the sociologists arguing for their theory against that of the subjects of their study. In so doing they will tend to dismiss these subjects as politically naive, unsophisticated, or ill informed; none of which, of course, the sociologist is.

It would appear, then, that there are severe practical difficulties in the way of the successful application of Lukes's proposals. And yet a very strong part of his case is that his three-dimensional approach can yield solid investigative work. To demonstrate this, he points to the findings of Matthew Crenson. Crenson's (1971) study is of the history of air pollution as a political issue in Gary, Indiana. The nub of his argument is that Gary is, to all intents and purposes, a one-company town. U.S. Steel is the town's major employer. Because of its dominating position Crenson feels that U.S. Steel's 'power reputation' prevented air pollution from becoming a major issue, and ensured that when pollution regulations were framed, they were neither costly nor very effective. In tracking through the issue, though, Crenson found that U.S. Steel never actively involved itself in opposing the formulation of regulations. But, for Crenson, this inaction is itself significant. 'What U.S. Steel did not do was probably more important than what it did do' (Crenson, 1971, p. 77).

Crenson's puzzle is how to explain why other towns of much the same size and industrial shape as Gary developed air pollution legislation while Gary did so only belatedly. His answer is that since it is obviously in U.S. Steel's interest to delay the formulation and implementation of such legislation because of the costs which it would incur, then it must, somehow, have been U.S. Steel which prevented the issue from arising except in an attenuated form. This, despite the fact that U.S. Steel repeatedly said that it would take neither a positive nor a negative stand towards the issue, but would conform to whatever local regulations were enforced. This being the case for Crenson, it must have been its 'reputation for power' unsupported by 'acts of power' which enabled it to control the legislation which emerged. Well, we all know what Crenson is getting at here. He means that members of the local authority and the legislature were frightened of the possibility that pollution legislation might make Gary's steel plants less economic to run, and hence U.S. Steel might withdraw investment and gradually run them down. This feeling of what U.S. Steel might be likely to do acted as a constraint on the proposals that were made. That the company had a vested interest was never denied by U.S. Steel. But they did nothing to promote that interest. It is this inaction and its consequences that Crenson refers to as 'unpolitics', whereas we might prefer to think of what happened as an instance of the normal estimation of the political gains and losses *likely* to follow upon the initiation of a policy programme. Crenson's case, in the end, has the same flaw as all the other studies which we have examined. The essentially political claims and assertions which individuals make in the course of promoting their own positions are taken as 'objective sociological descriptions' rather than the moves in the political game which they are. The hinge of the book is the assertion that since U.S. Steel knew about the proposals from the outset, in their failure to act overtly they mobilised bias and generated latent conflicts. But how does a corporate entity like U.S. Steel take such action? And how could we observe it? To demonstrate that this was indeed what happened, Crenson would have to show how U.S. Steel's managers and executives lobbied for their case, and hinted at and alluded to what company decisions might be if the proposals went ahead, and how politicians were able to make the inferences which they did. The examination of these things could hardly be called 'unpolitics' since it is the very stuff of political life as we know it. But Crenson offers us very little of it, which is a pity. If he were to do so he would be providing serious and detailed ethnographic descriptions of the nature of political life.

## Describing the Political Game

So far we have been pursuing the empirical investigation of power. We have ended up by saying that the best we can hope for is the ethnographic description of political life. This might look like settling for second best, but it isn't. The giving of ethnographic descriptions is a very tricky business indeed. We have arrived at this position because we have been unable to find a way of being demonstrably certain or precise about the distribution of power. Whenever we tried to find out 'Who Governs?', the investigative tools we used turned out to be inadequate. Perhaps there is a moral to be learned here. Perhaps it is the question itself that is causing all the trouble and not our incompetence in finding the answer. If we were to review the whole project differently, instead of feeling that we were settling for ethnographic description, we could make that the object of our investigations.

As we saw right at the start, lying behind the connection between the investigation of power by the study of decision-making is a supposition that power consists in control over decision-making, and that this is concentrated in the hands of a few. The task was to locate this group and describe what they do. But perhaps we might make more progress if we dispensed with this supposition as the starting-point of our investigations. What would happen if we set out from the assumption that no one exercises central control because there is no central control to exercise? If we were to do that we might be saved the embarrassment of continually having to bend our model of centralised control and rational organisation to fit the kinds of empirical data that we can discover. We could also stop worrying whether the distortions introduced into the model have become embodied in the data we collect. In the case of Crenson and Bachrach and Baratz, we have seen that this worry is a very real one. So, what other way is there to think about political life that is not bound up with power, hierarchies of control and the expression of dominating interests?

One suggestion that was made a long time ago emerges from a proposal to view the local community as an *ecology* of games. In the paper in which he makes this suggestion, Norton Long (1958) proposes that it is time to get away from the idea that communities should be viewed as highly integrated, tightly woven, systematically produced structures of interrelated activities. Instead we should see them as environments in which a whole range of different games are played. One of these games would be political. Rather than thinking of political life as the unfolding of a master design or preordained programme which is expressed in central control, and so on, Long suggests that we should think of the political game as itself made up of a variety of sub-games played within the local environment. Within these games, individuals are striving to achieve the ends which they want within the framework, and with the resources, which the games make available. In taking the actions which they do, individuals take into account the strategies which they feel other players are following, the other games that they are involved in, the resources which are available, how far 'ahead' or 'behind' they are, and what has to be done 'to win'. The competition which the idea of 'the game' invokes is competition to get decisions taken in a particular way, competition to get interests promoted, to get policies implemented, set aside, or defended. The whole compendium is a fluid network, an *ecology*, of relationships of strategic interaction with individuals taking part in many games at once, playing one game off against others and covering one set of strategies by others. Whatever stability, predictability, orderliness emerges to political life emerges as the unintended outcome of the pursuit of the aims which individuals have. It is not the working out of some inner or master logic.

Using this idea as a starting-point for investigations of the political game, we can immediately begin to discriminate many, closely inter-related sub-games, the business game, the banking game, the media game, the civic organisation game, the consumer action game, the welfare agency game, and so on. The play within each game is defined by sets of locally known and observed rules which have been developed over time, and which are used to regulate play and keep the score, determine appropriate strategies to be operated, and so forth. An example here might help to show what we mean.

There has been a great deal of debate about the location of the third London airport. Do we need one or will an extension to both of the existing ones suffice? And, if we do need one, where should it be sited? The debate over the issue could be used to focus the range of political games being played. Whatever decision is made will not be made on the basis of simple air transportation criteria, projected growth figures, cargo and other freight handling requirements, ease of passenger access, and so on and so forth. There are also engineering requirements to be met. British Airport Authority's administrative staff will wish to influence the location because they will have to sell it to customers, deal with the public outcry, raise the money from central government. Local authorities will be concerned because of the impact it might have on their environments, the attraction it might be to new industry. Local amenity groups will seek to protect the interests they serve. The media will see the issue as one which will, perhaps, increase their sales or popularity or influence. Local politicians will see the debate as one which may have important local consequences for them. Central government will seek to minimise costs and to have an effective decision implemented as soon as possible with the minimum of fuss. Those involved as advisers to the various parties will seek to make as good an impression as possible on everyone and so enhance the possibility of further future contracts without jeopardising the cases that they are making in this instance. Whatever the constraints and restraints that emerge in the process of decision-making, they are constraints and restraints which the participants impose upon themselves and each other. They respect the need to get some sort of decision made in as orderly a manner as possible. They agree to minimise the public embarrassment they cause each other and do not allow disagreements in one sphere to spill over into others. By developing, respecting and innovating upon these, they produce rules of the game which gradually become determinable. We do not have to start out with a theoretical stipulation of agreement on and sharing of these 'rules of the game' but can, instead, look to see how they emerge in the course of events.

The use of the metaphor of games enables us to appropriate another concept which is surprisingly underused in political sociology, namely, the idea of a negotiated order (cf. Chapter 6 above). We can ask how it is that the orderliness, the respecting of the rules, is brought about and reproduced by the things that the actors themselves do. How are images and definitions of the nature of the game and the parties involved projected and sustained, amended or changed? What kinds of types of actors are involved? What types of strategies do they follow? How do individuals convey information about their aims and how do they control access to such information by the arts of impression management? What resources are used to define the possibilities open to individuals and the courses of action which might be followed? How is time used to promote or pre-empt particular policies by the use of such notions as 'premature action' or 'the pressure of events'? How do myths and political rituals shore up and legitimate channels of action in the use that is made of them? How are significant events such as the Depression or Dunkirk used as legitimating devices? How is reputation managed and used as a political resource? How are categories used to mobilise support for or against particular policies? How does a particular vocabulary emerge and gain currency?

In looking at any or all of these things we would be looking at how political actors sought to win the day, get their aims achieved, strike bargains and ensure practicable decisions were reached. In talking about types of actors, types of actions and types of strategies played, and the ways that they are played, we would be forced down into the real world of the hurly-burly of political life to see just how it was organised as the practical, orderly phenomenon which we know it is. Norton Long's suggestion might provide us with a way of giving sociological descriptions of the conduct of politics. What it would not enable us to do is *measure* power. But then, as we have seen, we are no closer to that goal now than we were twenty years ago.

# References: Chapter 9

Bachrach, P., and Baratz, M. (1970), *Power and Poverty* (London: OUP).

Crenson, M. (1971), *The Unpolitics of Air Pollution* (Baltimore, Md: Johns Hopkins University Press).

Dahl, R. (1961), *Who Governs?* (New Haven, Conn.: Yale University Press).

Dahl, R. (1971), 'A critique of the ruling elite model', in A. Pizzorno (ed.), *Political Sociology* (Harmondsworth: Penguin), pp. 126–35.

Freitag, P. (1975), 'The Cabinet and big business', *Social Problems*, vol. 27, no. 2, pp. 137–52.

Johnson, R. W. (1973), 'The British political elite 1955–1972', *European Journal of Sociology*, vol. XIV, pp. 35–7.

Long, N. (1958), 'The local community as an ecology of games', *American Journal of Sociology*, vol. LXIV, no. 3, pp. 256–61.

Lukes, S. (1974), *Power* (London: Macmillan).

Miliband, R. (1969), *The State in Capitalist Society* (London: Weidenfeld & Nicolson).

Mills, C. W. (1956), *The Power Elite* (London: OUP).

Polsby, N. (1979), 'Empirical investigations of the mobilisation of bias', *Political Studies*, vol. 27, no. 4, pp. 527–41.

# Further Reading

Bailey, F. G. (1971), *Gifts and Poisons* (Oxford: Blackwell).

Barth, F. G. (1965), *Political Leadership among Swat Pathans* (London: Athlone Press).

Bell, R., Edwards, D., and Wagner, R. (eds) (1969), *Political Power* (New York: The Free Press).

Boissevain, J. (1974), *Friends of Friends* (Oxford: Blackwell).

Cohen, A. P. (1975), *The Management of Myth* (Manchester: Manchester University Press).

Goodin, R. (1982), 'Banana time in British politics', *Political Studies*, vol. XXX, no. 1, pp. 48–58.

Hall, P. M. (1974), 'A symbolic interactionist analysis of politics', in A. Effrat (ed.), *Perspectives in Political Sociology* (Indianapolis, Ind.: Bobbs-Merrill), pp. 35–91.

Kerbo, H., and Della Fave, C. (1979), 'The empirical side of the power elite debate', *Sociological Quarterly*, vol. 20, pp. 5–22.

Lukes, S. (1978), *Essays in Social Theory* (London: Methuen).

Parry, G. (1969), *Political Elites* (London: Allen & Unwin).

Plamenatz, J. (1973), *Democracy and Illusion* (London: Longman).

Schmidt, S., Scott, J., *et al.* (1977), *Friends, Followers and Factions* (Berkeley, Calif.: University of California Press).

Stanworth, P., and Giddens, A. (1974), *Elites and Power in British Society* (Cambridge: CUP).

Strauss, A. (1973), *Negotiations* (San Francisco: Jossey-Bass).

Urry, J., and Wakeford, J. (1973), *Power in Britain* (London: Heinemann).

# Chapter 10

# The Social Realities of Development

## JULIAN LAITE

The term 'development' is too general to apply to the varieties of social change occurring in the Third World: Africa, Latin America and Asia. Moreover, 'development' implies progress and economic improvement, which are not occurring in many countries of the southern hemisphere. Problems with the term 'development' have led to the growth of a number of perspectives on international socio-economic change, and four such schools of thought will be outlined here: developmentalism, dependency, modes of production and political economy.

Developmentalism (Kilby, 1971) views the world as progressing from an *un*developed state to a developed one, and uses the examples of Britain and America as the models for transition. Here, modernisation involves urbanisation, industrialisation and democratisation, this last necessitating the rupture of traditional value systems and the inculcation of striving personal motivation. This perspective was to some extent formed during the period of post-Second World War global reconstructions, as old empires collapsed and America sought to create a new world order.

The discrepancy between this theory and the fact that many countries in the new economic order were not modernising led to the emergence of a new, critical school of dependency theorists (Frank, 1969). Using Marxist concepts, they argued that the main features of Western capitalist 'development' were the 'dependency' of satellite nations in the southern hemisphere on the advanced metropolis nations. Dependent on America and Europe for capital technology and markets, satellite nations were drawn into unequal trading relations with the metropolises which led to a flow of wealth from the satellite, and its consequent *under*development. So, the poverty and lack of growth characteristic of satellite nations occur not because they are in an *un*developed state, outside the international economy, but rather because they have been exploited by the richer nations and systematically *under*developed. Within the poor nations, these external dependency relations are reproduced as the metropolitan towns exploit the satellite countryside. This school has further elaborated the theory of a world system (Wallerstein, 1974), made up of a global network of metropolis–satellite relations. The system originated in the sixteenth century when European imperial expansion began with the conquests of India and Latin America. The global system now has a centre comprised of Europe, America and Russia, a semi-periphery of some developing countries, and a periphery of exploited satellites. Global capital accumulation flows to the centre.

Critics of this dependency school also draw on Marxist concepts, concerning modes of production (Roxborough, 1979). They point out that Marx defined social systems according to their relations of production, whereas dependency theorists overemphasise relations of exchange. Also, the dependency school does not attend adequately to the process of class formation, nor the role of classes in the Third World. Focusing on production relations enables us to distinguish various modes of production around the globe which, although linked, do not form one world system. The major elements in a mode of production are the labour form, the nature of capital accumulation and the role of the state. In the capitalist West, the bourgeoisie accumulates capital through exploiting a proletariat and the process is facilitated by individualised property relations underwritten by the state. In a peasant mode of production, however, unpaid household or communal labour may be used, capital and land may be dispersed through festivals and rotation, and property may be held in common. Given such differences in modes of production, then, the relations *between* modes are very important. For example, a peasant system may resist encroachment by capitalism, or a capitalist class may 'freeze' a peasantry in a traditional mould so that it can recruit cheap labour from among those peasants.

Formal models of modes of production stipulate labour forms, class crystallisation and production relations, employing categories and concepts which on occasion do not fit well the processes and social structures in Third World countries. This formalism has been criticised by sociologists and anthropologists seeking a more flexible use of political economy concepts advanced by both Marx and Weber. Rather than defining modes of production and labour forms *a priori*, the political economy school (Roberts, 1978) first identify the operations of local socio-economic forms and then relate them to the international economy. The emphases are on indigeneous responses to situations of structural dependency, and regional processes of capitalist expansion and class formation.

So, there is neither one accepted theory of development, nor agreement about the nature of global social change. The advanced nations have different socio-political systems whilst the poorer nations are experiencing a variety of changes. In order to establish a perspective on the international economic order, this chapter will outline the political systems of the West, the Soviet Union and China, dealing with their emergence. Then the analysis will move to contemporary processes affecting the Third World, of industrialisation, urbanisation, working-class formation, political authoritarianism, social change among the peasantry and the growth of the informal economy. Whilst this chapter focuses on the Third World, it must be remembered that such changes are linked to, and are occurring among, the advanced nations.

## Three Development Models: Capitalism, Statism and Agrarian Socialism

These are three main models of development: the capitalism of Europe and America, the statism of the Soviet Union and the agrarian socialism of China. A fourth way has been tried by countries such as Cuba and Tanzania, but they have run into difficulties and so adopted one of the former paths. In the West, we think of the capitalist model as the 'normal' path to development, involving industrialisation and urbanisation. In order to understand the social changes occurring during development, it is useful to highlight the main elements of these models.

The British example is held by many to be the classic case of capitalist development (Hobsbawm, 1975). During the seventeenth century commercial classes emerged which struggled with the land-owning aristocracy and took control of the state. Instigating agrarian reform, they alienated agriculturalists from the land, using the Enclosure Acts, and dissolved rural communities. Concurrently, new technology was developed in mining and manufacturing, which was labour intensive. Displaced agricultural workers migrated to the towns and became a labouring proletariat in the new factories. By the end of the nineteenth century two major classes had crystallised in Britain: the working class, and the propertied and professionals of the middle class. Each class developed its own culture and institutions whilst the first industrial revolution was consolidated by the export of manufactured textiles and machinery throughout the British Empire. The American and European experiences of capitalist development differ from this classic case in terms of their rate and relative importance of different economic sectors, but urban-industrial cultures have come to dominate in these regions also.

The Soviet development experience too is of the establishment of an industrial society, although by different means (Nove, 1969). Before 1917 there was some capitalist development in agriculture and industry in Russia. Yet when the revolution occurred in that year, Russia comprised only 20 million workers and 180 million peasants. Having seized the state, the Bolsheviks had the dual problems of developing industry and transforming the peasantry – the 'awkward class' – into modern farmers. At first, from 1921 until 1928, private enterprise in towns and country-side was permitted, in order to feed the urban workers. Then, from 1929 Stalin used state power to reorganise agricultural production. Food and labour were requisitioned from the peasantry. They resisted, and reduced food production, but deportations and the transformation of communities into state farms broke that resistance. The industrial sector was favoured through state planning. Huge industrial plants were built and new towns were developed. However, the agricultural sector has remained a constant problem for the Soviet leadership, with poor productivity and production below targets.

The Chinese model of agrarian socialism placed the peasants at the heart of the development process (Worsley, 1975). Again, China experienced some capitalist development from 1912, when Sun Yat Sen seized power and the old feudal order ended, until 1949, when Mao Tse Tung established the socialist revolution. During the first decades of the twentieth century communists and nationalists collaborated, but soon Mao was banished to work with the peasants in Southern China. Under attack from nationalist armies, Mao's peasants undertook the Long March to the North. On the way the Red Army preached socialism and re-organised villages. Once in the north the communists strengthened and defeated first the Japanese and then the nationalists.

China was overwhelmingly a country of peasants and immediately after the revolution they took control of their villages. The development problem was to get these peasants to co-operate and so raise agricultural production. The first attempt to solve this was by co-operativisation, from 1952 to 1958. During this phase the peasants were organised into teams of self-help groups. This was followed by communalisation, involving the establishment of 24,000 huge communes, imitating the scale of Soviet development projects. These were far too large, floundered and in 1959 were replaced by 78,000 smaller communes. The commune became the focus of development, the strategy that of self-help. Peasants smelted iron in their backyards, built dams and transmitted innovations from commune to commune. The national irrigation system was reshaped and surpluses produced. However, the social structure of the communes ossified, with technicians, the Communist Party and the Red Army con-trolling power. To combat this Mao initiated the Cultural Revolution in

1966, during which mainly young people descended on the communes and denounced the leaders. Despite this ideological initiative, China is today faced with the problems of a lack of sufficient surplus to provide for industrialisation and a lack of modern technology.

Clearly, these three models show that socio-economic development entails major socio-political transformation, including civil war, class struggle and the establishment of new political systems. They also show different development paths. Industrialisation and urbanisation were embarked upon by the middle class in Britain and the state in the Soviet Union, but rejected in China. Agrarian organisation was dissolved in Britain, struggled with in the Soviet Union and strengthened in China. In the West, development was achieved with ideologies of modernisation and profit, but in China and the Soviet Union with ideologies of communism, socialism and nationalism.

These models are of more than historical interest. They represent possible development paths for the Third World (Worsley, 1967). Since the Second World War some countries, such as Algeria, Vietnam and Cuba, have attempted socialist transformation, whilst Chile and Argentina have adopted authoritarian militarism to ensure industrialisation. China itself is moving towards a more commercial system. The ideologies of nationalism and national liberation have been important in these attempts. Some countries have been successful in their development efforts. Brazil and South Korea are industrialising, whilst Hong Kong and Singapore are commercially viable. Mexico and Nigeria were developing until troubled by oil crises. India's industrial sector has developed. In the Soviet Union, the Ukraine and Siberia are prosperous. Oil reserves have helped Arab countries lay down industrial infrastructures.

However, in the West this development is uneven, in two ways. First, in 'developing' countries the gap between rich and poor remains, or has widened. Economic growth is not accompanied by the redistribution of wealth. In Brazil the middle classes and some workers have prospered, but many rural workers and city dwellers live in abject poverty. In South Africa the *apartheid* system results in a high standard of living for the whites, but pauperisation for blacks. Secondly, many countries have not 'developed'. For many people in the southern hemisphere, one cannot speak of an improvement in living standards since the Second World War. In India increases in food production go only to feed the increase in population in the rural areas. Large-scale industrialisation is not occurring in such countries. Rather, there is limited industrial development as multinational companies extract minerals or process manufactured goods. Urban migration is not into industrial work but to the 'informal economy' of peddling, street-hawking or car-washing. Migrant populations are housed in the huge squalid shanty-towns which surround major Third World cities.

As we noted, some social scientists see this lack of development in the capitalist international economy as arising, not from the lack of contact between Third World countries and advanced nations, but because of that contact. That is, the relation between the poorer nations and the richer ones is crucial for development. In the West that relation is mainly a commercial one, although there are political considerations too. The poorer nations are enmeshed in trading relations with the richer nations which heavily influence their development potential. The relation is discussed more fully in the following section on economic development in the international capitalist economy, and then analysed further are the issues of agrarian organisation, migration, urbanisation and the structures of political systems.

## Economic Development

Most poor countries in the southern hemisphere were once colonies, parts of European and British empires from the sixteenth century. In the twentieth century these political empires have been replaced by economic ones, dominated by America. Imperial expansion affected both colony and central power. Initially, this expansion was mercantile, for trade. Spanish, Dutch and Portuguese explorers and traders brought Latin America and Asia into an international economy, and trade was in high-value commodities such as spices, silks, precious metals and slaves. Some colonies were plundered, whilst the gold flowing into Spain caused inflation.

After mercantilism came colonialism. Trade required imperial outposts whilst Europeans realised the value of land and conquered labour in the Empire. In seventeenth-century Latin America and nineteenth-century Africa labour systems were devised to control the indigenous populations. The Spanish crown introduced the system of *encomienda*, whereby Spanish conquerors were given the right to control the indigenous labour on their new lands, in return for protecting these natives and paying taxes to the crown. In South Africa, the British introduced a series of Acts restricting Africans' access to land, whilst taxing them. This meant that Africans had to migrate to the mines and plantations in order to find the cash to pay the taxes. In India there was not direct labour control. Rather, the British imposed a system of individual taxes on peasants, which in some cases were paid by an intermediary group of *zamindars*, who were able to strengthen their control over villagers.

Under colonialism there emerged groups in the colonies which controlled that crucial relation with the imperial centre. They did this by controlling export commodities and in return the centre guaranteed their dominant position in colonial society. These colonial groups and economies became dependent on central markets and power, and for many countries that dependency continues today (Furtado, 1970). Exporting one major commodity to America or Europe is their only source of foreign currency, which in turn is used to buy modern or even intermediate technology. For some countries such as Peru, Chile, Bolivia, Namibia and Zambia, the commodities are base metals. For others such as Kenya, Ghana, Argentina and Guatemala the commodities are agricultural products such as sisal, ground-nuts, beef, or fruit. The prices of these goods are set in New York and London and they fluctuate markedly. Such fluctuations may be short run, so that a brief boom in prices will not sustain economic growth, or long run, such that poor countries will follow rich ones into major recession. Even the economic cycles of poor countries are dependent on the cycles in rich ones.

In such circumstances splits may develop among the colonial middle classes. Some will see their interests lying in servicing the dependency relation with the centre. They become local brokers for foreign interests, running the banks, finance houses and haulage companies which facilitate currency transactions and the transportation of commodities mined or farmed by multinational companies. Some among the local middle class will want to control the commodity themselves. This national bourgeoisie will struggle against the dependent international bourgeoisie in the poor country, to control the state and thus taxation and subsidies related to the commodity. Such splits help to explain the nineteenth-century Independence movements in Latin America, as local, nationalist bourgeoisies came to power.

One example of this process is Peru, and one exception is Brazil, the latter one of the West's most rapidly 'developing' nations. A colonial elite was established in Peru in the sixteenth and seventeenth centuries which by the end of the nineteenth century had become an oligarchy of powerful families, controlling land and finance. They offered no serious resistance to American domination of Peru's mining industry in the early years of the twentieth century, even though metals became Peru's most important exports. Rather than competing with the Americans the oligarchy preferred to invest in construction projects. Mining became an enclave sector, with a low spin-off of profits or technology into the economy, even though profits for the Americans were very high. Attempts by the nationalist bourgeoisie to compete in the mining sector were given little help from the state. The nationalist reaction came with the growth of political parties and a reforming military government in 1968, which in the early 1970s nationalised mines and plantations. However, low metal prices due to the world recession during the 1970s and 1980s have meant that Peru has been unable to proceed with a development strategy based on the mining sector.

For many years Brazil was dependent on the export of coffee. Grown in the state of Sâo Paolo by large landowners, it was the dominant export by 1890. The coffee producers of Sâo Paolo became economically and politically powerful. They recruited European labour on to their estates and linked ancillary investments, such as railway construction, to their coffee interests. The immigrants provided labour for further manufacturing investments and a market for manufactured goods. Sâo Paolo became so rich that in 1930 President Vargas, head of the central government in Rio de Janeiro, was obliged to curtail the power of the business community there. Vargas used the power of a strong central state to build on the industrial base in Sâo Paolo, through controlling imports and investing in heavy industry. Brazil diversified and expanded during the 1960s and 1970s, on occasion using high coffee prices to accelerate development plans. Now, Brazil has a large domestic market of 80 million people which can sustain growth. However, she also has large foreign debts, and the wages of the poorer classes have been held down, in order to finance expansion. The Brazilians' success has been partly due to the fact that, at the crucial period in the 1930s, a strong state was able to separate Brazil from the international economy in order to lay down the investment needed for economic development.

## The Rural Sector

The vast majority of people in the Third World are agriculturalists (Long, 1977). Over 80 per cent of the population of China, India and Africa live and work on the land. In Latin America the proportion is lower, around 50 per cent, but still agriculturalists are the largest group in the working population. Whereas the dissolution of the agrarian population occurred early in the capitalist model of development, the rural sector presented major problems in the Soviet and Chinese models leading to major divergences in their development paths. The problem remains today and is acute for Third World leaders: What to do with the agriculturalists, the largest block in society?

Three forms of production exist in the Third World agrarian sector and each has implications for development strategies: small-holdings, communities and plantations. The first two embrace the peasantry, the bulk of the agricultural population, whilst the last accounts for the most important commercial crops.

Peasants either work individual small-holdings or are members of a community, or even tribe, with land rights held in common and the produce accruing to individual families. In both productive forms the unit of production and consumption is the peasant household. Land is worked with family labour. All contribute and there is usually a division of labour by sex and age: the women perhaps winnowing and weeding, the men leading the oxen, the children scaring off birds and foraging for firewood. The family does not receive wages and consumes most of the produce. The remainder is marketed in exchange for essential items such as salt and oil. In Latin America, long colonised, the family is the main peasant social institution, whereas in Africa, more recently colonised, tribal organisation is still important. Some villages are still communitarian, with planting, harvesting and grazing done by all community members together, but with capitalist penetration it is increasingly the case that while land is still held communally, it is worked by families separately.

Commercial crops are grown on large farms – plantations or *haciendas*. These require much less labour than the family farm, use more advanced technology and specialise in particular products: beef and cereals in Argentina, sugar in Fiji, and cotton and tea in India. The large landholders are usually politically powerful and in India and Latin America can continue to impose feudal-like working conditions on their labourers. Rather than being paid wages, workers are rewarded for labouring five days a week for the landowner by being allowed to work for two days a week on a small plot owned by the landowner but whose produce accrues to the labourer. So, the landowner is able to take the price of the product as nearly all profit. The commercialisation of agriculture is now spreading rapidly in the Third World and peasants also are beginning to specialise in commercial crops when the price is high. On occasion, the price is unstable and the peasant loses badly because he may have no subsistence crops to fall back on. On occasion, large-scale agri-business can pressure peasants into either leaving their land or renting it out for commercial exploitation. The current development of the Amazon Basin in both Brazil and Peru is an example of this.

Social change is occurring among this mass of humanity and there are three main causes: political movements, agrarian reform and population growth (Wolf, 1970). The political example of the Chinese Revolution has changed the attitudes of social scientists and politicians towards the peasantry. Peasants used to be viewed as traditional and conservative. The developmentalist school saw them as an obstacle to development, clinging to practices and beliefs at odds with modernisation. However, the examples of the Soviet peasantry and the Chinese Revolution have shown that peasants can pursue their political interests in two major ways. The first is political uprisings, which have occurred in Mexico, China, Algeria, Cuba and Zimbabwe. With appropriate leadership, the logistic difficulties of organising peasants can be overcome, armies can be formed and state power can be seized. At a local level, peasants organise amongst themselves and invade the land of large commercial farmers. The second political strategy is for the peasantry to turn in on itself, reduce production and resist changes. This looks like conservatism, but for the peasants it is a means of defending their rights to land and produce against outsiders.

Agrarian reform, the second source of change, is one type of outside intervention. It may take the form of land redistribution to the peasants, but this is very rare. Otherwise, agrarian reform means either institutional or technological change. On occasion, central governments expropriate large private landowners and then run the plantations as co-operatives. Usually, this results in state officials replacing the management, and workers continue to be excluded from decision-making. Technological changes are aimed at raising the productivity of the peasantry by introducing new crops, fertilisers, irrigation schemes, tractors and credit agencies. Sometimes the results are successful, sometimes not, but in either case there are social consequences.

The most dramatic increase in agricultural productivity due to technical change has been the Green Revolution. New hybrid strains of wheat, rice and other crops were developed by aid agencies and then introduced into Third World countries through package programmes including seeds, planting techniques and fertiliser. At first, production of these crops soared. India is a good example of the introduction and consequences of the Green Revolution. New strains of wheat and rice were introduced into some areas and nearly all the farmers who used them experienced increases in yields. However, in the wheat areas the larger farmers were more successful than the small-holding peasants and so the relative position of these latter agriculturalists declined. The same was true in the rice areas also, where farms of over 20 acres did much better than small-holdings. Moreover, the peasants found that the new seeds required irrigation and fertilisers, which they could not afford. So, the consequences of the Green Revolution in these areas have been to increase the differences between social classes in the countryside. Large farmers have used their increased income to compete more efficiently against small peasants, have purchased their land and now employ them as labourers. In villages in Southern India this polarisation has reinforced the caste system, emphasising the differences between social strata, and increased dependency relations as the landless depend on the rich farmers for subsistence and work. It is thus not surprising that peasants will seek to maintain their forms of organisation to resist this sort of change.

The third cause of social change in the countryside is population growth, currently at around 4 per cent per year in the Third World. Medical advances have brought down death-rates whilst birth-rates have remained high. So, the size of families is high and populations are young – in Mexico over half the population are under 25 years old. The birth-rate remains high because the family, particularly in the rural areas, is the main form of social security. As parents age, so they need their children to support them. However, these large families require increased access to the means of subsistence.

In itself, population increase is not detrimental, for it can be a source of labour and a domestic market. Britain and America developed with rapidly increasing populations, and some countries in Africa and Latin America feel that their populations are not large enough. The problem in the Third World is population growth with limited economic resources and constraining political systems. Politically powerful land-holders resist attempts by peasants to encroach on their land. So, the peasants must colonise new land, or subdivide their family plots, or migrate. Colonisation is an important feature of development. Just as the Soviet steppes and American West were colonised, so today are the Amazon Basin and Argentinian interior. Elsewhere, however, little new land is available and so subdivision of plots occurs. As the family land is divided among the children, so any one person's plots become small, and they are scattered, since he is left some by both parents. Family squabbles occur over the inheritance and the plots become too small to support a family. So, one member may be left in charge of the family plots while others migrate.

## Migration

The current migration of people to the cities of the Third World is one of history's great mass population movements (Laite, 1981). Each week, thousands of people arrive on buses and trains and they need to be fed and housed in already teeming cities. The causes and consequences of this migration need to be understood in the wider context of capitalist development.

Initially, the causes of migration may be divided into those which 'push' people off the land and 'pull' them into the cities. The main push is rural population growth, but there are others. Technical change usually requires less labour due to the use of machinery. Natural disasters such as drought and earthquake affect many. Commercialisation and the growth of agri-business put pressure on peasants to sell or rent their land. Low wages and hard working conditions in the countryside offer little to young people. Such people are 'pulled' to the towns by the possibilities of jobs and wages, the higher standard of living, the accessibility of education and the chance of a more 'modern' life-style of cinemas, television and department stores.

However, the structure of the migratory process shows that it cannot be explained in terms of objective forces acting on passive populations, causing them to move. Rather, different groups interpret the pressures on them and the opportunities available. Populations are not pushed out of the rural areas by poverty alone, for the poorest rural areas do not have the highest rates of emigration. Nor is it only peasants who move to the metropolises. Rather, it is small-town dwellers who move to the large towns and peasants who move to the small towns.

There are various types of migration. Seasonal migration is by peasants whose own harvests have finished and who want to work in the harvest of the nearby plantation. There is cyclical or circulatory migration, whereby peasants may work for a short number of years in a mine or town and then return to their village. Step migration involves a migrant moving first to a small town, then a provincial centre, then to the capital. Stage migration is when each step is taken by a succeeding generation. All these migrations can be short distance, as in Latin America, where it is only a few hours' journey from countryside to capital, or long distance, as in Africa, where temporary mine-workers will travel thousands of miles. Increasingly, direct migration is occurring, involving a direct move by peasants to the capital city. All these types of migration are undertaken for a variety of reasons and so similar 'push' or 'pull' factors can be responded to in different ways.

Migrants face several problems. A major one is whether to leave the family behind in village or provincial town, or to call family members to join them. The move itself requires being housed and fed in their destination, particularly in the first weeks while they look for work. So, most migrants know of lodgings or even work in their destinations before they move. On arrival, they go to the house of a known person which may be a kinsman or someone from the same village or region, called a *paisano* in Latin America, *amakhaya* in South Africa. The migrants maintain contact with their village, supporting families there or relying on village produce to subsidise their stay in town. In town they must maintain contacts with the people they trust, to help them find work and with whom they can socialise.

Migration thus has several consequences, arising partly from attempts to solve these problems. The first consequence is demographic imbalance between countryside and town. Although in most regions total rural population does not decline with emigration, due to overall population growth, migration changes the population structure. Usually, it is younger people who migrate, the men to mines and cities, the women into domestic service, resulting in the towns being full of able-bodied people, but the villages containing populations of old people, or mainly women.

The second consequence, related to the first, is the threat of social breakdown in decaying villages, where the absence of young people might have a stultifying effect on new ideas, and in towns, where the presence of many young workers threatens social and political disorder. In fact, the reverse is often the case: migration strengthens social networks and institutions. The problems of migration are tackled by recourse to kin and village links. Family structure is not transformed from an extended to a nuclear type, as occurred to some extent in Europe and America. Rather, a complementary family system is developed, in which rural and urban family members complement one another, working family lands, earning cash and educating children. Aging parents maintain a village presence for the migrants, ensuring continued family access to village land. Wives, resident in the villages, are responsible for planting and harvesting, using cash remitted to them by their migrant husbands to hire labour. In the town, kinship links are strengthened as a distant cousin is asked to provide lodging and news of work. Migration thus occurs within extensive social networks and reinforces them.

A third consequence of migration is the formation of clubs and associations in the towns, and examples from Africa and Latin America serve to illustrate this. Tribal associations are formed in African towns, which have several functions. Some originated in burial societies, which organised proper burial of the tribal dead in the town. The associations organise dances and their leaders may even act as arbitrators in urban disputes. In Nigeria they even provided a basis for political parties. So, in Africa urban tribalism is developed to cope with migrant's urban problems. In Latin America, villagers and *paisanos* form clubs to help them maintain trust relations with known people in the towns and to maintain links with the village. The urban clubs are used to raise cash for a school roof in the village, or buy school books or help repair a bridge there. On occasion the club can bring political pressure to bear on a metropolitan politician, to win patronage for the village.

Migration is thus an attempt by Third World populations to solve the problems raised by capitalist development. As we have seen, a major characteristic of that 'development' is its instability. Faced with unstable economic change, indigenous populations attempt to maintain links across a range of economic sectors, just in case any one sector should fail. Networks are spread across the peasant, commercial and industrial economies which can be activated when problems arise. Usually, migration is seen as a 'transitional' phenomenon, for that was its status during the early capitalist development of the advanced nations. However, in the Third World it is transitional neither in the lives of individuals nor nations. Individuals spend their lives voyaging and organising their social relationships around that process. Nations have large migrant populations which are unable to find employment in the limited industrial sectors. Since industrial expansion is limited, there is not a move from a peasant culture to a working class culture, in which migration is transitional, as there was in the West. Rather, in the medium term at least, the labouring populations of the Third World lead migrant lives.

## Industrialisation and Working-Class Formation

Industrialisation in the Third World is uneven. There are different phases and types, as well as some common properties. The first major similarities are the dependency of Third World industrial sectors on American and European technology and markets. Secondly, poorer nations must compete at home and in the advanced countries with American and European corporations, some of which, such as Ford, Esso and Philips, have sales larger than the gross national product of Third World countries.

This dependency and competition also have some common consequences. Technological dependency may mean importing capital so advanced that it has to be installed and serviced by the West, as with nuclear power stations in Brazil. Or, machines may be so productive that they satisfy domestic demand and put out of work artisans who previously supplied products such as shoes, furniture, or textiles. Machines relevant for Third World requirements may not produce goods of a high enough quality to compete in international markets. Dependency on foreign markets renders poor nations susceptible to price fluctuations and the tariff policies of advanced nations. The Americans use their import quota system on commodities such as sugar, to political advantage.

The flow of Western capital into Third World economies illustrates these dependency relationships. The flow is either in the form of aid, or direct investment. Aid is a minor component and industrial aid is usually comprised of a loan by the international banking system to a poor nation, which uses it to develop projects in conjunction with multinational corporations. Direct investment is independent multinational investment in the southern hemisphere. Such investment occurs because raw materials are there, labour is cheap and some local markets, such as Brazil's, are profitable. During the 1970s the multinationals invested heavily in the Third World, generating industrial development in Brazil, Mexico, Nigeria and South Korea. The problems with this sort of development, now faced by those countries, are that they now all have very large foreign debts and the profits of industrial production are either used to pay off debt interest, or accrue directly to the multinational corporation.

As well as these common characteristics of industrial development, there are also important differences in its phases and nature. In some countries it occurred early, and is now generalised, in others it is more recent and limited. Early industrial development in the Third World occurred in the final quarter of the nineteenth century, in railways and mining. Railways were built by the British and Americans in Mexico, Peru, Brazil, India and Southern Africa. They linked towns, mines and ports, requiring large amounts of labour that either was recruited locally, or gangs of imported, indentured labour, such as Chinese 'coolies', were used. Occasionally linked to railway construction came investment in mining. New pumping and drilling technology enabled unprofitable mines to be expanded and the ores transported along the railways. The wages, sales and profits of these investments spun off into further manufacturing investments in textiles, furniture and food-processing. The period 1890 to 1914 saw considerable industrial development in the Third World.

However, this early industrial investment was often 'enclave' development, an extrusion of international capital into the local economy with limited employment and profits repatriated to corporations in the advanced nations. Such enclave investment does not lead to the further expansion of industry and manufacturing. Rather, colonies became industrially dependent on America and Europe and after the First World War were severely hit when the international economy went into the Depression of the 1930s. Reduced production was maintained in the core countries but ran down in the periphery. An exception to this pattern was Brazil, which embarked on a policy of import substituting investment, putting up tariff barriers against imports and subsidising domestic investment to replace those goods.

After the Second World War there was a second phase of industrial development as old empires broke up and American capital flowed to the

Third World. Whilst investment in basic industries such as mining continues, and oil investment became increasingly important, yet the major switch was to investing in manufacturing and, more recently, agribusiness. Manufacturing in the Third World is now often the assembly of machine parts made in America and Europe. Agri-business is the short-run production of crops whose prices are high, and is often ruinous to local ecology. This new investment flowed into the more profitable sectors of Third World economies and countries such as India found their leading sectors dominated by foreign capital.

As well as these phases of industrial development, the two types of general and limited industrialisation can be identified. As a result of both foreign investment and national capital accumulation some countries are industrialising, and quite rapidly: Brazil and Mexico are examples where industrial growth may now be self-sustaining and their social structures transformed. Even in South Africa industrial expansion has led to a new search to incorporate labouring blacks into white-dominated society. In many other countries industrial development is still limited to mining, construction and manufacturing assembly. Peru, Bolivia, Zambia and Ghana are examples of this. Even India, which has a large and modern industrial sector, has only a relatively small proportion of its labour force employed in industry, the great mass of the people still working in agriculture and living in rural areas which have been little affected by industrialisation.

A major concomitant of industrial development is working-class formation (Lloyd, 1982), whose extent depends on the type and nature of industrialisation, the origins of industrial workers and state policies. There are two processes involved in working-class formation. The first is proletarianisation, the 'freeing' of workers such that they can sell their labour on the open market and so combine with capital. The second is class formation, the development of social institutions and a consciousness particular to the working class. Where the first process is now widespread throughout the Third World, the second is more limited.

Countries experiencing general industrialisation, such as Brazil and Mexico, have a high proportion of industrial wage-workers in their total working population. These workers found trade unions, perceive that they have general interests in common with other groups of workers and support political parties and workers' candidates in elections, as in the 1982 Brazilian elections. Countries with enclave industries have only 10 to 15 per cent of their working population in the industrial sector, with many of these in the enclave. Enclave workers may feel isolated from other groups in society and may become a 'labour aristocracy', identifying their interests with those of industrial employers, protected by state policies and offering limited support to the struggles of other workers. Industrial workers in Mexico were for many years an example of this. However, in many cases enclave workers are migrants who maintain their social and political links with the peasantry.

The origins of industrial workers may be urban or rural. In Brazil and Argentina most workers are urban based, whilst in Mexico, India, Peru, Nigeria and South Africa there are urban-based railway workers, dockers, textile, steel and oil workers. These labourers come from working-class communities with traditions of trade unionism, political representation and communitarianism. On the other hand, many industrial workers are recent rural migrants. These workers are being proletarianised, for the subdivision of family lands or the commercialisation of agriculture has led them to migrate and become dependent wage-workers. Yet they maintain their ties with the rural sector and their rate of turnover in industrial work is high as they are either laid off or they go to work in the commercial sector. They struggle to establish trade unions which, because they are in the crucial export sector, can be very powerful, but that struggle is greatly influenced by state policies.

State policies may help or hinder working-class formation. Governments committed to, and experiencing, general industrialisation may subsidise the industrial sector, encourage formal workers' organisations and incorporate them into the state political machinery to ensure stability through coercion, banning trade unions, controlling workers' wages and continually circulating labour, as occurred in Brazil, Argentina and South Africa. In countries with limited industrial development the industrial sector is often the crucial export sector and so governments seek to control workers again through either repression or incorporation as a labour aristocracy. The lack of a generalised working class means that the government can isolate particular groups, as has happened in Peru, Bolivia and Chile. The preoccupation with stability by Third World governments arises from their need to guarantee to multinational corporations that their investments will be profitable, that there will be no interruptions of production, sharp increases in wages, or threats of nationalisation. However, migration to Third World cities is not only into the formal industrial economy and so the process of urbanisation must be explored more fully.

## Urbanisation

An urban explosion is occurring in the southern hemisphere (Roberts, 1978). Indeed, the shanty-towns and squatter settlements around the major cities seem to be the hallmark of the 'development' process. Millions crowd together in abject poverty, in cardboard and tin-can shacks, with no facilities and seemingly little hope. In India the old die on the streets, in Latin America children are barefoot and homeless. At first glance the shanty-towns appear as a blight on the nation's economy and locations of social breakdown and disorder.

Urbanisation is the rate of increase of that proportion of the national population which lives in cities. The proportion of urban dwellers in Latin America is 50 per cent, increasing at 5 per cent per decade, while in Africa and South-East Asia it is 20 per cent, increasing at 4 per cent per decade.

By the end of the twentieth century 2 billion people will be living in Third World cities and towns. The major increases occurred up to 1960 and there is some evidence of a slackening rate of growth now. Within the continents there are national variations: for example, 85 per cent of Uruguay's population live in cities, but only 40 per cent of Ecuador's. This urbanisation is unbalanced in several ways. First, capital cities are growing most rapidly and becoming megalopolises. Mexico City is now probably the largest conurbation in in the world, containing 17 million, while seven cities in Latin America have over 4 million people. Secondly, there is a lack of medium-sized cities, since most industry and administration are in the capital. Thirdly, urbanisation is occurring without widespread industrialisation.

The causes of urbanisation are population growth and migration, whilst the cause of metropolitan domination is the tendency towards centralisation in Third World countries. In the capital cities are concentrated most of the state's administration and much private investment, excluding primary raw materials. Not only are the Ministries of Education, Labour and Interior in the capital, but also the minor arrangements for taxing and licensing have to be done there. It is in the capitals that multinational companies invest in manufacturing, for there is a resident labour force and it is easier to deal with central government in the capital.

Some of the consequences of urbanisation have been dealt with in the section on migration. Outlined more fully here are examples of the social, economic and political consequences. One social consequence of urbanisation is the development of new urban-based social networks. Whereas in Britain industrialisation generated working-class communities, the shanty-towns are not characterised by homogeneity of occupation or class. Migrants in the metropolis are strangers to one another and so the urban process is one of 'organising strangers'. Received initially into kin networks, individuals do not then involve themselves in secondary associations based on co-operation and trust, such as mutual benefit societies and consumer co-operatives, but they rather establish personal relations of exchange and compromise. To obtain jobs or access to housing and schooling, individuals seek out a patron who will be able to help them, become his client and are in his debt. This is a family strategy which minimises risk and does not lead to generalised trust relations outside the family. The culture of the shanty-towns is thus family, rather than class, oriented, and it appears that migrants are reproducing peasant culture in the towns (cf. Chapter 8 above).

The widest economic consequence of urbanisation is the growth of the 'informal' economy. The 'formal' economy is the one of registered, bureaucratic firms, paying wages. The 'informal' or 'black' economy is made up of itinerant workpeople often working for themselves as mechanics, porters, waiters, car-washers, boot-blacks, lorry-drivers and street salesmen. Illegal activities such as gambling, prostitution and tax-evading are also included in this sector. It is to this sector that most migrants come, even if their work there is temporary whilst they await an industrial job. It is estimated that over half the working people in Mexico City are in the informal economy. At first glance it appears that the informal economy is parasitic, merely servicing the formal economy.

It is argued that shanty-town dwellers are 'marginal' to the cultures and economies of poor countries. The marginal masses are seen to have traditional values and social structures and to be excluded from the central, formal economy. Studies of the shanty-towns and the informal economy show this view to be mistaken. The poor somehow feed, house and employ themselves, producing services for which there is a demand. Moreover, they are relatively well educated and desire education for their children and jobs for themselves, which is why many migrated in the first place. Indeed, the shanty-towns of the Third World have been characterised as 'slums of hope', rather than of despair.

In Accra, the capital of Ghana, half of the labour force are self-employed, whilst one-quarter is unemployed, living in shanty-towns. Tribal groups control occupational entry, such as the Hausa controlling meat-trading. The migrant Frafras, unable to find a foothold in factory employment, work in the informal sector of building, shoe-shining, petty crime and trading, in which they specialise in fowls, craftwork and bread, accumulating some capital. In Latin America shanty-towns are usually the result of a land invasion by squatters from a nearby settlement. There is thus an invasion committee which then seeks to procure light, roads and sewage facilities from the state. The people in the *barriadas* quickly set about establishing schools and looking for work after the invasion.

The informal sector and the shanty-towns are thus not marginal to the process of capitalist development, but an integral part of it. The informal economy is made up of petty-commodity procedures, contracting their services and using both household and wage labour. Economic surplus accrues to the household and families can expand their interests into one or more lorries, restaurants, or sweetshops. The informal economy is a sector of primitive capital accumulation, in which a 'reserve army' of labour is fed and housed, available for work in the formal sector. The shanty-towns are not characterised by uniform proletarianisation but by a multiplicity of occupations and different types of labour relations.

The political consequences of urbanisation are both local and national. Locally, inhabitants struggle for amenities and become the clients of a political patron who can provide these through the municipality. This patron is in his turn the client of a national politician who can make resources available to him. Such links support the national political phenomenon of populism, the establishment of political leadership without a party system, through popular appeal. National politicians use the system of patron–client dependency relations to bring pressure to bear on local ward political bosses to mobilise the urban masses in their support. Rather than rely on a political party a military figure in command of resources can use those resources to activate a chain to mobilise support for himself. In Argentina, Juan Peron used this system. During his period as Labour Minister he was able to patronise some labour leaders who in turn supported him when he made a bid for power. The Peronist Party came into being after he was President.

## Political Systems

A range of political systems exists in the Third World, related to both local and international economies (Alavi and Shanin, 1982). In general, there is a variety of interest groups aiming to control the limited local resources and the crucial relationship with the advanced nations. This struggle for power does not necessarily result in democratisation. Authoritarian measures can be used to control key sectors, and the institutions of labour can be suppressed. Indeed, democratisation did not automatically follow in the three major development models either, which experienced the rise of Fascism in Germany, Spain and Italy, the Stalinist era and the close control of power by both Soviet and Chinese Communist parties. Despite the sensational revolutions and coups in the southern hemisphere, authoritarianism is a major political development there.

The industrial development at the time of the nineteenth century changed the political situation in many Third World countries. During the nineteenth century colonial aristocratic elites had controlled land and the export of agricultural and mineral products to Europe and America. With industrial development emerged commercial and industrial groups seeking to control the state in their own interests. These groups became also the spokesmen for the newly urbanising and industrialisation masses. Political parties were founded, particularly ones with nationalist and socialist ideologies. The Russian Revolution, then the Chinese, gave a tremendous boost to socialist parties, even though creating splits in them. Perhaps the more important ideology, however, has been nationalism, which has united groups in a desire to bring about the end of colonialism. This political liberation has occurred due to the demise of the British and French empires after the Second World War, and armed national liberation struggles. The problem facing Third World countries such as India, Algeria, Cuba, Vietnam and Zimbabwe is that such political liberation has not resulted in economic liberation from the constraints of international economies.

In Latin America, once the country of revolutions, militarised regimes have held power during the 1960s and 1970s. In Brazil, the military took office in 1964 and have controlled the presidential elections ever since. The military have used the state to collaborate with foreign capital, outlaw trade unions and repress wages. Although allowing some political freedoms in 1982 the military continue to control the presidency and important sections of the national budget. The picture is similar in Argentina. In Chile the military, with American assistance and support by the middle class, overthrew a socialist president in 1973 and continue to rule. Again, foreign capital is favoured and the working class and their institutions are repressed. There is now a 'militarised southern core' in Latin America. In 1968 Peru attempted radical reform through military intervention, which lasted for ten years, but the experiment failed and Peru has returned to parliamentary elections, with a guerrilla movement and a failing economy. Cuba's guerrilla movement succeeded in 1959 in breaking the power of the American-backed sugar oligarchy but American policies limited Cuban development and she turned to the Soviet Union for assistance. Cuba is now a one-party state and her social institutions are heavily sovietised. Elsewhere in the Caribbean and Central America, peasants are waging liberation struggles against American-backed regimes in El Salvador and Guatemala. The recent successful struggle in Nicaragua has run into economic problems and again an increasingly authoritarian stance is being adopted by the army. Only Mexico, of the larger Latin American countries, has achieved development with some democratisation. Yet this has been through incorporation, for again Mexico has been virtually a one-party state since the 1930s which has set out to incorporate peasants and workers in state administration bodies.

Africa contains many one-party states. In Zambia and Tanzania concerted efforts at democratisation were attempted after de-colonisation. The Tanzianians embarked on the *ujamaa* programme of co-operatives and collectivist villages to try and raise agricultural productivity. However, both countries ran into trading difficulties with the advanced capitalist nations, and groups' interests are subordinated in more autocratic development plans. In Nigeria, where oil wealth brought rapid social change, a civil war was followed by military takeover. Libya has a one-party state implementing an Islamic development plan with oil reserves. South Africa, through the policy of *apartheid*, deliberately restricts the access of Africans to housing and productive land. Mozambique has instituted a one-party system after the long war of liberation against the Portuguese.

South-East Asia also is marked by authoritarian regimes. Vietnam has a one-party system in which the military play a major role after the liberation struggle in the middle 1970s which they have exported to Cambodia, breaking the previous Chinese-oriented regime. Military takeover occurred in Indonesia. India is the most important country with democratic institutions, yet the crises of rising population and low agricultural productivity forced Mrs Gandhi, the Prime Minister, to take increasingly authoritarian measures until her overthrow. Reinstated, Mrs Gandhi is still faced with India's huge development problems. Neighbouring Pakistan has had a repressive military government since 1977.

One political problem for poorer nations is that power is competed for by minority groups – the industrialists or large land-holders or exporters – and when one group takes office, its authority is not legitimated by the other groups. The office-holders are seen as pursuing their own minority interests and so their continual coalitions, policy changes and the sabotaging of plans. In this situation the military take power in order, as they see it, to restore political stability and force groups to co-operate. Moreover, the military see themselves as representing a force for modernisation and efficiency in otherwise backward economies.

The one group in society which is in majority is the peasantry, but they are perhaps the most difficult group to organise and to sustain political power. Peasant revolutions do occur – in Mexico in 1910, China in 1949, Vietnam in 1973–4 and Mozambique in 1975. With forceful leadership peasants will support national liberation struggles. However, their aims are often short run, including the expropriation of large land-holders or the expulsion of foreign armies, and once in power it is difficult for the leadership to sustain political momentum. After liberation key commodities re-emerge as crucial to the local economy.

When minority groups are in power, the peasantry are seen as a 'problem'. The strategy is to raise agricultural productivity and then use the increased surplus to invest in industry, but both producing and then expropriating that surplus are difficulties most Third World nations have not overcome. The short-run tactic is to gain control of the state to erect tariff barriers, levy taxes, organise subsidies, nationalise industries, or control labour organisations. In themselves these are not long-run development programmes and do not resolve the dilemmas posed by continuing dependency relations.

The three development models outlined at the beginning of this chapter represent political alternatives to the Third World. More than this, most Third World countries are within the political and economic orbit of the West, the Soviet Union, or China. Just as Nigeria and Brazil are within the international capitalist economy, so Cuba and Hungary are in the Soviet COMECON and Tibet is a satellite of the Chinese economy. For poorer countries linked to America and Europe, their problem is to attempt development in an international economy dominated by the advanced nations and multinational corporations. Political attempts to break out of that international system, through liberation struggles, meet with resistance from the core countries, and even when such attempts are successful, the Third World nations may find that it has changed one political orbit for another.

## Conclusion: Perspectives on Development

It is clear that the lack of modernisation in the Third World is not due, as the developmentalist school argues, to a lack of the right values or social structures on their part. Rather, as we have seen, these countries find themselves in an international system which limits the accumulation of capital in the poorer countries and hinders development. As we say, with the peasantry, the 'traditional' social systems found in the Third World may often be a defence mechanism against aggressive intrusion by foreign agencies. It is also clear that the dependency school has overemphasised the level of domination of the advanced societies. Brazil, Mexico, Nigeria and the Arab oil countries are all examples of how the relation with the centre can be renegotiated by peripheral countries and how some can even establish successful development programmes. The dependency school also, by focusing on 'metropolises' and 'satellites', did not provide adequate explanations of the process of class formation in Third World countries, either of bourgeois groups implementing dependency relations within the satellite nations, or of proletarian and peasant groups resisting such exploitation.

Rather, it is clear that there are different forms of production around the globe, linked by international markets. Such forms are those outlined by Marx – capitalist, peasant and petty-commodity. However, formalising such forms into a Marxist analysis of modes of production raises certain problems. Not the least of these is the lack of fit between these modes and their labour systems, and the social relations of production found in the Third World. A capitalist mode of production is characterised by proletarian labour, a peasant mode by household labour and a petty-commodity mode by contract labour. However, research reveals that in the industrial, agricultural and urban sectors of the Third World there are a variety of labour systems in operation. Also it is as yet unclear how these labour systems will crystallise into the bourgeois, propertied and proletarian, unpropertied classes central to Marxist analysis. That is to say, it is difficult to see many Third World countries as transitional between one development stage and another. Their social, political and economic structures, though splintered, seem stable in the medium term, for their position in the international economy is relatively unchanging.

However, whilst there are problems in fitting the formal structures outlined by Marx, to conditions in the Third World, yet the political and economic processes highlighted by both Marx and Weber are occurring in the Third World and influencing social organisation there. Proletarianisation in both industrial and rural sectors is increasing. The primitive accumulation of capital occurs in both town and countryside, and importantly in the informal sector. Commoditisation and commercialisation are occurring as land, labour and products are alienated and exchanged for cash in markets. Property relations are altered as the state intervenes to nationalise companies or expropriate land-holders. Life-styles are developed to cope with the exigencies of unstable economic development. Political economy analysis, through focusing on these processes, is now beginning to make statements about the social relations of production, the formation and dissolution of social classes, political strategies and the relations between regional, national and international economies. It is these processes, too diverse for the term 'development' which comprise international social change.

# References: Chapter 10

Alavi, H., and Shanin, T. (eds) (1982), *Introduction to the Sociology of Developing Societies* (London: Macmillan).

Frank, A. G. (1969), *Capitalism and Underdevelopment in Latin America* (New York: Monthly Review Press).

Furtado, C. (1970), *Economic Development of Latin America* (Cambridge: CUP).

Kilby, P. (ed.) (1971), *Entrepreneurship and Economic Development* (New York: The Free Press).

Hobsbawm, E. (1975), *The Age of Capital* (London: Weidenfeld & Nicolson).

Laite, J. (1981), *Industrial Development and Migrant Labour* (Manchester: Manchester University Press).

Lloyd, P. (1982), *A Third World Proletariat?* (London: Allen & Unwin).

Long, N. (1977), *An Introduction to the Sociology of Rural Development* (London: Tavistock).

Nove, A. (1969), *An Economic History of the U.S.S.R.* (Harmondsworth: Allen Lane).

Roberts, B. (1978), *Cities and Peasants* (London: Edward Arnold).

Roxborough, I. (1979), *Theories of Underdevelopment* (London: Macmillan).

Wallerstein, I. (1974), *The Modern World System* (New York: Academic Press).

Wolf, E. (1970), *Peasant Wars of the 20th Century* (New York: Harper & Row).

Worsley, P. (1967), *The Third World* (London: Weidenfeld & Nicolson).

Worsley, P. (1975), *Inside China* (Harmondsworth: Allen Lane).

## Further Reading

Frankel, F. (1971), *India's Green Revolution* (Princeton, NJ: Princeton University Press).

Lewis, O. (1980), *Pedro Martinez* (Harmondsworth: Penguin).

Mangin, W. (1970), *Peasants in Cities* (Boston, Mass.: Houghton Mifflin).

Oxaal, I., *et al.* (1975), *Beyond the Sociology of Development* (London: Routledge & Kegan Paul).

Sandbrook, R., and Cohen, R. (1975), *The Development of an African Working Class* (London: Longman).

# Name index

# Subject index